JAMIE'S EXTRAORDINARY ADVENTURES

Jamie's Extraordinary Adventures

Copyright © 2020 by Brian Robinson. All rights reserved.

No part of this publication may be reproduced, stored in a retrieval system, or transmitted in any form or by any means, digital, electronic, mechanical, photocopying, recording, or otherwise, or conveyed via the Internet or a website without prior written permission of the publisher, except in the case of brief quotations embodied in critical articles and reviews.

ISBN: 978-1-7366722-3-5 (print)
            978-1-7366722-4-2 (ebook)

Printed in the United States of America

JAMIE'S EXTRAORDINARY ADVENTURES

BRIAN ROBINSON

Table of Contents

Synopsis 1
Introduction 3

Chapter 1 5
Chapter 2 12
Chapter 3 22
Chapter 4 35
Chapter 5 42
Chapter 6 59
Chapter 7 65
Chapter 8 71
Chapter 9 76
Chapter 10 87
Chapter 11 94
Chapter 12 99
Chapter 13 105
Chapter 14 111
Chapter 15 121
Chapter 16 135
Chapter 17 142
Chapter 18 147
Chapter 19 152
Chapter 20 157
Chapter 21 163
Chapter 22 174
Chapter 23 184
Chapter 24 195
Chapter 25 220
Chapter 26 233
Chapter 27 239
Chapter 28 253

Synopsis

In the late eighteenth century the main Hero called Jamie Heslop. He qualified at the young age of fourteen as a Midshipman. This young man showed extreme ingenuity to solve problems or meet challenges in making the impossible possible.

When finding out his Father was murdered at sea by henchmen, hired by his vicious uncle Zak and his evil stepmother Edwina. Under the misapprehension they both would inherit the Heslop shipping fortune. Jamie fearing for his life, he takes one of his late father's ships with his friend Kate. The only ones he could trust to man the ship were the young children, from the orphanage some having severed on a ship with his late father. Their destination is an island in the Indian Ocean using a map given to him by an old seaman friend. After setting sail he discovers forty black slaves chained up in the ships hold. They would also become dedicated loyal friends. The long journey helps all of them to develop skills to turn them into able seaman, some learning other different trades. But the other most important thing was they all had to learn the art of swordsmanship. They all would become an elite band of fighters, having been taught by a beautiful orphan tomboy called Sam.

On this perilous Journey, they would encounter many dangerous situations, including storms, an erupting volcano, becalmed seas, shortage of water and food. One of Jamie's first dangerous sea encounter was when his vicious uncle Zak, who wanted Jamie dead. In another incident, he comes under attack from a notorious pirate called Nancarrow wanting his ship and crew. Using his ingenuity in both attempts, Jamie repelled disabling both ships, without firing a single shot or loss of life. They all would find out in the future, the Wrath from these two encounters.

Reaching their island, they soon established themselves, building homes farming the land. Then after a violent storm, they find a English shipwreck on one of the smaller islands. After boarding the wreck, among other things they discover a wanted posted. It read their skipper is wanted for murder of his dear friend. Jamie vowed to clear his name when he gets older but for now he had to keep a promise he had made to his late father. Firstly he turned his attention to find the plantation owners on the mainland, whom had taken some of his loyal crew's families for slaves.

On one such encounter before sailing back to their Island Jamie was amazed to see Zak's ship moored up in a harbour. Catching Zak's crew off guard, they seized his ship and sailed back to their Island. Only to find Nancarrow wanting revenge had attacked their island. Sadly a few of his crew he had left behind some had been killed along with their livestock. Jamie knew it was only a matter of time before this evil Pirate would return to kill them all, so he had to prepare everyone. Nancarrow did return, but this time with Zak and Edwina on board wanting their ship back. Jamie cleverly responded with his elite band of fighters. The outcome of the battle enabled him to return back to England to clear his name. That would only be after one more last big escapade. Once back in Portsmouth, establishing his innocence, then finds out his father maybe alive in Ireland. Desperate to uncover the truth, he sets sail for Ireland leaving his girlfriend Kate behind expecting to be back in a few months.

Introduction

Almost a year ago in my ancestral cottage well buried deep behind clutter under the stairs, I made a fantastic discovery, there was this 18th-century copper strongbox, bearing the initials CC! Now CC you may ask, perhaps this might have been hidden away from a Relative from the past. What secrets would it hold inside? I found a Diary and journals in very good preserved condition. Being eager to find out whether CC is a relative and if so how did I become a Riley. After reading everything being so amazed I have now decided to write my first book. So I have combined my version along with what is written in the diary and journals, and take you on a journey of a lifetime beginning with CC first entry.

Chapter 1

One hot September afternoon a young fourteen year old girl walking home across a village green, heading towards her was this magnificent horse with a young male rider. When passing each other unfortunately she let out one hell of a sneeze Achoo. The horse spooked reared up throwing the rider into the air then hitting the ground with an almighty thump. The poor girl did not know whether to laugh or cry, seeing this young man red faced getting up rubbing his bum, but luckily none the worse. She apologised politely, 'sorry Sir are you okay.' Being so embarrassed muttered. 'I am fine madam.'

Then all of a sudden they both looked at each other and burst out laughing, that's when she saw his captivating smile for the first time. 'Madam my name is Jamie; I'm very pleased to make your acquaintance.'

She curtseyed. 'My name is Catherine but sir, please call me Kate as everyone does.'

Kate had also had noticed his eyes were a gentle blue, glistening in the sun and he was very handsome. Nerves got the best of her so told him. 'It was nice meeting you, sir.'

Then she began to excuse herself with a short customary curtsey and turned to walk away.

He did not want to lose the opportunity to see her again so he suddenly asked. 'May I walk you home but only if you stop calling me Sir.'

She gave him a lovely smile before telling him. 'Well Jamie there is no need too I just live down that path and I was just going home before I made your horse jump so there is no need to walk me home.

'You sure did make me and my horse jump, the main reason I had just been to the graveyard to put flowers on my late mother's grave and my thoughts were miles away.'

Poor Kate looked a bit depressed. 'I am sorry for your loss Jamie; I know the sadness you bear because I lost both my parents when I was very young, I am being brought up by my grandparents. They both love me and treat me like a mother and father. They have lived in that cottage for many years, sadly they are getting old now and when they die, I will probably live there for the rest of my life too'.

He expressed sorrow for her loss and understood, 'I am sorry you lost your parents Kate but happy that you have such caring loving grandparents. Unlike you Kate I have my father but sadly he remarried not long after my mother died to a woman called Edwina. I hate her so much even though I try so hard to please her; she is so very evil to me and all the servants.'

Jamie quickly changed the subject talking about his problems. 'Kate what you just said about living in that cottage forever, you never know what's going to happen in life just think positive. Who knows things might change for you from now onwards if you believer in fate. Also, I might see more of you as I only live just over there, at the top of the green in the Manor house with those big iron gates'.

Kate sudden becomes tongue-tied in his presence, and a bit embarrassed and a silence fell between them. Even Jamie was trying to think of something, as he didn't want to lose the opportunity to meet her again and blurted out. 'Kate I am going to fly my kite on this green tomorrow mid-morning if the wind was favourable, would you like to join me.'

'Jamie, I would love to, but I don't know how to fly a kite'.

'I will show you how to do it, as my mother always told me, there's always a way around a problem. Sadly I have to go now as well because my father will be home shortly and I need to discuss something with him'.

He was secretly hoping his father was going to say he had finished with the Merchant Shipping academy for good and that he would take him to the West Indies the following week. As he mounted his horse he looked back over his shoulder and called to Kate,

'I will see you mid-morning tomorrow. I have really have enjoyed meeting you Kate. "Achoo"'

'Oh Jamie, are you okay'

'I will be fine.' Galloping away with a big grin on his face, Kate smiled at him and waved. She enjoyed their meeting as much as he had done. Her thoughts turned to Jamie; he was so down-to-earth, not at all like most boys with well-to-do father's, who thought they were so much better than everyone else was.

Jamie trotted down the Manor's long drive, which was lined either side by flowers and huge elm trees, leading to a large house he lived in called Compton Manor. It was impressive, with grey stone walls and several tall red-brick chimneys. It had been built almost 200 years earlier for a minor earl, that had been much smaller back then, but a succession of owners had built an addition east and the west wing. His father had purchased the property when he had married his mother, and they had hoped to fill it with children. Unfortunately, this had not come about, and Jamie remained a much loved but an only child. When he arrived home the stableman took his horse, his little dog, Peggy, was waiting at the big oak front door. His nanny, Mary, who had looked after him since his mother had died, opened the door, pulling him quickly into the large hallway. It was a beautiful room, with thick-red embossed wallpaper and a huge fireplace at the far end stacked with logs ready to be lit when the winter closed in. Mary was fifty years old and had never married but loved Jamie as if he were her son. There were a few grey hairs sprinkled among the red hair that had once been lustrous. She was always very proper, and Jamie had never seen her dressed in anything but her maid's uniform and apron.

'Jamie, you are late. Hurry along now you must take a bath and get into clean clothes before Edwina discovers you're are late back. I will make an excuse for you, so go on and get ready'.

About an hour later, Jamie heard from upstairs the front door open, and Mary was greeting Mr Charles Heslop with a good evening. He was a tall, handsome man in his mid-forties with long fair hair tied back with the customary black bow. His light-blue eyes sparkled with energy, and his kind and generous nature shone through. He was well liked by all his servants, all the workers at the shipping company; he never had any problem also operating his ships, as he was known to be a fair and honest captain.

Edwina emerged from the drawing room to greet Charles and kissed him lightly on the cheek, saying, 'Good Evening, Charles. As soon as you clean up, my love, dinner will be served'.

'Edwina, please, I have told you before to call me Jim'.

'No!' Edwina exclaimed. 'You should be called Charles, in front of the servants'.

'All right, so be it. Charles, if it is only, in front of the servants if it will keep the peace'.

Jamie came running down the stairs excited and hugged his father. He blurted that, 'I met a girl today from this village, and her name is Kate.' 'Slow down son and tell me about her after dinner and I also have a lot of good news to share with you too'.

Jim went upstairs and quickly changed from his usual working attire of heavy breeches and high boots, quickly washing in the bowl of hot water one of the servants had left ready for him. He soon joined Edwina and Jamie in the small dining room. Dinner was usually a quiet affair as Edwina disapproved of discussing business matters at the table and Jim was always full of the day's work. Jamie wanted to hear everything about the shipyard but waited patiently until he was on his own with his father, not wanting to antagonise his stepmother's anger. When they had eaten and the servants had removed the plates, Jamie and his father got up. Jim put his arm around his son and they went into the library to talk. They settled themselves into a pair of large comfortable leather chairs, and Jamie poured his father a glass of port. 'Father I would like to ask you a question if I may.'

'Go ahead son. 'Why, did you look so miserable at dinner.'

'I dislike being called Charles as much as your mother hated being called Dorothea. She preferred being called Dorie, so why does Edwina say Charles?'

'Because she is a snob father,'

'I don't think so son'.

Jamie had been thinking for a long time about speaking to his father regarding his stepmother but had been putting it off. He wanted to tell him about the arguments and shouting he often heard between Edwina and his father late in the evening after he had gone to bed and about the way Edwina treated the servants and the animals and that she always treated Mary dreadfully and had no time for him at all.

Jamie decided to summon up the courage to talk to his father about Edwina. 'Father, do you love Edwina?'

'That's personal, my boy. Why do you ask that question son?'

'Because I never see you both being affectionate towards one another, and sleeping in the same bed, as you and Mother were'.

'It is not the same, my son. We have a friendly relationship and I wanted to make us a family again.

'But, Father, I was happy the way we were'.

'I take it you do not like Edwina'.

'We have our ups and downs sometimes,' replied Jamie tentatively. 'Jamie, for my sake, could you try to get along with her?'

'I will try, Father. 'With that, Jamie decided that it was best to leave the conversation for now, as he could see his father was getting upset talking about her. Jamie then told his father about him meeting Kate, to whom his father replied, 'Son I am really happy, for you to have made a friend locally, and we will talk more on this later, but I am sorry to have to change the subject, as we have more pressing things to discuss tonight Jamie'. Jim had a lot to say to his son about his next trip. 'My son I am taking you with me to the West Indies. The reason your fourteen now and you have passed all your midshipman exams and ships navigation courses as well, I am so proud of you.'

'Farther I do not know what to say, I am thrilled to bits.' But in the back of his mind thinking about how he is going to tell his new found friend they won't see each other for months. So he decided to wait for the right opportunity.

'My son there will be two ships on this trip. Captain Temp and his crew would be sailing the Earl of Cornwall and I have just completed the purchase of a brand new ship I recently required. Which I want you to name son because she is going to be your ship one day when I retire, relax and do some fishing'.

'Father, I do not know what to say! I'm surprised and honoured, can we name her after my mother. Jamie always said that if he ever owned a ship, he would call her the 'Lady Dorothea' after his Mother.

'I knew you would call her that, my boy'.

On Monday, they decided to christen her with that name. But they knew that it will not go down well with Edwina and they both would be in trouble.

'Young man I am going to blame it on you, just to keep the peace!' 'They both said it together and laughed and laughed..'Father, that's nice of you to blame me'.

Father and son fell about laughing and then his father took another sip of port and memories of past times came flooding back. Believing this was the end of their conversation, Jamie rose from the chair to make his way to bed, but his father said,

'Hold on there, I have not finished with you yet' Son I want you to take note of how this ship operates at sea, as its important' Jim said in a stern voice.

'Of course, I will father follow your instruction.'

Jim in a softer voice 'If we get the time on our new ship my son, let's see if you can beat me at sword fencing'.

'No problem father I came top of my class at fencing this year father'.

'I see then I will look forward to you beating me then.'

Jamie was eager to listen to hear what else his father had to say.' During the last year, I have been taking young children from the orphanage to sail on our ships. We have been teaching them to become merchant seamen, and then when the ships return sadly I have to return them all to the orphanage until the next time. The main reason there is a shortage of merchant seamen as a few of our seamen already have joined the royal navy. So my son bright and early Monday morning we will take the carriage to Portsmouth docks and I want you to go alone to the orphanage '

'I can do that father' 'It will be a good experience for you son'

Jim wants his son to see how the other half lived in squalled and have nothing in the lives and to see what these places look like, as a boy of privileges. He told Jamie that the orphanage was no more than a mile away from dockside and he was to speak to Mr Humphrey the man in charge. He wants Jamie to inform him that they were setting sail on Friday and request the boys that Charles had trained before. Also telling Jamie he needs an additional twelve boys and four girls, payment fee as normal from Heslop Merchant Shipping will follow all was explained in the letter Jamie was to hand over. However, Jim knows the boys did not see any of their pay as it went into Mr Humphrey pocket, but they enjoy the experience. An annual retainer fee is paid to keep these children from going to the wool mills when they come of age, Jim wanted the chance of taking them on as trained seamen when they are older.

'Son I think it is a great experience for your new friend, Kate too. Maybe she would like to accompany you to the orphanage. So, ask her in the morning if she would like to go with you? She could also christen the ship, because of the ships name will be in a woman's name, but let us keep it a secret from her for now. I think it's an excellent idea even if I say so myself', laughed his father 'Oh yes, Father that's a great idea I can't wait to see the new ship and I will ask Kate tomorrow'. 'Now it's time for you to go to bed, my boy'.

'Yes, Father, I am going now. I am looking forward to Monday. Goodnight, Charles Oh sorry, Father,' and received a clip round the ear for his cheekiness.

Chapter 2

Jamie woke the next morning, stirring lazily; he suddenly remembered he had arranged to meet Kate with his kites. He rushed to his bedroom window and pulled back the heavy blue velvet curtains. He was delighted to see a stiff breeze blowing. He hurriedly pulled on his breeches and shirt, through on his jacket; straighten it as he ran down the sweeping staircase to the kitchen. Mary was already preparing his breakfast as he quickly told her about meeting his new friend Kate. She smiled and nodded giving her approval, and filling happy for him.

'Not so fast young man. You will get indigestion, what time are you meeting Kate today.'

'Not until around eleven auntie but I thought I might practice for a bit on my own, It's been a while since I flew the kites'.

Regardless of Mary's warning, Jamie ate his bread and cheese, with a thick slice of ham quickly. He gulped his cup of milk, preferring that to the customary tea, thanked Mary who was standing there rolling her eyes at him and ran into the boot room to pull on his long brown leather boots. He flung open the door in a hurry and rushed headlong into his father.

'Whoa! Son, what's the big hurry?'

'Oh father I am going to meet Kate about Monday and show her how to fly a kite'.

'A Kite what next, why don't you on this lovely morning take Kate for a picnic on the beach, that's a way of getting to know her better than flying Kites son,' his father trying not to laugh. 'Use the old dirt track that leads to the beach, you can take the horse and buggy, but you must keep away from those cliffs'.

'Thanks, Father that's a lovely idea, but I thought Edwina would be using the buggy today to see her brother'.

'I will have a word with her. She can use the carriage instead. You go and tell the coachman to saddle up the buggy and I will tell Mary to prepare you a picnic basket'.

Jamie was delighted as he ran out to tell the coachman. Then whistled for his dog and ran off fast towards the village green but to his surprise, Kate was already waiting by the main gates. 'Hello, Jamie that's a lovely dog! What's its name?'

Jamie was a bit slightly out of breath, but he managed to say, 'Hello Kate this is Peggy. She is a Staffordshire terrier, I also have two cats at home, called Molly and Spike and my father allows me to take them all with me when we go sailing, as they are all good ratters'.

Then after he got his breath back he explained. 'I am going with my father to Portsmouth docks on Monday, two reason my father wants me to go to the local orphanage to select some young children to use as deckhands on his ships, as they are sailing on Friday. The other reason is my father has just brought a new ship so they will be having a Naming Ceremony called a ship's christening to give the ship a name. It's part of a tradition of naming a ship is a way of bringing the ship good luck, my father let me decide the name so I have decided to call the ship The Lady Dorothea, Kate I would like to come with me as well."

'Jamie, that's lovely, your mother would have been so proud of you calling it in her name'.

'So Kate, would you like you to come with us on Monday if you can?'

'I would love to go, Jamie, but I will have to ask my grandparents permission first. I'll just run over and ask them now. Can you wait here for me?' She ran off across the green, in only a few short minutes returned with a smile on her face and out of breath but managed to say.

'They don't mind as they have met your father before and so admire him for what he is doing for the community, especially paying to keep the village vicarage school running'.'

'Wonderful! We will be leaving early Monday morning, is that alright? When we have finished at the orphanage, we can go and watch the new boat being christened.'

'That's fine. I will be there'.

'I hope you don't mind, but there has been a change of plan for today. Instead of flying kites, I am taking you for a picnic on the beach if that is alright with you'.

'That's lovely my Grandparents know I am with you today, but Jamie I would have liked to fly a kite'.

'So you shall Kate'.

Luckily, there was a young boy on the green flying his kite, and Jamie asked if he could borrow it for a few minutes. The boy handed it to Jamie, and whilst it was in the air, he gave it to Kate, he asked her shyly. 'May I put my arm over your shoulder to help control it'?

Kate agreed and soon got the hang of it, but she was surprised at how strong the kite pulled her when the wind was blustery. Jamie looked at Kate and winked, 'I think I'll tie you to that kite, but then I'm sure you would have taken off with it'.

'I am sure I would,' she replied with a smile, enjoying herself. 'Come on, Kate; time to go for that picnic'.

They returned the kite to its owner and went to Jamie's house. As they got to the stables, the coachman said,

'Sorry Sir, Lady Edwina wants the buggy today, so I'm getting the carriage ready for you, your food basket is inside'.

Jamie thanked him, and just as he was about to find Kate, who had wandered off to the stables to pet the horses. Suddenly He was abruptly halted in his tracks by a sudden shout coming from a nearby window.

'Take the carriage you little brat'

He knows by the voice, it was Edwina shouting but ignored her. Kate overheard and was astounded, remembering what Jamie had said, she too guessed it was Edwina shouting, but decided not to say anything to Jamie. 'Can I sit up there next to you and Peggy? Kate asked after coming out of the stable.

'Sorry, Kate, but it is safer for you to ride inside the coach'. She reluctantly agreed as he made sure she had got into the carriage. He climbed up onto the seat with Peggy; the coachman passed him the reins, telling him to be careful.

They set off towards the sandy beach. Jamie took his telescope with him in the hope of spotting the new ship. He knew the best view would be near the edge of the cliff. He was reluctant to disobey his father's instructions, but curiosity got the better of him. 'Kate, I am going over near this cliff to see if I can see the new ship so it's going to be a lot bumpier leaving the track.'

However, just as the carriage was negotiating a slight incline it caught a pothole, unnoticed by Jamie, preoccupied with his father's new ship, the bolt harnessing the carriage to the horses had jumped out. Jamie had no choice but to let go of the horse's reins leaving him and Peggy sitting on top of the carriage. By now the two horses trotted off luckily all they wanted to graze on the long grass. Jamie was horrified as he felt the carriage start to run back down the slope towards the cliff edge. He shouted at Kate to jump out, but she was too terrified to jump. Screaming hysterically in the back of the carriage when she realised what was happening. He struggled to keep control of the coach's handbrake, as it was his only chance of slowing down the carriage. His concern now was where the carriage was heading. He knows they wouldn't survive if they went over the cliff. Still wrestling with the brake the carriage headed nearer and nearer the cliff edge. Jamie gasped in horror as the carriage was about to plummet down to the beach he had no option but to jump off when all of a sudden the carriage juddered to a halt. The wheel had wedged up against a large rock, leaving the coach underneath him perched precariously on the edge of the cliff. Kate was sobbing uncontrollably and pleading for help, too terrified to move. He carefully climbed down with Peggy, realizing that the coach could dislodge, and quickly opened the door. As he leaned towards a distraught and tearful Kate, he felt the coach start to tilt and quickly withdrew. He knew he had to get Kate out quickly before disaster could strike. A petrified Kate was unable to move and Jamie knew he had to do something fast. So he shouted to Peggy and told her to jump sit into the carriage. 'Sit and stay Peggy!' Jamie commanded as he patted the seat just inside the door which was the opposite end to Kate, to counterbalance the weight. Peggy did as she was told. Then Jamie leaned in again towards Kate and this time the extra weight from Peggy was enough for him to grasp Kate's hand and pull her through the open door to safety, leaving the carriage teetering on the edge of the cliff. Jamie called to Peggy and she obediently jumped straight out. The carriage had now settled from its rocking motion and sat tantalisingly over the cliff edge. Peggy ran over to Jamie, who was comforting Kate to console her and tried squeezing in between them both.

She said in a loud embarrassing voice 'You can let go of me, Jamie, and your dog. I am fine now' As she smoothed her dress down and patted her hair, trying to regain her composure. Neither of them was hurt other than the exception of a few bruises and scratches. Kate was very impressed at Jamie's quick thinking in rescuing her, using the dog to balance the carriage.

'Kate, I am going to try and save the coach'.

'Please Jamie, be careful'.

Jamie looked around for the pin from the carriage.

He found it and noticed the safety pin had come adrift. He backed up the horses, very carefully hooked the shaft on to the carriage, replaced the pin, and then fixed the safety pin in firmly.

He led the horses forward; there was a lurch, and the carriage came back away from the edge, once the carriage was back on the track, they climbed in to make their way to the beach.

Jamie was a bit worried then said to Kate. Please do not say a word to my father or anyone else'.

She smiled at him. 'You have my word. I will not tell a soul. I will say the bruises and scratches happened when I tripped and fell into some bramble bushes and that you rushed to rescue me'. They both burst out laughing.

When they arrived on the beach, they laid out the picnic but they didn't have much appetite and picked at the food before them. Peggy sat beside them wagging her tail and looking at the tasty offerings. Jamie gave her the rest of the food and she gobbled it down in no time. Kate wanted to ask Jamie about his stepmother as she had noticed he gets uncomfortable when he mentions her name, especially what she heard at the stables earlier. 'Jamie I would like to know more about your stepmother if you do not want to talk about her I understand.'

'Kate it is fine I do not quite understand but for some the reason I have this filling I need to confide in you, it will not make me fill so much alone any more.'

'Jamie I will never betray your confidence and never judge you even if I was a mere acquaintance, I always would keep your secret, and promised not to betray your confidence.'

He then began to tell her about his troubled life at home.

Edwina, is my stepmother and her brother, Zak my uncle, they dislike me intensely more so, when my father is away at sea, or when my father is not looking. Edwina eyes narrow and her lips pout when his father gives me more attention than her and he hears his name being mentioned when they argue sometimes. She makes me clean out the animals when we have servants to do that. If I was to do anything wrong to upset her, she would lose her temper and send me to bed without food. If it were not for Mary my nanny, sneaking food into my bedroom, I would go hungry. Other times my Father gives me responsibilities at the dockyard to teach me things. Zak thinks it's undemanding him and his face turns to thunder and gets ready to explode. After my father has gone to sea, Uncle Zak gets his own back on me and makes me clean the office in the dockyard, and all other menial work just like Edwina makes me do. I cannot tell my father as Zak would denial everything.

Kate, I was Secretly told on good authority that he overcharges the customers most of the time and divides the money between himself and Edwina he also makes a lot of blunders, like not sailing our ships on time and sending the wrong bills to the wrong people.

He also brags about how he could do a lot better, and if it were not for him, the company would go broke. Zak lies quite often to my father. Telling my father that when he goes out to meet new customers when he returns if there have been any problems while has been away. Zak would sack the ones involved for being incompetent even though it's his mistakes.

'Jamie how do you know all those things about Zak and Edwina.

'Because it is all true Kate, it was related to me by a loving family-trusted friend, called Captain Temp, who made me promise not to say a word to his father. This was because if Zak and Edwina were to find out they would make my life even worse when my father is away. They would, certainly do the same to Temp, as some of those who work for my Father could turn against both of us, as many of them are Zak's loyal paid friends'.

Kate then asked, 'who is Captain Temp.' 'Temp is a lovely old man; he works for my father and my late grandfather for many years and is a competent Captain and family friend. He knows all about Zak, being untrustworthy and that he can be very convincing when he wants to be with his lies'

Kate suddenly realised it was getting late, and the afternoon was becoming chilly.

'I have to be going home soon as my grandmother told me to be back on time for tea or it will be cleared away, but I don't think I can eat much more.' She said laughingly

'Oh sorry, Kate, I didn't realize the time, it sounds as if your Nan is strict with you'.

'Yes, she is, but not really and I don't mind as I love them very much'.

Jamie trotted back carefully, watching the track for more holes. When they arrived back to the village green, Kate noticed Edwina's buggy heading back to the Manor in the buggy, she was heading straight for them, from behind and overtook the carriage at the last minute, and in doing so, Edwina gave them a thunderous look as she passed them by. Kate was about to put her head out of the carriage window and thought better of it when she saw Edwina. Jamie pulled the horses to a stop outside Kate's cottage and got down to help Kate. She asked him if he had noticed Edwina's look, but Jamie shrugged it off saying.

'She is often ill-tempered and probably been to see her brother again. She does every Saturday afternoon when my father has a nap'.

'Can I call on you tomorrow, Kate?' Jamie asked hopefully.

'Sorry, Jamie but I can't, a doctor friend of my grandparents from Portsmouth is coming to the village tomorrow to teach me about herbal medicines and how to use them for healing. He comes every other Sunday, so I can't put him off'

'That's ok Kate, that's a good thing to learn'

'Thank you, Jamie, I have to go in now.'

'Don't forget early Monday morning. Jamie shouted out'

Kate turned to wave, thinking what an adventurous day it had been and how lucky they both were, and Jamie was such a nice young man.

Jamie was thinking, exactly the same thing about her, as he gave the horses a little slap and headed for home. He was right about Edwina and she had been to see Zak. She was furious with her husband calling the new ship after his late wife. Although Jim and his son had wanted to keep it a secret about the Lady Dorothea, Edwina had been listening at the door as always and overheard everything they had been discussing.

Edwina had talked Jim into marriage not long after the death of his beloved wife, Dorothea, at a time when he was very lonely and vulnerable. She had looked every part of the dignified woman she portrayed. Her fair hair had been piled, neatly on top of her head in fashionable curls, her manners were impeccable, and her dress sense was immaculate. Gradually, her standards had reverted to her inherent personality. She rarely washed her hair, her manners became slovenly, and she put on large amounts of weight, she cared not and her temper had increased.

Edwina was in the foul mood when she saw Zak. 'Just in time for tea sis'

Edwina muttered something under her breath.

'Now sis what's up with you?'

'You know full well what's wrong'

'Ah, the damn Heslop's I'm sick of them too'.

Zak works in the Heslop shipping office in Portsmouth. He got the job when Jim married his sister, as a family obligation. Jim did not really get on with Zak, but put up with him, for Edwina sake, but did not trust him. Zak didn't think he was being paid enough, but Jim paid him a fair wage.

Zak was unlike his sister always dressed in formal attire, cotton breeches with the fashioned style coat, of the time. His fair hair tied back, a curled lip and his chin thrust forward with narrowed eyes. Irresponsible and selfish by nature and tries to get what he wants through crafty and mean actions.

'You heard about the ship sis?'

'Of cause I have, I am sure they are going to get this young wench Jamie's just met to christen their new ship as well. 'It's about time you sorted them out'

'Give me time sis. I am working on it.

'We both have been planning this for ages so how much longer do I have to put up with all this'?

'I know sis.' By now Zak was getting irritated with his sister.

'Still, want to go ahead with killing them both?'

'Of course, that's why I married him, was it not, to get our hands on his money; I want it done sooner than later'?

Zak has have been planning quite a while to get rid of Captain Heslop and his son. The latest plan was to tamper with the carriage to look like a carriage accident.

'The brat was going to take his wench for a ride in the buggy today. So I told him to take the carriage, just in case I had a big argument with the coachman'.

' Sis I have no idea if my man has sorted the carriage out or not as I haven't spoken or seen him.. Anyways, it wasn't supposed to be used until Monday'.

'Just get on with it Zak'

'I am Sis!' Zak was getting more irritated with Edwina and she was getting more frustrated with him. 'If it doesn't work, I have a better idea to get rid of them'.

'How? 'Edwin said eager to find out.

'Trust me? Make sure you kiss that husband of yours goodbye for the last time when he and his boy set sail on Friday'

Edwina got up and left smiling, thinking of how things were going to be without Jim and the brat in her life. Then deciding how she and Zak will change things around at Crompton Manor.

Zak thoughts were only about the money, and having the best shipping company in the southwest of England, and how he will be able to sail ships to anywhere he pleased. Asia, China, and the best place of all are in Africa where he can acquire many slaves to fill his ships, and then sell them in America or the West Indies. This will make them very rich.

Zak went to find his associates in a dockside Tavern, as prearranged, to plan his despicable act upon Captain Charles Heslop and his son. He knows he can rely on them to do his dirty work. He signalled them over to a quiet corner in the so he could go over the plan with them.

'Right lads make sure you report for duty on the right ship? I will be watching from a distance. It's the Lady Dorothea, you have to sail on as there are two ships on this trip and they are both leaving on Friday's high tide. He paused.

Looked around to check no one was listening in on their conversation before continuing. 'Bide your time to get it right as you can't afford to bundle it. I suggest you wait for bad weather one night as everyone will be busy as most of the crew will be below deck. Make sure the coast is clear and you get Jim and his son together on the deck so you can throw them both overboard. There is always the return journey, so pick the best time. When you return and the deed is done I will pay you five gold guineas each '.They all agreed and shook hands with Zak. 'So I'll see you scum bags on Friday, but keep away from me as I don't want anyone to know you're connected in any way to me, got that?'

The four men nodded their assertion, moved away to another table go over the plan of their devious act, also on how to spend their reward. Zak sat a while longer, before he got up, to make sure nobody was watching and left the Tavern.

Chapter 3

Sunday morning dawned, and there was a knock on Jamie's bedroom door.

'It's Mary. Jamie Are you awake?'

'Yes auntie', Jamie replied sleepily.

'Your father wants to talk to you after you had breakfast and to tell you he will be in the study'.

'I will be down in ten minutes'!

Jamie jumped out of bed, dressed quickly, after washing in the bowl of cold water that made him shiver. He rushed downstairs and said 'good morning' to Edwina. She knew Jamie was meeting his father, so Edwina made sure he ate every last piece of his breakfast before he could leave the table so that he would be late. When he had finished eating, he asked to be excused; she made him wait for an answer and then said, 'You may go'.

Jamie got up and straightened his attire. He then hurried off to the study, apologising to his father for his tardiness. Jim nodded in acceptance and said he needed to discuss the new ship. 'Have you changed your mind?' Jamie frowned and looked very worried.

'No, son, it's nothing like that'. 'I wanted to tell you the history of the ship and all of her specification'. Jamie sat down to listen with a big sigh of relief.

Jim told his son, that she is the sister ship of HMS Endeavour, which Captain Sir James Cook sailed on when he made his epic voyage around the world in 1768 and went on to say he had the pleasure of meeting him and his ship in Portsmouth harbour before they left. The two ships are identical except for their canvas sails. However the new ship has a new type of canvas sails, which are made from a lighter material that comes from the Netherlands. Fewer sailors would be needed when rigging or de-rigging the ship, so instead of the usual seventy seamen, only fifty would be needed to man the ship, which means the ship will take on more cargo. When we return from the West Indies, we are going to use the ship to trade in Asia with China, Java, India, and some small islands. As she will be ideal when we trade with some of the larger islands in the Indian Ocean because India is now going to be under the British Empire and will be colonised by the British, that means taking cargo over and fetching cargo back, and a lot of money is to be made. This is the reason why this ship was purchased was that she had already been ship-rigged and sturdily built with a broad, flat bow, a square stern, and a long box-like body with a deep hold. A flat-bottomed design makes the ship suited for sailing in shallow seas, especially in the islands where the coral is shallow and there are no docking facilities. This allows her to beach easily for loading or unloading of cargo and basic repairs on sandy beaches. The ship has a longboat and two twenty-eight-feet sweeps to allow the ship to be rowed if she becomes becalmed or unmasked. She also has a yawl and two pinnacles.

Jim also told Jamie, about a group of beautiful coral islands in the Indian Ocean that their good friend, Captain Temp had told him about and one day the three of them the dog and the cats will go and explore these islands for themselves.

'So when I have made a lot of money with this ship, I promise that one day we will go'. Jamie grinned at his father, and his heart was bursting with excitement not only with the thought of the adventure in front of him but also with love for his father.

Monday morning had arrived. Kate was ringing the bell on the big oak doors of Crompton Manor. She was wearing her best Sunday outfit of a simple blue cotton day dress that was as blue as the morning sky, with a matching bonnet that had two ringlets of her black hair curling down the sides of her face. Her beauty was apparent even at her young age. As she stood there waiting, she glanced around again at the size of the house and gardens. Then she looks up at the morning sky bright and clear with a few soft clouds drifting like wispy curls of hair and thought, it was going to be a lovely day. She turned as Mary answered the door, and Kate introduced herself and asked for Jamie.

'Please come in Kate, he is expecting you. I will tell him you are here, please wait.

Kate was amazed at the beautiful things all around her as she waited in the large entrance hall while. Mary went off to find Jamie. He came rushing down the stairs taking Kate by the hand and pulling her through the front door and over to the stables, telling her as they ran that they had to leave right away. The coachman and Jim were already harnessing up the horses to the carriage. Jamie introduced his father to Kate; she had suddenly become very shy.

'Hello Kate, I am so pleased to meet you, I've heard a lot about you,'

Jim put her at ease and made her welcome, he had the same captivating smile as Jamie had, Kate shook his hand and said she was happy to meet him too.

'Come on, you two, get in because I am the coachman today, so hold on tight,' Jim hurriedly ushered them into the carriage as the time had already passed and they had a lot to do today.

It took about an hour to reach Portsmouth docks; Kate and Jamie got out of the carriage and were thankful to stretch their legs after the long ride. Jim pointed to a cobbled road directly in front of them and said to Jamie,

'Remember what you have to do?' Jamie nodded. His father gave Jamie the letter, for Mr Humphreys.

'I will see you both later as I have other business to attend to'.

They set off up the narrow road, without a care in the world. They passed many shops, yards and houses, and there seemed to be people everywhere. Jamie stopped outside one of the workshops.

'It's a blacksmith's Kate! Jamie exclaimed. Don't you just love the smell of the hot shoes going on to the hooves of the horse'?

'Well I have smelled better things in my time' she said with a chuckle.

When they got within sight of the orphanage, Kate told Jamie.

'I am a bit concerned about what it may be like inside'.

'I am as well this is the first time for both of us, but then look on the bright side, we are helping some young boys and girls to better themselves'.

Kate agreed. They approached the large metal gate with thick strong iron hinges. There was a chain attached to a bell, and Jamie pulled on it. The bell rang loud and clear. They waited, and very soon, an old looking man appeared, opening the gate halfway just enough to stick his head out. The man was only about five feet tall with a hump on his back, which gave him round shoulders and stooped posture. His face was long with ridged lines running all different ways, making him look very evil. Suddenly he shouted at them in a harsh voice.

'My name is Sid what do you want?'

Jamie trying not to get to near the man because of the way he smelt, their noses started to wrinkle up and they tried to hold their breath for a minute. His clothes were nothing more than rags and had not seen soap and water for months.

'I have a letter to give to Mr Humphreys from my father Captain Heslop; I am here about the orphanage boys that work on his ship'.

The man opened the gate fully and told them to go to the office pointing to a door about a hundred yards away. Both Kate and Jamie were a little nervous as they walked across the yard to a small wooden door. Jamie knocked, and a voice told them to come in. Sitting behind a desk was a big fat fearsome-looking man eating a whole chicken. He was ripping off lumps of meat and stuffing them into his already full mouth. This was obviously Mr Humphreys, the proprietor of the orphanage. The room was airless and smelt of body sweat and stale food. Trying hard not to wrinkle their noses again, Jamie and Kate introduced themselves to him. They both could not stop staring at the man and were amazed at how huge his body was. He looked like an enormous egg with arms and legs coming out of it. His face and chin were so fat they could not distinguish where his chin ended and his neck began. It was impossible to tell how tall he was as he was sitting behind the desk, but observing that he was a big man, Kate felt sure his legs would not stand the weight of his overweight body.

'I have been asked to give you this letter from my father sir,'

He handed over the letter to him but before Mr Humphreys opened the letter, he spoke to Jamie. 'You must be Captain Heslop's son.' As bits of chicken and saliva came out of his mouth.

'I know your father quite well, he is a shrewd man'.

Then he carried on reading the letter and shouted out to the man that let them in.

'Sid, take these visitors to the workrooms and show them the twelve Heslop boys who had worked for him previously as well as…'

Jamie quickly interrupted before Mr Humphreys finished his sentence.

'Mr Humphreys, can we chose the other twelve extra boys and four girls ourselves that we need please Sir'?

Mr Humphreys nodded his consent, and they bade him good morning and followed Sid. He led them up a narrow hallway into a dark cramped room; where they saw the children sitting at the tables, sewing mailbags destined to deliver mail on large ships going to the colonies. What they saw horrified them; these poor children were wearing filthy rags as clothes and showed signs of being beaten.

They all needed a good wash and a decent meal. Jamie questioned the man called Sid when he noticed filthy straw pallets in the corner of the room where the children obviously slept.

Jamie was soon to ask. 'Why are these poor children kept like this?'

Sid shrugged his shoulders and informed them.

'Sir the children live sleep, and work in their rooms during the night, we lock the door, in case they tried to escape. The children might not realise it, but they are better off in here than outside on the streets'

Jamie turned his back on Sid and did not answer him, as he was so disgusted. Then he addressed the children.

'Who wants to come and work on Captain Heslop's ships for about six months'?

Every child in the dirty, straw ridden room had their hand up 'Me! Me sir!' they all shouted with a look of pleading in their young eyes as they were desperate to be picked. Sadly, Jamie knew they could not take everyone and the task of having to choose laid heavy on his heart. Firstly he asked Kate to pick out the four oldest and strongest girls for cleaning work then shouted out an order.

'I want the twelve boys to come forward who have worked for Captain Heslop'.

Twelve boys stepped forward eagerly, and then he selected twelve more. He found the decision harder than he had expected but chose the sturdiest-looking boys he could. Kate had picked out her four girls, and Jamie then addressed all the children they had chosen.

'I want you all to be ready at five o'clock Friday afternoon'.

'Yes sir' they shouted, congratulating each other for being chosen. Kate and Jamie bid the children goodbye. It was hard not to notice the ones not chosen having tears in their eyes, as Sid shouted at them all to get back to work. They stopped at the office on their way out to speak to Mr Humphreys, who was still eating, and told him they would be back for them at five o'clock on Friday afternoon. Mr Humphreys nodded.

'Tell your father I agree to the terms of his letter,' as he was still spitting food everywhere.

Jamie could hardly control his anger, as they walked through the yard and out of the orphanage gates, Kate started to cry.

'That was horrible Jamie I wanted to take them all the poor things,'

Jamie promised himself that one day, he would help all of them although he did not know how he was ever going to achieve it. He put his arm around Kate,

'Do not forget what we talked about on the way up here. At least, we are helping some of them'.

'Suppose you are right Jamie, but…',

'No buts, now, Kate, I can see why he is called Humphreys.' trying to lighten the mood.

'Why is that Jamie?'

'You see Kate, with a face like his; he will always have the hump!'

They both started laughing as they walked down the road. They had only gone about halfway down the cobbled road when they saw many people on the road looking up at a terrace house; pointing, and shouting, and some were screaming.
'Help! Help Me!' a woman was shouting,
'My two children are in there'.
They both ran to the house and saw the ground floor was ablaze. Jamie looked up and could just see two small children at the window. Someone shouted to the children to go to the back of the room. The two children must have heard, as there was no way anyone could get to the window or up the stairs as it was all ablaze. Jamie said to Kate in a strong voice.
'Please wait here and not move as I will only be a couple of minutes, no time to explain.'
He ran off, and within a few minutes, he returned running with 'The Towns Blacksmith' they had seen earlier, and he was now carrying a large hammer. Jamie and the blacksmith ran straight to the neighbouring house. Jamie kept shouting to the man,
'Follow me quickly there is little time'.
They ran straight up a flight of stairs into a room adjacent to where he thought the children would have gone. 'Now,' said Jamie to the blacksmith.
'Quick as you can knock a hole in this wall, big enough for me to crawl through'.
It only took the 'blacksmith' twenty seconds to make a hole big enough for Jamie to crawl through. The room was dark and full of smoke, he suddenly heard children crying. 'Don't be scared! I am here to save you now.'
He followed the sound of crying and found two children huddled together in the far corner of the room coughing as the smoke was black and thick, but otherwise seems fine, but were very frightened. The main thing was they were alive!

He quickly got hold of them and pushed them through the hole to the 'blacksmith', who pulled them all to safety. Jamie thanked the man, who had the two children under his arm.

'You go first,' Jamie shouted, 'I will follow you'. The blacksmith rushed down the stairs with a child under each arm, and he emerged from the front door. There was an almighty cheer "It's the blacksmith" someone shouted as the children's mother ran across to greet him, crying with relief; she gave him a big kiss as she took the children from him. The crowd picked up 'The Towns Blacksmith' and put him on to their shoulders. Shouting and singing, as they took him down the road to the local tavern for a beer as 'The Hero of the day'. Jamie waited to everyone had gone, then appeared from the side of the house and ran across the road to Kate. She had not moved from where Jamie had left her.

'What did you do to rescue them, Jamie?'

He grabbed her hand and swung her around. 'Quickly we have to go. I will tell you on the way'.

People were still passing buckets along a row of people from the communal pump to put the fire out. It was almost under control when the man who lived in the room of the neighbouring house arrived.

'That was close. When he finds a big hole in his bedroom wall, all hell will let loose,' Jamie said to Kate as they hurriedly ran down the road.

'So that's how you did it. You're amazing Jamie'.

Kate was very impressed at how quickly and effectively Jamie had rescued the young children. What a hero! She thought to herself. With a big smile, he looked at her and said.

'You know the saying, "Where there is a will, there is a way" but promise me, you will not tell anyone about what happened.

'I won't tell a living soul,' she replied with a smile on her face.

The pair laughed as they trotted down towards the harbour. As they approached his father's office, Jamie started getting excited. 'I am really looking forward to seeing the ship my Father has just brought.

I wish one day he would let me be in charge of her when I am older or when I can prove to him, I am good enough'.

'That's not a bad thing, Jamie. But you have to wait to the time's right for you and him'

.Jamie looked at her and nodded, thinking how sensible she was. They arrived at the office near the harbour and found Jim waiting for them.

'How did you both find things at the orphanage?' He enquired.

'It was terrible father to see the conditions those poor young children have to endure. We found it quite distressing, and that awful man, Humphreys, infuriated me'.

'Well, Son, I wanted to show you both how lucky you are in life and to appreciate what you have'.

'I always have, Father'.

'So have I, Mr Heslop,' agreed Kate.

Changing the subject, Jim said with a smile.

'Right, come on, you two we have a lady to christen., pick up that bottle of champagne, my young man and let's get on with it, '.

Jim went into the next office and asked Zak if he would like to go with them. Unfortunately, Zak was mumbling away to himself and appeared buried under mounds of paperwork and declined. Jim gathered up the pair of them and strolled off to the ship.

'Hurry up you two? We are meeting Temp there'.

As they were hurrying off to the ship, moored at the quay, Kate asked Jim, 'why Zak didn't want to come?'

'He is a miserable so-and-so,' Jim replied with a big grin on his face that made Kate and Jamie chuckle. When Jamie saw the ship up close he was amazed by how beautiful it looked, then right away asked if they could go aboard.

'No, my son, you know it's bad luck to go aboard before we have christened her, come on we go down these steps into that small boat then we have to row out to the ship's bow to christen her'.

As they started to get into the boat, they heard a shout 'Wait for me'. It was Temp trying to hurry, best he could down the harbour steps, with his leg given him pain, waving his walking stick and saying 'I wouldn't miss this christening for anything'. He had worked for many years as a competent sea captain in Jim's fleet. His face was sun bleached, from the many sea voyages over the years, his beard was grey and short, and the hair that remained on his head had turned grey as well. He was a loyal, honest, and a pleasant man, known for his fairness and honesty among mariners and reached the grand old age of sixty-five years.

'Temp, this is my friend Kate'.

'Hello Kate, nice to meet you'.

'Likewise,' Kate replied as they started to sit down on the boat. They pushed the boat out and then Jim started to row across to the ship. As they got to the bow Mr Heslop then gave Kate the champagne and said, 'Now, young lady would you do us the honour that champagne bottle that you are holding, we want you to smash it against the bow in a minute, right there! Jim pointed, 'and say these words' "I name this ship the "Lady Dorothea" and then say' May God bless this ship and all that sail in her.'

Kate was terrified and excited at the same time. She stood up and nearly fell over, as she was so nervous. Shuffling towards the ship's bow, carefully, not to rock the boat too much as the last thing she wanted was to tip the boat over. She kept repeating the words to say in her mind. Then Jim said, 'NOW KATE'! She said the words and smashed the bottle of champagne against the wooden bow, nearly falling over backwards and tipping the boat, and then all of them said together, 'God bless you Lady Dorothea'. They rowed the boat back to the quay steps and climbed out both Jamie and Kate eager to board the ship.

'Right son you two have a good look around the new Lady Dorothea, but only for an hour.

Both were so excited, Kate had never been on a ship before and was amazed at how big it was. While they were looking around the ship Jim had been giving out orders

Temp do you know a place I can buy potatoes, and carrots because I found out that Captain James Cook took a lot, of vegetables on his voyages to stop illnesses like scurvy and only two sailors became ill and later recovered. Jim wanted to prove the theory, by taken vegetables with him on this trip, storing them in barrels of peat, just to see if they lasted the journey, which keeps them from drying out. If it worked then I will use them on his long journeys to India and beyond.'

.Temp replied. 'I heard that too Jim, you should find these vegetables at the marketplace, by the church'.

'Thanks, Temp, good man 'I will go there in the morning, for now, could you make sure that her name is painted on the hull by tomorrow,'

'Ay-Ay Captain, certainly leave it with me'...

'Right I am going across to the office to instruct Zak, regarding the cargo for Friday, so both ships will be ready to sail on the high tide, all being well.'

Over an hour had passed before they were all back together. They bid farewell to Temp and went to collect the horse and carriage for the journey home.

Jamie said to his father, 'This definitely has been the most exciting day for Kate and me'.

His father smiled saying that 'My son it has been a pleasure'

When they arrived at their village, Jim pulled up at Kate's grandparents.. Kate looked at Jamie and his father and asked if they would like to meet her grandparents tomorrow, as they had offered them both an invitation, Jamie was first to reply.

'We both would like that very much shall we say noon'?

Jim quickly butted in., 'Hang on a minute there young man, I'm sorry Kate, perhaps when I come back from the West Indies? I am too busy, as we sail on Friday.'

She was happy that at least Jamie was coming.

Kate waved goodbye, thanking Jim for taking her along. 'My pleasure Kate and thank you as well for christening my ship.'

Jim and Jamie returned home to find the coachman waiting in the stables to take the harness off the horses, so on their way back towards the house. 'It is a shame Kate is not sailing with us on Friday, she would be good company for you'.

'It would be wonderful if she could to father I have not told her yet I am going with you'.

'I see that's a bit naughty son, however so why don't you ask her to sail with us?'

'Can I father? Kate is training to be an herbalist and maybe be helpful to us'.

'Yes, she could be very helpful son'.

'I will ask her tomorrow and let you know father', Entering the house, Jim turned around to his son.

'You know I think Kate is good for you. She is a very nice young girl, and you have an invite to meet her family'. He grinned as he added, 'When's the wedding then?'

Be quiet, Father' Jamie replied, as he became red-faced.

'Come on son, enough of this banter let us have our dinner.' Jim puts his arm around his son.

'Father, I love you'.

'I love you too, Son'.

The following day just before noon, Jamie set off to meet Kate's grandparents. He knocked on the door, Kate asked him in, and she introduced him to her grandparents. 'Take a seat young man'. Kate asked if he would like a cup of tea, to which Jamie accepted. Her grandmother seated herself opposite Jamie. 'I hear your father is sailing to the West Indies on Friday'.

'Yes, I am going with him as well. Then to his astonishment, she asked him something.

Can I be so bold as to ask you, if it wouldn't be a problem to take my granddaughter with you?'

Being relieved he quickly answered. 'Of course not a problem Mrs Clayton'

'We both want her to have the experience as we are too old to take her anywhere, and she needs to start being independent of us.'

Jamie did not know what to say as it came as a surprise and he had expected to ask them. He had to be calm even though he was so excited, knowing she might be sailing with him, clearing his voice with a cough he said. 'I would love to take Kate, Mrs Clayton. I am sure my father will be pleased as well'.

'Would you ask her now? But please do not say it was my idea'.

When everyone was sitting down, Jamie asked Kate the question but Kate was upset.

'Well I never so when were you going to tell me I would not see you again for six months or more.

Jamie's face had turned bright red and mumbled to her. 'Sorry, Kate I did not tell because I was hoping my father would take you with us, which I am sure he will.

Kate now understood his reason not to tell her.

Any way even if I could, I can't. I can't leave my grandparents alone'.

Kate's grandmother was soon to reply.

'Do not to be so silly Kate you must go we will both be fine, we have friends and neighbours if we needed help. It's a great opportunity that is hard to come by my child.'

'We both never have regretted letting your mother go off on adventures when she was about your age, then before she married she had seen life to the full, so you have to do likewise my love.'

Kate relented a little but was not sure about it, she looked at Jamie and said 'Are you sure? I won't be in the way?'.

'Do not worry about that. There is plenty of work available that you can do on board like maybe scrubbing the decks, and also don't forget your medical box'

Kate looked horrified for a moment and then released Jamie was joking, as the biggest smile came across his face. Mr Clayton sitting in his rocking chair burst out laughing saying. 'Spoken like a man Jamie' then they all had another cup of tea. Mr and Mrs Clayton wished them both good luck with their venture and a safe return.

Chapter 4

Before they knew it, Friday morning was upon them, the carriage fully loaded and standing outside the front doors of Compton Manor. The morning was chilly after last night's rain and the sky was still grey from the rain clouds. Jamie and his father said their goodbyes to everyone, put on their coats and made their way to the coach. Jamie jumped in the carriage with Peggy. Jim shouted up to the coachman. 'Everything loaded my man'

'Yes sir, the cats are in their baskets inside' Jim got in beside Jamie,

'Let's go and get Kate, my son.'

Jamie was hanging out the carriage window, showing the coachman the way to Kate's house, by using his hat and waving it around, as they arrived, Kate was coming out of her grandmother cottage with her grandparents. They loaded her belongings into the coach. Kate had tears in her eyes as she waved her grandparents goodbye from the coach as they set off to Portsmouth docks. During the journey, Jamie's father told Kate that she would have the boatswain's cabin but would have to share it with the two girls from the orphanage, and Temp also was organising the boatswain's cabin on his ship for his two girls. Jim's plan for getting there early was for Jamie and Kate, to explore the ship fully and sort out their sleeping quarters, then in the afternoon collect the children, and bring them down to dockside and get them ready for embarking.

Upon arriving, Jim told the coachman to take their luggage to the ship and make sure it was taken on board before returning home, the coachman nodded his head, and the three of them went into the office.

Jim asked Zak.' Is everything on board?'

'Yes, even what you bought and paid for the other day was delivered this morning; the ship's manifests are in order if you would like to check them, captain? '

Zak had loaded everything Jim instructed including the extra cargo he requested. The ships cook had already stored away all the fresh vegetables that Jim had ordered from the market the other day. 'Anything else you require?' Zak said with a little irritation in his voice.

'No, Thank you, Zak, that will be all, what would I do without you?' with a smile that had a thin line of a smirk in it. Nothing much passed Jim by, and he knew, Zak all too well. Zak thought likewise and replied.

'Well, you might need a partner one day.'

They looked at each other and gave a half-hearted smirk. No way thought Jim. He knows all about Zak actives, but put up with them for Edwina sake. 'Zak, just one thing more when I am away can you advertise to find families or companies that would like to colonise India as it is now under English rule? That's our next project'.

'Will do, Jim,' thinking to himself he was, going to do that anyway and, addition to that he had his own project he had in mind when Jim was out the way as he was free to do what he wished.

'Now, let us all have a cup of tea before we get on with preparing to sail.' said Jim.

Zak excused himself on the pretext of double-checking the ships were fully loaded and ready to sail, but he was checking his associates were all on board ship. After they had finished, Jim turned to Jamie and told him.

'Leave Peggy and the cats in the office for the time being, now off you two go I have work to do. Go on board and settle in and have a look round and sort things out, don't forget our young sailors.'

'No father I won't forget.' With that, Jamie and Kate left, eager to go on broad again and settle into what would be their home for the next few months. Zak returned, passing Jamie and Kate on the way out and had caught the tail end of what Jim had said.

'Jim what the hell are you taking kids again for? Surely, it is better to take men'.

'Look here, Zak, those kids will grow into good merchantmen one day.'

'Well Jim I still think it is a waste of time,'

'That's a matter of opinion,' Jim replied sarcastically.

Later that same afternoon, Jamie and Kate walked up the narrow cobbled road to the orphanage. The sun was still shining along with a light breeze; their hearts were filled with excitement at the thought of the adventure in front of them. They quickly hurried past the blacksmith shop; on reaching the orphanage gate they rang the bell. Sid opened the gate and let them in, telling them to follow him. He then leads them down a long corridor passing some of the children, in deplorable conditions. Some were crushing what looked like bones. In another room, young girls were sewing up ships sails and sailors clothing.

This formidable building, Jamie sadly thought it must be worse than a prison. Sid stopped in front of an unpleasant cold and dark room, where they found Mr Humphreys and the children they had selected all lined up and ready to go. They had no belongings with them other than the filthy rags they stood up in Jamie told the children to follow him. Jamie wanted to get Kate and the children out of there as soon as possible. He shook hands with Mr Humphreys and headed out the orphanage, and down the road towards the dock. Some walked, some skipped, and some even danced, then everyone ran the last few yards. Jamie understood the way they felt but needed to rein them in, then in a loud voice.

'Whoa...stop, listen carefully... when you're all on board, you all must all stay in their allocated sleeping quarters until the ship is well out to sea, and then the captain will send someone to call them up on deck'.

Jamie now wanted to divide the children into two groups. 'Attention. Hands up the boys that have sailed before?' Jamie waited for hands to go up. 'Right now, split yourselves into two halves, six in each group? Jamie waited patiently'.

'Now take six new boys, into each of your groups with two girls'? He waited patiently again.

'Now this group wait here,' pointing to the group to his right. 'We will be back for you shortly'

'Right you lot follow me' Jamie and Kate took them on board the Lady Dorothea. He showed the boys where they were going to sleep and reminded them to stay in their cabin until they were told to go on deck. Kate did the same with the two girls. Then he and Kate returned to the rest of the youngsters to take them on aboard the Earl of Cornwall.

On arriving Jamie cheekily asked Captain Temp to come aboard. Permission granted Master Jamie was Temps reply.

'Good evening, captain these are your children for your voyage'.

'Good evening children. Store them away below deck Master Jamie and I will speak to them when we are underway'

'Aye, aye captain' all of them grinning. Jamie and Kate took them below deck, when they returned back on deck the first thing Jamie was dying to ask Temp. 'Captain what was it my father brought, that is now on board your ship.' Temp smiled and told him. 'Are that will be the potatoes and carrots to see how long they keep onboard the ship, that's all.

Jamie thanked him, wished him a safe journey, then they both disembarked.

They met Jim heading up the gangplank he asked. 'Son is Temp ready to sail and have all the orphanage children settled in? Jamie told him they were, but he remembered he had to go and get Peggy and the cats from the office Jim said. 'Know son they were already on board in the lower deck.' Once they had all got on board they were met by the Bosun.

'Welcome aboard cap'n' Mr Thompson said with a big smile.

'Thank you, Bosun, can you make ready to set sail'

'Aye-Aye cap'n Then the Bosun shouted. 'All ashore that's going ashore' and all the crewman wives and families disembarked down the gangplank. Then the call was heard from both ships, as they get ready to sail, it was hard, heavy work as Kate watched in amazement at the amount of rigging, and sails that they set, within two hours, the lady Dorothea and the Earl of Cornwall raised anchor and set sail out of the harbour into the open sea.

The wind was favourable as they got under sail. Jim explained to Kate and Jamie, 'While we are at sea, I want you both to call me captain like the rest of the crewmen...not Father or Sir.

'Yes, cap'n,' they both replied with huge grins on their faces.

The captain smiled back at them and said. The children can go on deck now, but only for a while.' It was getting late when they reached the open sea, and the captain let the children have a good look round under the watchful eye of Jamie and Kate. Then made sure they were back in their sleeping quarters safely, and tomorrow, they could start their chores. Jim requested that later on that Jamie and Kate join him in his cabin for dinner and a chat.

'I want to see you both. Let's say nine o'clock'

'Yes, captain,' Jim walked off to inspect his ship. Kate and Jamie kept an eye on the children until it was time for them to leave the deck. After the children had eaten they took them all below to their bunk beds making sure they all was well. Then later on Kate met up with Jamie both commenting how well dressed they both were.

Kate asked. 'What does your father, oh sorry, I mean, captain, wants to talk to us about?'

'I haven't a clue. My guess is as good as yours.'

They knocked on the captain's door. A voice told them to enter. 'My, you are both looking smart, come and sit down you two and make yourselves comfortable.'

After they had eaten, the captain told them what it would be like in the ports around the West Indies 'Listen carefully it's going to be rough in the harbours you have to stay at his side at all times and that all the orphan children must stay on board. Because there are many undesirable people walking about in the harbour, beggars, thieves, and muggers. Crewmen loading and unloading cargo, and some will be trading with slaves brought over from Africa and sold to work on the plantations. It was deplorable the way they treated those poor people, and all he could do was turn his head the other way.

'Now the other main reason for this meeting..., and please Kate do not mention a word to anyone about what I am going to say to my son.'

She promised, feeling a little embarrassed to be privy to such confidences.

He turned to his son and, with a serious expression on his face.

'Jamie I want you to promise me, that if anything happens to me, never let Zak trade in slaves all anyone else do this terrible thing. Plus try to stop the slave trade whenever you get the chance, but please be careful.'

Jamie promised, 'Nothing is going to happen to you father. I mean, captain...please do not talk like this.

'Son you never know what's around the corner, especially when you're at sea months at a time but I am sure I live to a ripe old age, son'.

He didn't want to worry his son but had to prepare him. He went on to tell him he made a Will and it was lodged with a solicitor called Mr Westgarth.

'I did not know captain' He was feeling sad knowing that one day; his father would not be there for him.

'I am sorry Kate, but I had to tell my son what to expect and that I would like him to carry out my wishes'.

'I understand that captain, 'she replied. Then she changed the subject quickly and thanked him, for the warning now we know what to expect when we docked.

At that, Jim called it a day, stood up and walked them to the cabin door. They said their goodnights and made their way to their separate sleeping quarters, Jamie to where some of the boys were, Kate to the boatswain's cabin with the two girls. Kate found the two girls giggling and asked them, what was so amusing? They explained that they were having a problem getting into the hammocks. Every time they got in, it tipped over, and out they fell. Kate quickly undressed and put on her nightgown and decided to show the other two how to do it. She gently eased herself over the edge of the hammock and promptly fell out the other side. They all collapsed into fits of laughter. It took them a while, but eventually, they got the hang of it and were fast asleep in no time. They were exhausted with all the activity of the day.

The next morning, Jamie was up early and knocked on Kate's door, asking her if she was up. 'Just getting ready, see you on deck, Jamie!'

He climbed the wooden ladder, opened the hatch, and put his head out of the door. There was a steady breeze, which meant the ships should be making good progress. He saw his father already on deck giving orders and directing the crew. Jamie felt a surge of love for this man and walked towards him. Jim greeted his son commenting on how good the sails of the new ship were; it only took six men on each yardarm instead of twelve. Jamie noticed four men staring at them oddly; one with a patch on his left eye and smoking a pipe, the other had a facial scar covered slightly by his beard. The other two looked strangely, dirty looking and rather sly. As he stared back at them, they looked away, but Jamie felt unease, he did not remember seeing any of these men before, did a double take, before turning his attention back to his Father and listening to his father instructing the men. The four men are Zak's henchmen, on the ship to do the unspeakable deed of killing Jim and Jamie. The one with the patch over his eye was nicknamed Popeye and was the ringleader. He had a fat face pockmarked with scars from smallpox. They all had long dirty hair, which had been bleached by the sun and smells like dead fish.

Chapter 5

The day sped by; everyone on board was busy. The weather was holding, and there was a good stiff breeze. Excitement ran around the whole ship, as they grew accustomed to the ship's movement. The girls were in the galley, been taught to cook, clean, and wash clothes. The boys were been shown by Jamie, everything they needed to know about sailing the ship: how to tie knots, what ropes were connected to the yardarms as well as de-rigging and rigging them, and which sails to use in different winds. Later on in the afternoon, Jamie and Kate were resting on the deck, watching the sun sparkle across the water. Kate turned to Jamie,

'The young children are really enjoying being here. It is such a lovely adventure for them.'

'Yes, I have noticed they seem happier. It is a shame it will come to an end when we return home Kate.'

The captain strolled up and asked if they had had a good day. They replied they had, although very tired.

'Jamie, let's see how good you are. Have you noticed anything different with Temp's ship?'

'No captain. Should I'?

'Well, if you look at her sails, she is not using one of her main topgallant sail.'

'Why is that, captain?'

'That's because she is a faster ship than ours. Otherwise, we could not keep up with her.'

'Do you know why we sail together, Son?'

'Yes, captain. It is for protection against pirates but we have double gun power now.'

Jim said that is correct, as there are a lot of pirates where we are going. Jamie asked if he would show him and the boys how they load and fired the cannon. Jim said he would tomorrow, two of the boys Mitch and Joe Ben, have already, been taught how to fire a cannon already and a swivel gun when they sailed the first time. We will see tomorrow if they still remember how to fire one.

'Now, I want you to get ready to try and beat me at sword fencing. If you win, I will call you my young man, not my young 'son'

'You may start calling me that now, captain' Jamie said with a big smile.

'Ah-ha, that's only if you win my boy'?

Jamie told his father he would be ready within half an hour, called his dog and left to get his sword and a stout leather jacket for protection.

It was not long before they were both on deck and ready to start, with nearly all the ship's company there to watch. They crossed swords and stepped back.

Someone said, 'On the third count, start fencing. One... two... three,' then the cheering started. Jamie was defending for about ten minutes. He then began to back away, stumbled on some rope, and fell into the arms of one of the girls. He found himself staring up at a cheeky face with large green eyes and beautiful long golden sandy hair. 'Sorry, miss...'

'That's fine, handsome. You can drop into my arms any time'.

Jamie jumped up and carried on fencing. They fought over every inch of the deck, jumping across ropes, leaping over barrels, and dodging rigging when Jim started to tire. By this time, Jamie was getting the upper hand, and Jim shouted out,

'I submit, young man.' The crew cheered, and a huge roar bellowed throughout the ship.

'Well done, young man!' Jim put his arms around, Jamie, saying. 'Jamie, you are really a young man now. I am very proud that you are my man. You fought brilliantly. Your late mother would be proud of you.'

'Thank you, captain.' Jamie said with pride in his voice.

Kate, the two girls and all the young boys congratulated Jamie, as Jim shouted out,

'Come on, you scum-bags. There's work to be done.'

They all smiled and shouted, 'Aye, aye, captain.'

Some of the crew scurried to return to work. The younger ones carried on with their jobs. Jamie turned to Kate. 'What is that girl's name, the one I fell on?'

'She is called Sarah, but everyone calls her Sam, because of her sandy hair, she is a bit of a tomboy and undoubtedly could give you a run for your money in a sword fight. She is very pretty and about your age even if she does dress as a boy. I feel a twinge of envy, her beautiful long hair and the freckles sprinkled across her nose. She seems to be good at everything she attempts, but she has such a good sense of humour you can't help but like her'.

'Very interesting,' he said with a grin.

'Kate, before you go, I have noticed you've been teaching the two girls to read and write in their spare time. Would you mind doing the same for the boys?'

'I'd love to. I didn't ask you about this because you were always giving them something to do, like taking them up on the yardarms and showing them how to raise and lower the sails.'

'Your right Kate but I was only carrying out captain's orders, but I will find the time for you to teach my boys, to read and write it will be great for them.'

They went their separate ways to oversee the children but met later at dinner. Jim again congratulated Jamie for getting the better of him with the sword, and they all laughed. Then after they had finished dinner Jim told them both.

'Our two ships are going to dock at a big island called Cuba and unload the cargoes from both ships. Most of it is important equipment for the plantations, and they, in turn, will be trading with their sugar, tobacco, cocoa, and coffee beans. Jamie, I must repeat again that you and Kate must stay with me at all times when we go ashore.'

They both assured him they would, and as they turned to leave, Jim said to Kate, 'Could you stay a minute? I have something to tell you in private.'

Jamie was curious about what Jim wanted to talk to Kate about but obeyed his father and left the cabin. Jim asked Kate to sit down.

'Kate, don't worry. It is just a chat about my son. I can see he likes you a lot. I just want to say I am so pleased you are friends. You both seem to be so happy with life. It makes it easier for me knowing he is happy when I go off sailing.' Kate got up to leave when Jim continued, 'Just before you go Kate... please don't tell him what I am going to tell you. I think he will make an excellent captain, but for now, I want him to enjoy life before he takes command of a ship.'

'I won't say a word about it, captain,' she smiled and left.

It was not long before Jamie caught up with her and asked what his father had wanted to talk to her about. With her hands on her hips and looking at him squarely in the eyes, 'mind your own business as it was a private matter between the captain and me'.

She turned abruptly on her heels and walked away; leaving Jamie standing with his mouth opens in astonishment. The following day, the captain summoned Mitch and Joe Ben on deck along with Jamie, The hardships of the orphanage, showed neglected, ill-treatment, and deprivation, upon these boys. Mitch was tall and thin as was Joe Ben or JB for short, but was slightly shorter. Despite what they had suffered, both were eager to please and learned everything with ease. They were reintroduced, to Mr Thompson, the boatswain although; Jamie had met him several times before. He was a likeable man in his late forties, always wore a hat to cover up the lack of hair on his head but made up for it on his face. The captain told the boys in a stern voice.

'I want you all to go with Mr Thompson, Mitch and JB can show my son what you have learnt about firing a swivel gun and cannon.'

They went with the boatswain to the armoury; both of the boys showed Jamie what they had learned about firing the cannon, and the swivel gun. The boatswain pushed the swivel gun and the cannon partly pocking out through the porthole and prepared them for firing. Stand well back lads and watch,' said the boatswain.

They kept well back with their fingers in their ears to avoid the recoil from the cannon. There was an almighty bang as it emitted clouds of smoke, making them all cough.

'Now for the swivel gun lads,' again he loaded it and fired a shot. Jamie stood up and said 'That was not as noisy as the cannon.' The boatswain laughed and replied,

'I have been told to practise this with you boys once a day until we dock. Cap'n orders.'

As the days passed, the weather stayed in their favour, so they made good time. Within a few days, they would be close to the West Indies, and everyone on board had been told to look out for ships, as there may be pirates about. Lookouts were posted from the crow's nest day and night. The four men whom Zak had hired were getting concerned about the weather not being in their favour for the assassination of Jamie and his father, but as Zak had said to them, there was always the return journey. The two ships had good luck and did not encounter any pirates. One evening just before dusk, they entered Havana Harbour. They had been at sea for seventy-two days and had timed it just right and just missed the rainy and muggy season of the tropical climate of Cuba and now it was dry and relatively cool. Jamie asked JB if he would look after his dog Peggy and his cats the next day as he was going ashore with the Captain. JB readily agreed as he liked Jamie's pets. The captain put out an order for all the crew to assemble on deck. When everyone had arrived, he addressed them all.

' We are weighing anchor in about an hour, it will be dark and no one is to disembark until the morning that is for their safety and in the morning only a few of them will disembark at a time. He goes on to say, that most of the crew are aware of what the situation is here, but the new members of the crew and the younger ones need to be told about Havana Harbour and the dangers of docking here. This is a slave port and sometimes slaves will escape under the cover of darkness, as it's a lot easier for them to hide and then make their escape. That's why it's dangerous when the sun goes down in the harbour. Slaves hijacking ships, seek out anyone carrying a gun or knife, even if they die doing it. They have taken people hostage, using them as a shield, all because they are desperate to escape by any means possible so for those reasons, everyone must stay on board until the morning, and the youngsters must stay on board at all times. 'So the only one to leave the ship tonight is me and the docking crew who will go ashore and dock the ship safely and then return on board to keep watch, but everyone needs to be vigilant at all times. Dismissed and stay safe'. OH, just one other thing I will be going aboard the Earl when she docks just to make sure they are all fully aware of the situation'.

Aye-aye captain came back the reply the new members of the ship's crew, plus the orphans, looked worriedly at one another, fearful of being perhaps being killed by slaves. They soon dispersed and went about their jobs while the tricky business of docking the ship with everyone staying vigilant at all times.

When the Earl of Cornwall had docked also, Jim went aboard, only to find some of Captain Temp's crew had fallen ill. Temp told Jim it had only happened two days ago. Some of the sick men were responding to treatment, so he did not think it was serious.

Jim asked if his doctor was coping, and Temp replied that he felt he was so far. Jim told Temp to address his crew with the same instructions that he had given his crew and made it clear to Temp that if any more men fell sick, he let him know right away. And that it would be better if only a few men went ashore the next day to unload the cargo, Temp agreeing with a nod of his head.

Early the next day, they started to unload the cargo on to the quay and then on its way to the holding warehouses that had been allocated to them in the port. Jim, Jamie and Kate had disembarked and were heading to the harbour offices to meet up with the harbour master whom Jim had dealt with in the past.

His name was Mr Dave Sayers. He was a fat man, who smelled sweaty and stared at them through narrow green eyes. They shook hands, and Jim introduced Jamie and Kate. Jim told him he would like to trade again for sugar, coffee, cocoa, and anything else he had in exchange for the cargo they were unloading. He went through their inventory, emphasizing he had a lot of machinery for the plantations as well as tools and some clothing.

'Yes, we can do a deal, Jim. All we have to do now is agree on the trading amounts and see if there is going to be money involved. By the way, have you any slaves on board? They're fetching a good price now.'

'No, I don't deal in slaves,' was Jim's quick reply.

'Ah well, that's a pity. I'll have to make do with what you've offered me then Jim.'

Mr Sayers and Jim came to an agreement on the trading goods and they agreed to help each other unload and load the cargo. Both were happy as no money was involved. They said their goodbyes and went on their way. As they went outside, Jim told Jamie and Kate to stay close as he was going to show them around the harbour. Kate and Jamie had been looking forward to this, as they had heard so many stories about its vibrant atmosphere. Kate was amazed. She had never seen anything quite like this in her life, slaves working hard and a master whipping those who slacked.

She was soon to say in a harsh voice, 'I think it's terrible the way they are treating those slaves. Look at that beastly man. He is using a whip on them.'

'I know, Kate, but there's nothing anyone can do about it until they change the law.'

Jim pointed out, not liking the situation himself.

'Captain I hope it is soon and they should change the law for the poor orphanage children as well,'

'Yes, I agree with you young man. It's a harsh world we live in.'

They walked around for a while watching the ships being unloaded and loaded. Spotting a Tavern, they stopped for a drink.

When they were sat with steaming mugs of coffee, Jamie said with a big broad smile, 'Captain, are the potatoes and carrots keeping in good condition whilst in storage?'

'How did you know that?' Jim replied. Jamie smiled and replied, 'A little bird told me.'

'That bird's name must be Temp then.'

They all laughed. 'Jamie, do you know why I am doing it?'

Jamie jokingly replied, 'Probably because when you retire, father, not only will you go fishing you'll farm as well'

'Ha-ha, very funny young man'.

Jamie and Kate could not stop laughing, they laughed so much that they were not listening to Jim trying to speak.

'Stop laughing, you two, and listen to what I have to say. When we return to England, the next journey is to India and that could take six to eight months at sea before we get new supplies. Eating fresh vegetables will stop the crew from getting scurvy. So if my potatoes and carrots stay fresh on this journey, I will definitely be taking them with me on the journey to India.'

'Captain I was told the same thing by my Sunday school teacher about eating fresh vegetables, like carrots and potatoes, but also sauerkraut on long voyages, as it helps to stop scurvy,' Kate added.

'Yes I've heard that too. Come along both of you, I need to get back to my ships to make sure everything is going to plan. Go aboard and make yourselves useful as I'm going to see if any of Temp's crew is getting over their sickness.'

He remembered what Kate had said about her herbs medicine and maybe she could help in some way but put it to the back of his mind for the moment. He knew Temp has his own doctor of sorts on board trying to help. Therefore, he was going to see how he was performing. I hope that he had found out what the illness was and whether it was an infectious disease. If it was an infectious disease, he didn't want Kate or Jamie anywhere near the Earl. He also didn't want Temp's crew infecting his crewmen either. So he had kept his distance from the ship and insisted both crews stayed away from each other and the ship's as much as possible to stop it spreading to the Lady Dorothea. He turned to make his way over to the Earl. Everyone had been working hard on the ships, unloading and loading the cargoes. When both ships were loaded with their new cargo, Jim heard Captain Temp had sent one of his crewmembers over asking him to come over to see him. He still hoped everything was fine with Temp's ship. They were catching the high tide in three hours' time. He left instructions that nobody leaves the ship, and to make sure everything is ready to sail as he wanted to leave the harbour without delay'

'Aye, aye, captain.'

When Jim arrived aboard the Earl, wearing a mask around his mouth, he enquired as to the whereabouts of Captain Temp. The first mate informed him that captain Temp was in his quarters awaiting your arrival. Jim went down to the captain's quarters only to find poor Temp ill in bed. 'How are you "old man"?

'Could be better Jim'

'Will the ship be ready to sail tonight?' asked Jim concernedly.

'Yes, all is ready apart from a few items that the crew are seeing to now'

'Temp, I am going to have a word with your boatswain just to make sure.'

'I'm afraid he has gone to his quarters with the same illness... so has the doctor' Temp replied reluctantly. With that, Jim started scratching his head, pondering over what they should do.

'Do you have anyone other than the second mate to take charge of the ship, Temp'?

Temp replied that he hadn't. Jim knew the second mate on his own did not have enough experience, and he didn't really want to put anyone else at risk of becoming ill. He paced up and down, still scratching his head and pondering what he should do. Then he thought there were two people he could send over but didn't feel comfortable doing this. But didn't have a choice, they were young, fit, strong and healthy enough to not catch the disease.

He would have to send his son and Kate, as they have experience in both problems.

Temp, this is what I am going to do. 'I'll send over my son and his friend, Kate. She has had some medical training and can help those who are sick. My son, as you know, is quite capable of taking over as junior captain along with the help from your second mate until all of you have got over this illness.'

'Thanks Jim for the help'

'I will send them over straight away. Get back on your feet "old man".

Temp was feeling better already now the problem had lightened. He lay back in his bed with a big grin on his face. Jim left, concerned as to whether he had made the right decision then believing that a problem had been solved but. Before he left the ship he looked around just to make sure everything was ready for sailing. He told the second mate he will send Jamie over to work with him and a young girl called Kate to help with the sick. He then left and hurried over to his ship, calling his head boatswain. 'Find my son and Kate. Tell them to come to my cabin straight away.'

The boatswain went off in search for Jamie and Kate, who both immediately went to Jim's cabin, giggling along the way, unsure of what was going on but not concerned, as they were just happy to be on this journey.

When they arrived, Jim told them of the problems with the illness affecting Temp and his head boatswain and that he wanted Jamie together with Temp's second mate to take the captaincy of the ship, running it jointly until the men were well enough to work again. He asked Kate, would she mind taking over from the doctor because he was also ill?

They were both delighted to help and looked forward to the return trip ahead with anticipation. Jim thanked them both and told Jamie a couple of things about what he had to do on the way to England, such as what time they were to set sail shortly. This was important as the sea is unpredictable, and leaving at the wrong times could bring all sorts of problems. Kate and Jamie rushed off to pack their things. When they were both ready, Jamie went to see JB and asked him to look after his pets again. He also asked him to make sure the young girls, boys kept learning, and to make sure they obeyed the captain's orders at all times. Just before they were about to leave, Jamie's father gave him a letter to give to Temp. Jim was proud and saddened as well as he realised his son was growing up fast and he had to let him go, but he was still that little boy who was innocent to the world in his eyes and wanted to keep him safe. Jim squeezed Jamie hard and told him how proud he was of him and said his goodbyes. He then turned to Kate, gave her a hug as well, and wished them both a safe journey home.

One of the four men whom Zak had hired to kill Jamie saw them leaving to go on to the other ship. This was not part of the plan. He then spoke to the other three men, and they agreed that they would continue with the plan to kill the captain when the opportunity arose but they would have to deal with Jamie another day. Jamie and Kate boarded the Earl.

The second mate greeted them warmly. 'You must be Jamie, and you must be Kate,' he said with a nice smile. 'They call me Spider, but I will make sure the crew call you Skipper and me Bosun.'

Spider was about thirty-five, very thin with many lines etched on his sunburned face. He was a cheerful person, who always looked on the bright side of things but with much experience of sailing. Jamie and Kate looked at each other and exchanged a secret giggle. Spider had long grey hair, which looked like it had not been washed for years. It was so matted that it looked like a spider's web, which was probably how he got his name.

Spider ordered the crew to show Jamie and Kate to their cabins. Kate met the two girls who she had picked to go on this voyage and asked them how it was going. They said that it would be better if there were not the sickness aboard, even with that, it was better than the orphanage. After she had arranged her belongings, she asked the girls to take her to the men who were sick. She was appalled to see that the men were in a dark and dingy place and that they were very sick. Kate was afraid that this was too much for her, but she had to at least pretend. That she knew what she was doing. She immediately instructed the two girls to open all the hatches and doors to let in the fresh air. Then she told the girls to fetch fresh water and towels whilst she checked the men's pulses and asked questions about their illness. Kate was doing a great job. The crew warmed to her and always did as she asked. Jamie, on the other hand, went on the top deck to join Spider.

They had agreed to work in two shifts, but for now, they had to get the ship ready to sail. Jamie was excited to be a part of this, and as he was a junior captain, he needed to gain the respect of the crew. He worked hard and prepared the ship for sailing, and it wasn't long before the anchor was raised and the ship was unmoored. They were off... slowly behind his father's ship. With Spider and Jamie giving out orders, it was working out quite well. The two ships left the port, and it was not long before they were at full sail.

When the initial rush of the open sea had calmed down, Jamie and Spider sat down to discuss how they would work the shifts between them. It was agreed to have half of the crew doing the first six hours under Spider and that Jamie would do the second six hours until morning. They then agreed to take it in turns thereafter doing eight-hour shifts so the men would be well rested between shifts. They arranged to meet in the ship mess room after each shift to give the coordinates and discuss any problems. Jamie was too excited to sleep, so he went to see Kate. 'How are you coping?'

'Fine, Jamie. I might know what is causing the illness. I am sure it is food poisoning'.

Kate found out the men had all the same symptoms. All complaining of stomach pains and diarrhoea, that would have given them a fever. She was making sure they drink plenty of water and keep warm. She told Jamie they remember eating smelly meat, which she didn't think was cured enough. Jamie looked concerned. 'Kate, I hope you are right. I will find the bad meat and destroy it.' Kate told Jamie that the men should be fine in a few days and he would be at full-crew capacity again. Jamie went to find Temp to tell him of Kate's findings. He told Temp what Kate had said, that it might be food poisoning, which was good news as then the crew would soon be better and the ship would be in full sail. Temp was delighted, 'If that's the only thing wrong, Master Jamie then that means all of us should be fine in a few days.' Jamie agreed. Then within a few days, all the men had recovered from their sickness and had returned to work. Jamie gave the letter to Temp and in doing so asked him how the orphanage children were performing on his ship. Temp said that he was delighted with them all, especially one girl who had made him a very good soup and that some of the boys loved going up the mast, helping the men with the rigging. He also said that they would be welcome aboard his ship anytime, and as for Kate, he could not speak highly enough of her for what she had done for himself, and the rest of his men and Jamie remembered he had a letter from his father to give to Temp when he felt better. So when Temp and Jamie were alone, he gave Temp his father's letter but told him it wasn't important and open it when he felt better. When Temp found the time to read the letter, it contained orders as to what he should do when they had sailed clear of the pirate-infested waters. He was ordered to go full sail to go and get to Portsmouth first, to unload his cargo and get

Zak to arrange the sale of it all, including the cargo aboard the Lady Dorothea. The letter continued to say the next journey would be to India and if he could help Zak to organise the loading of the new cargo that he should have already stored in the warehouse.

After a few weeks, after having left Cuba behind them, Temp called Jamie to his cabin and told him the contents of the letter. Jamie noticed a violin in a cupboard and asked him about it, 'Does it play?'

'As far as I know, it does.' Temp changed the subject and explained that he thought the weather was going to get stormy that night because being an old sailor he could predict the formation of the clouds and reminded Jamie to keep the boys in their cabins if it happened. Jamie replied that he would make sure and asked Temp if he would mind telling him about the islands in the Indian Ocean, especially the one he told his father about. Temp grinned. 'You have been talking to your father.' I said to your father that if we ever get time, one day, we all should go there. But unfortunately, like everything else, we have never had the time, and I'm getting too old'

Temp told Jamie, he had a map and was going to give it to him and his father when they got back to England as it was in his cupboard at home we will have to be careful with it as its very old. The map Temp remembered, gave navigational references as to which route to take. It also said what the place was like. His memories of the map were a little vague, but he remembered some of it. He continued to explain that they are called the Keeling Islands. Because they had been discovered by captain Keeling around the year 1610 but had remained uninhabited since. The islands consisted of two atolls and quite a number of coral islands, but there were two larger ones. Altogether, they covered about five square miles, the most northern one being the smaller of the two. Both the big islands had coconut palms and other vegetation covering them. The other small islands had the same vegetation surrounded by a clear blue sea full of fish swimming around the coral reefs. Temp said that he saw no reason for these islands to be any different and that they sounded like paradise. He explained that Jim had bought the Lady Dorothea so that it would go through the only entrance into those islands, if they were all to go there one day; they could sail right up close to the beach to collect the coconuts from the trees. He described the islands with a great passion it was obvious that he was disappointed that he may never see it. Jamie was impressed and curious; he thought it was the best thing he had ever heard. He pictured his father and himself running around the island, swimming in the sea, and fishing with nothing and no one to worry about apart from themselves.

'Wow! It sounds wonderful,' Jamie said dreamingly.

'Jamie, before you go… the map does not mention anything about drinking water, but from my experience, if there's vegetation, fresh water must be there.'

'Thanks, Temp, for telling me all about the islands,' but he insisted that Temp would be going with him and his father one day.

Temp nodded his head and smiled. They went on deck to see what the weather was like and looking up at the sky, they observed it was very grey with dark black clouds.

'Jamie It doesn't look good. I want you to tell all the crew that there is a storm brewing, and once the wind gets up, the ship's bell must be rung, and I expect all hands on deck.'

'Yes, captain,' but for now, he really wanted to see if his father's ship was in view, so he looked through the telescope but could not see him. Temp looked at Jamie and realised he was getting upset. 'Your father's ship is probably a day behind us by now.'

'Yes! Captain you could be right.'

'Jamie, I know you like to help, but when the storm hits, I want you to look after the youngsters below and check that the valuable cargo isn't getting wet.' Jamie was upset, but an order was an order, and he unwillingly agreed. He went below to look for Kate and found her sitting with the other girls. 'It's good having you all here. A storm is brewing and my advice to you is not to eat too much now' said Jamie.

'Why is that, sir?' one of the girls asked.

'You'll find out soon enough all of you must not leave the cabins until it has passed.'

He went off to tell the boys the same. Two hours had passed when he heard the ship's bell ringing and Temp shouting out, 'All hands on deck!'

The storm had begun; the sky darkened, and the wind lashed against the remaining sails. The ship was heaving in the swell, and seawater was washing over the deck.

The sails had to be hauled in and secured. The crew were battling the elements and struggling with the wind. All but the forestaysail remained as it helped keep the ship on course. It was getting very dark, and the ship was rolling from side to side and heaving up and down. Some of the youngsters were frightened, and Jamie felt it was up to him to try and comfort them. He gathered them all together in the biggest area below deck, began to sing, and tried to get them to do the same. One of the boys asked Jamie if he had a fiddle or a violin that he could play. 'What is your name?' Jamie asked the boy with long ginger hair.

'My name is Alan, but everyone calls me Dingle. I think it's because I have Irish blood in me.'

'All right, Dingle,' Jamie chuckled. 'I know where there's a fiddle or a violin. I have seen one in a locker in the captain's quarters, but I'm not sure whom it belongs to, almost certain no one owns it anymore, so I'll try to ask the captain if we could have it.'

He knew that he could not go on deck but managed to get Temp's attention even though the wind was howling, and shouted at the top of his voice to him.

'May I borrow the violin?'

'Take it by all means and the dust as well. I am glad to see it go.' Jamie managed to find it, rushed back, and handed it to Dingle.

To everyone's surprise, the young boy played incredibly well. One of the girls began to sing, the children sang and danced to the music, and they forgot about the storm. With the ship's movement, it added to their laughter.

The storm lasted just over four hours, by this time, they were all ready to get in their hammocks, but the following day, it was back to the old routine for them all. Any spare time for the youngsters was taken up by Kate, teaching them to read and write as she had done with the others on Jim's ship. During the day, Kate found Jamie and asked,

'As there is a good breeze, would it be possible for them to fly a kite from the ship as it would be a lot of fun'?

Jamie had to think for a moment. 'I do not see any reason why not. All I have to do is to go down to the carpenter's workshop and make a couple up.'

'Wonderful.' said Kate. Jamie told her he would let her know when he had made them. It did not take him long, and he came back with the kites. Kate was waiting with excitement as she had really enjoyed flying them before with Jamie.

'We will have to go to the bow of the ship to catch the breeze,' said Jamie.

'Of course, the wind blows from the back of the ship. Oh sorry Jamie Stern,' Kate replied with a little grin. After a few attempts, the kites gained height, increasing in speed as they cleared the sails. Kate was getting a lot better at making the kite go left and right, gain height, and swoop down again. They were enjoying themselves so much they carried on until well into the evening.

The next day, all the youngsters were back to their chores. Jamie noticed that the biggest and strongest of the boys had taken the helm, closely observed by Spider, the second mate. 'Spider, how is this young man performing at the Helm?'

'I think he is very good, almost better than you were when you were at the helm and learning to do the same last year. So I have been led to believe,' Spider replied with a big grin on his face. Jamie ignored his remark but smiled. He turned to the lad and asked him to remind him of his name. He noticed he was a big lad for his age and obviously had thrived from being away from the orphanage. 'Mick,' he replied.

'Well, Mick, congratulations on doing a good job, and one day my father could offer you work doing this on his ships.'

'I wish he would because I hate knowing I have to go back to that orphanage, that Mr Humphreys could send me and the others up north to work in the cotton mills one day.'

'Not if my father can help to put a stop to it for you all, I promise you, Mick, I will do everything in my power to get you all out of there.'

Over the next few days, all the youngsters worked very hard; then one evening, the captain asked Kate if the young man would like to play the violin and the girl to sing again, but this time on the amidships deck.

The captain had heard the music and laughter coming from the youngsters' cabins during the storm and wanted to see them enjoying themselves but most of all for himself and his crew to join in. That evening Kate could not get them all together quick enough. Dingle would start playing the violin, with the rest of the orphan's singing and dancing. This became a nightly habit for the rest of the journey.

They crossed the northern Atlantic with no mishaps, avoiding a few icebergs and sorry to have left the warm climate of the West Indies for the cold winds as they sailed nearer to the English coast. Christmas came and went, no roast beef and plum pudding for them, just an extra church service conducted briefly by Captain Temp.

Chapter 6

The days flew by, and it was not long before a sailor shouted from the crow's nest, 'Land ahoy!' It was the English coast at last, and the ship proceeded along the coast towards Portsmouth harbour. Within hours, the crew were docking. The youngsters were not excited to be back and sorry that their journey together was ending. With a mixture of smiles and sadness, the children got ready to disembark, when the captain told them to wait a minute, as he wanted to say something to them before they left. He told them it had been a pleasure to have such young people on board and said 'You all have made my ship come alive on this journey. I hope I have the privilege to sail with you all again.'

The crew shouted to them loudly, 'Hip, hip, hooray!' and threw their hats up into the air. Temp made sure he shook hands with them all as Jamie and Kate led them off the ship. Most of the children hung their heads in silence, struggling to hold back the tear. Kate said to Dingle, 'I see you have left the violin in the cabin. I will take care of it until the next time.'

'I hope so madam,' Dingle thought to himself but was feeling too emotional to answer her. When they arrived at the orphanage, Sid opened the door and told the children to go to their workroom. Tears were stinging their eyes with the sorrow of coming back as they bid farewell to Kate and Jamie, who walked away also wiping tears from their eyes as they went to meet Mr Humphreys. Jamie told him that his father would bring the rest of the youngsters back and pay him what he owed him, once he had returned as his ship was about two days out. Mr Humphreys was not looking too happy as he was expecting to get paid but grunted that he had no option but to wait.

They both left not saying a word to each other as they walked back to the docks as they got to the office, they met Temp about to go in as well. As Jamie opened the door, Zak jumped up and was astonished to see him. He was taken by surprise.

'What's the matter, uncle? You look as if you have seen a ghost.' Zak coughed and spluttered, 'I thought you were sailing with your father?'

'I was, but then a problem arose, so we had to sail back on the Earl. Is it a problem, Uncle?'

'No, no, it's no problem at all,' he said, still trying to come to terms with seeing him.

Temp told Zak about the orders in Jim's letter. 'I don't know about any orders in a letter unless Jim's changed his mind. I only know the orders he gave me before he left,' muttered Zak.

'He said my orders were to get everything ready for the next sailing, to India, and that I have taken care of. Well, most of it.' Temp was getting annoyed.

'This letter says he has asked me to tell you to sell what is on board my ship and his straight away. Zak inquired as to what sort of cargo Temp was carrying and what sort Jim had on board.

Temp explained the cargo he had on board and that Jim was carrying pretty much the same. Zak told Temp. 'I can easily get a buyer for all the cargo on the two ships straight away.

Then with a bit of luck, both ships should be unloaded by early next week or at the latest at the end of the week.'

Thinking to himself, they were playing straight into his hands! Temp was getting irritated by now and told Zak.

'I will take charge of all this, once they have unloaded the Earl they can start loading it with non-perishable goods, which would not take too long at all. Both ships could be loaded by the end of the week, then a couple of days before they are due to sail, we'll load the main food and animals. This can be done provided Jim's ship returns in the next two days.'

Zak still in shock agreed without a mown, the three of them left Zak and returned to the ship. On the way, Jamie asked Temp if he was going to India with his father.

'No, I have decided not to, as I am too old to be an active captain, so when I have got both ships loaded and ready to sail, I am going to retire as I will not work in this dockyard under that the man.'

'Temp my faithful friend, I will miss you and so will my father '.

'Hang on a minute you are not getting rid of me that easy. I will always be around the harbour to see you and my friends. So I won't be gone for good'

They all ended up laughing, Temp patted Jamie on the back' When they arrived back on the ship, Temp went to supervise the unloading of the cargo. Kate and Jamie went to the cabins to clean and gather their clothes and belongings together. They missed the children and the hustle and bustle of the ship, now it felt like a ghost ship. Jamie began to think about Kate and her grandparents and he sensed she might be missing them. 'Would you like to go home to see your grandparents Kate?'

'I would rather like to stay here with you until your father arrives.'

He shook his head in approval and smiled at her. They both agreed to work on the ship for the next couple of days or until the Lady Dorothea docked.

Two days later one of the crew upon the rigging shouted loudly, 'It's the Lady Dorothea'. Kate and Jamie ran to the quarterdeck. Jamie grabbed a telescope and focused it on the Lady Dorothea. All he could see was there Flag flying at half-mast, he shouted to Temp. 'Why is their flag flying at half-mast? What does it mean?'

Temp rushed up behind him with Zak strolling behind him. Temp grabbed the telescope from Jamie and looked towards the Lady Dorothea. 'Someone's died, my boy,' Temp said in a loud voice.

With that, all went quiet. Everyone including the wives and children, rushed down to the quay to wait for the ship to dock. All of them were so anxious to find out who had died. Something was gnawing away at Jamie and he started to feel sick. Time was going slowly. Everything rushing by and he was standing still. The whispering started, the crew trying to guess who it was. All Jamie could do was waiting and pray that it was not his father.

The ship entered the harbour and slowly moved towards the dock area. As soon as Temp saw the head boatswain, he shouted to him,

'Where is your captain?' It seemed strange he wasn't on the deck, and fear started to grip him. The boatswain made a crucifix sign and shouted back. 'God rest his sou.'

All the crew and bystanders took their caps off, placed them on their chests, and lowered their heads. Jamie screamed out, 'Oh no! Please God, not my father!' He pushed his way to the front. Temp fell down as his bad leg gave way, and he buried his head in his hands, mumbling to himself, 'No...no...no.' Kate was trying desperately hard not to cry as she put her arms around Jamie, who was shouting.

'Why- oh- why- oh- why, in God's name, it was my father!'

Someone had helped Temp up, not speaking but trying to console him, the only way seamen knew. The ship finally docked. Jim's boatswain came down the gangplank and they all went off to the office to discuss what had happened Zak was the first to ask the Boatswain 'What the hell happened?'

'The Captain fell overboard during a storm and drowned.' He cleared his throat and continued to tell them what happened. 'The storm came in the early hours of the morning...it hit us hard, so all hands were on deck...I heard someone shout...'Man overboard'. I turned not knowing who it was. We couldn't see...the waves were still crashing on to the decks... I shouted to everyone as to who had fallen overboard.

One man shouted back that it was the captain. I asked if anyone had seen what happened. Two men shouted back saying they had seen Jim climbing the rigging when a huge wave hit him, then he slipped and fell into the sea.

Jamie and Kate were only half-listening as they were struggling to control their emotions with Jamie desperately trying to hold himself together. Temp looked up and pondered on what the boatswain had said, but he thought it didn't make sense. 'Why would Jim risk his life in a storm to go up the rigging?' Temp asked the boatswain.

'I don't know. I wondered that myself, but the one called Popeye told me Jim wanted to free a sail that was caught up,' he paused. 'I thought it strange because I had checked the sails, making sure they were secured. There weren't any problems...but one could have loosened. I am sure this man Popeye is genuine. He helped us sail the ship back to port and was very good at it, and he told me that a few years ago, he had been a captain.'

Temp still looked puzzled, feeling sure Jim would have not taken such a risk himself. Zak turned to Jamie, trying not to smile but delighted that at least part of his plan had come to fruition. 'I will get a carriage. I'm sending you both home.'

Jamie still couldn't believe that his father had died. His whole world had fallen apart!

'I do not want to go back home because it will not be my home anymore. It would only bring back memories.'

Kate turned to Jamie. 'We have a spare room if you like I am sure my grandparents' won't mind.

He looked at her with gratitude. 'That would be very kind if you are sure they won't mind.'

Temp suddenly remembered the cats and Peggy the dog. He told Jamie not to worry about them, as he would take care of them. It was not long before the carriage turned up and Kate and Jamie left. Zak stayed behind and shouted out to Spider to take the youngsters from the Lady Dorothea back to the orphanage. Zak gave him the money to pay Mr Humphreys. 'Don't tell him about Jim for now.' Zak glared at Spider. 'As you say, sir, but he'll find out sooner or later.'

Zak then turned to Temp. 'I want you to take the rest of the day off as you are too upset to work. I'll go down to the ship and arrange the unloading and storage.'

'That suits me fine, Zak.'

They left the office and went their separate ways. Temp had only gone a short distance when he suddenly remembered his promise to Jamie about the animals, so he turned around and went back to get them. As he climbed aboard, he saw Zak laughing with four men.

He thought it a bit odd as Zak had just lost his brother-in-law. After Temp had got the animals, he decided to have a word with the ship's second mate about the four men. He asked the mate to describe the men who said they had seen Jim fall overboard and was not surprised to hear they were the same men he had just seen Zak laughing with. Temp left the ship and was going home with the animals. When he overheard one of the crewmen talking to the harbour master about the night Jim died. He described the same four men, one being hook nose and Popeye, with a patch over one eye, and they both were there at the time Jim fell overboard. Temp started to thinking on his way home about everything he heard and been told and in his mind, he started to put things together. He decided to keep this to himself so as not to raise any suspicions, but it planted a seed for thought.

Chapter 7

Zak had arranged to meet the four men he had hired to kill Jim in his office to pay them, although they hadn't completed their task by not killing Jamie. Zak was not concerned, as he knew that his sister would now inherit everything. After he had paid the men with twenty gold guineas, he went to his lodgings to collect all his belongings to go and live with Edwina in Compton Manor.

During the next three days, Jamie never left Kate's cottage, still trying to come to terms with the loss of his father. By the third day, Kate decided to help him as best she could. She encourages him, 'Come on, Jamie enough is enough you have to do something, especially sorting things out with your father's company. Let's go down to the harbour to see Temp and have a talk about what your father would want you to do in these dreadful circumstances.'

' I suppose you are quite right, Kate. I have to get on with life, and Father would expect it of me to act like a man.' A neighbour was going that day to Portsmouth in his horse and cart, so Jamie and Kate jumped on to the back and settled down for the long and bumpy ride. The neighbour told them if they needed a ride back to the village, he would pick them up later at the harbour. They arrived at the harbour and managed to find Temp, who was organising the cargo for the ships Temp was so delighted to see him.

Jamie asked him if he would mind telling him what would be required of him now his father was not there and was willing to take on any responsibilities of the company. Temp as well felt that Jamie needed to talk about Jim and the future. They all decided to go to his house as it afforded them more privacy than the docks. Temp's house was close to the harbour, it was only a short walk away. Jamie was still very upset and each step felt like a million miles, they soon arrived and sat down with Peggy and his wanting to be made a fuss of. Kate quickly took control of the animals as Temp spoke 'Jamie, I spoke to the village vicar the other day here in Portsmouth about your father, he wants everyone to commemorate his life in remembrance of all he did for the community. He would like to hold a memorial service as this is the usual procedure when a sailor is lost at sea. It would be this coming Sunday at the village church at two, which would be a good few hours before the ships sail to India.' Jamie agreed nodding his head, he wiped his tears away and blowing his nose. 'Thanks Temp' Temp continued struggling with his own emotions. 'I think your father may have left a will.'

'Yes, he did Temp. He told me about it on this last journey, telling me what I would have to do if...' Jamie had to pause, weeping for a while. Kate offered Jamie a glass of water. He took a deep breath and carried on, 'My father told me about his will and said I was to go to his solicitor if anything happened to him. His name is Mr Westgarth, this is his address'

Temp looked at the address and replied. 'I know this man. He is a good friend of mine.' He hesitated for a second, looking at Jamie, 'You do realise Edwina and probably Zak will have to come as well.'

'Yes, I know they will have to come. After all, she was his wife and I expect my father has made provision for her and also for Zak to get some share in the business. 'I hope not,' Temp muttered to himself. 'What do you mean by that?' 'Forget it, Jamie' Temp said angrily. 'I just do not like Zak I think he is up to no good, but that's my opinion. If you have time, why wait, let's go over to see the solicitor now. It's only a fifteen-minute walk.'

'I agree, Temp let's go now, 'The three of them walked with determination to see the solicitor and managed to get an appointment at two o'clock the following day. Jamie agreed he would tell Edwina as he had decided to go home that night. 'Would you inform Zak of the appointment, Temp?' 'There's no need. He moved into your father's house three days ago after hearing about your father, so you can tell him yourself.' Jamie was still very upset, as Kate said to him,

'Perhaps Edwina needs some help to come to terms with the loss of your father.'

'Maybe, you're probably right, Kate.'

Temp then interrupted. 'Jamie, because both ships are sailing to India this coming Sunday, I have to make sure all the cargo goes on board by then, so tomorrow I cannot stay too long.'

Temp thought to himself that if Edwina got control of the company, he would tell Zak afterwards that he would not be going with the ship to India as he had decided to retire. He looked a bit glum as he thought that without Jim being around, what was the point anyways this would give him more time to spend with Jamie. He knew Zak wouldn't like it, but he couldn't care less. Then Jamie said, 'I know it is important to get the cargo on board because my father gave orders before we left England, instructing Zak to find customers and merchandise to take to India, so I know they must sail.' 'You never can tell, Jamie. It might be up to you after the will is read tomorrow to pick a captain for the ships. Let's wait for the outcome until after the meeting with the solicitor and find out then.'

Jamie decided it was time to reluctantly return home, take his pets with him and drop Kate off at her grandparents' cottage.

Temp headed back to the harbour to carry on with his work. He turned to Jamie and Kate, saying he would see them tomorrow, apprehensive of the outcome.

The neighbour waiting for them with the cart they climbed in. It was a cold and wet ride in the back of the cart they both huddled together under some sacking to keep warm, along with the animals. On the way back to the village above all the noise, Kate told Jamie what a wonderful time she had sailing to the West Indies with him even though it had been blighted with sadness, she told him how remarkable the children were and had now decided she wanted to be a teacher. Jamie had already realised this as he had watched her on the two ships with the younger children from the Orphanage. She was kind and fair to them. 'I think you will make a brilliant teacher Kate. I'm sure everyone would agree.'

Kate smiled, 'Thank you, kind sir, for that compliment. Jamie, I think it best if I do not come tomorrow. It's a private affair and I have a lot of things to do around the house.'

Jamie considered what she had said, although he was disappointed, he agreed it would probably be for the best.

'Jamie, whatever the outcome after tomorrow's meeting, I am sure you will want to go sail again on the Lady Dorothea. I am sure your boatswain friend Spider, will help you. I know everyone thinks you are good enough and your father said to me you would make a good captain.' 'When did he tell you that?' he said with emotion. 'We talked about it when we were sailing to Cuba.' With tears running down his cheeks he replied. 'I know my father would have taken me to Asia with him. If only he were alive today.' The dog could see he was sad and tried to lick him. Jamie pushed her away and cleared his throat. 'You may be right about sailing again, but I will make up my mind after tomorrow's meeting.'

Jamie was still feeling reluctant about returning but realised he had to face Edwina at some point. The cart arrived all too soon at Kate's house and they said their goodbyes. 'I'll come to see you after the meeting tomorrow. It will probably be in the evening, but I'll let you know the outcome of Father's will.'

'I hope all goes well for you, Jamie. See you tomorrow.'

Jamie made his way home, trying to control Peggy who kept jumping up at him, excited to be with him again. As he opened the door to the big house and entered the spacious hall, he looked around and thought he could still feel his father's presence. Edwina, coming from the drawing room to greet him so he thought but snarled at him instead, soon interrupted his thoughts. 'Thank you for not informing me of your whereabouts for the last three days, and make sure that those animals are left outside, and take your shoes off!' she bawled. She suddenly had a twinge of remorsefulness and added,

'I am sorry about your father. I am going to miss him as well.' She was trying to sound sincere and forced tears from her eyes, using her lace handkerchief to mask her true emotions. Jamie walked over to Mary and hugged her. Edwina did not like that, but she didn't want to be been seen reacting to it. Her face torn with anger and both of them felt her eyes on them. Edwina said to Mary sharply, 'I hope dinner will be ready in an hour and a half. Mary hurried off to the kitchen and left Jamie with his stepmother. 'Your uncle, Zak, will be home by then and he would like a word with you. He's living here now.'

'Yes! I know, I was told he had moved in three days ago,' he said very loudly. Edwina smirked, 'My goodness, the word does get around.'

Jamie wondered when would be the best time to tell them about the meeting with Mr Westgarth. Jim's will was being read the following day and perhaps Edwina and Zak were expecting a huge share of the business, but no one knows what was in the will. It was not long before his uncle arrived and they were sitting down to dinner. When they had finished, Zak turned to Jamie and told him what Edwina and he had decided. They were going to send him to the Royal Naval Academy, where he can complete his training to become a naval officer.

They also decided between them that they were going to close the vicarage school as it costs too much money to run it and stop paying the Orphanage as well as he didn't want the Orphanage children on their ships, as it was a waste of time. Jamie was furious. He was finding it very difficult to control his outrage but decided not to say or do anything, until after his father's will, was read, hoping he would be able to stop them.

Zak then explained to Jamie, 'Because your father did not leave a will, Edwina will inherit everything as his wife and we made the decision regarding the Academy we are sending you back to stop you from interfering in the business.' Zak scowled at Jamie and with that Jamie stood up and shouted, 'You're wrong. There is a will. My father made one.' Stuttering, he added, 'A-a-and tomorrow at noon, we'll find out who's got what. I am supposed to take you both to see Mr Westgarth, but to hell with it now! You'll just have to get Temp to show you his office. We'll see who stays or goes!' With that, Jamie looked at them and shouted, 'I'm leaving this house. I cannot stay here with you two'.

He rushed to his bedroom, packed a few belongings, got his animals and left to go to Temp's cottage. Zak was furious, shouting at his sister. 'Did you know about this? And why the hell didn't you say anything?'

'I knew nothing of this. My husband kept that very quiet.'

Unbeknown to them, Mary was listening outside the door. She had no liking for either Edwina or Zak and was very sad that Jamie was leaving. Mary had looked after him since he had been born, caring for and loving him like her son.

Chapter 8

Jamie walked out of the house with no regrets about leaving Edwina and Zak. How he loathed them! He walked and walked, lost in thought and sadness. Luckily, an old man in a horse and cart had been delivering goods to the village and was on his way back to Portsmouth before dark. The man was quite happy giving him a lift, Jamie quickly jumped in to the back with his dog and cats.. He arrived at Temp's house with his animals, cold, tired, and thoroughly miserable. He sat down and cried, shaking like a leaf. 'What the hell has happened now, my boy?' Jamie related to Temp what had happened and been said. Temp was furious. The more he thought about it, the more he was convinced Edwina and Zak had been involved in Jim's death, but still, he said nothing to Jamie. 'Jamie, it's getting late, time for bed. We will talk more about this tomorrow.'

Jamie asked if he could take his animals with him to bed. Temp did not mind in the least, knowing they would bring some small comfort. Jamie wearily retired and left Temp to his own thoughts. He wondered if Jim had put too much trust in Zak and Edwina and he prayed things would turn out fine the next day for young Jamie. Edwina and Zak had not slept well. They were worried about the outcome. By morning, they were in very disagreeable moods but thought the best approach would be to go to the docks and see Temp. Maybe, he would know something about the will. They arrived at the docks and sought out Temp. When asked what he knew about a will, he shrugged his shoulders and told them that he does not known nothing about it. Zak asked Temp for directions to the solicitor's office, he pointed the way for them. Temp looked at the time and left to collect Jamie. Temp had noticed that Zak and Edwina appeared worried about the outcome of the meeting.

Precisely at two in the afternoon, everyone seated at Mr Westgarth's table waiting for the reading of the will. Mr Westgarth was well dressed, wearing a wig as was the fashion, which made him appear even taller than his natural height. He made the usual formal introductions before he began.

'We are gathered here today for the reading of the last will and testament of the deceased Captain Charles Frank Heslop. At the time of signing this Will, he was of sound mind and well-being. It states I, Charles Frank Heslop, decree that my wife Edwina has full control of the house in which she now dwells. Edwina grinned but waited for more.

To Zak Armstrong, I decree that he has full control over the shipping company.

Zak was delighted as this gave him great power.

To Mr Temp Elliot, my faithful friend, I decree a monthly pension of twenty-two shillings when he decides to retirement. I also give him the responsibility of my son, as he is his godfather to ensure his well-being.

If my son Jamie Heslop has a dispute with the running of the Heslop shipping company or Compton Manor, he is to bring it to the attention of Mr Elliot and if it cannot be resolved between himself, Edwina, and Zak then Mr Westgarth will make the final decision.

The smiles soon disappeared from Edwina's and Zak's faces. There seemed to be some confusion as to what they had inherited. Had they inherited the mansion and the shipping yard in their entirety or were they just managing them? Mr Westgarth continued, Finally, I come to my beloved son, Jamie. I hope that I have made the right decision for him. Edwina and Zak are to take good care of my son until he reaches the age of twenty-one. When he reaches the age of majority, he will then be the sole owner of Heslop & son Merchant Shipping Co, and my estate known as Compton Manor. I pray that my dearest son will be happy with these arrangements and that my wife, Edwina and brother-in-law, Zak, oversee the company until he becomes of age. When Jamie becomes of age and inherits, he must provide for my wife and her brother. I have made this decision to enable my son Jamie to enjoy his youth, to do anything he wishes, and go anywhere and not to have undue responsibility. This is my will and testament.

Signed Mr Charles Frank Heslop, owner of Heslop & son Merchant Shipping Company

'Ladies and gentlemen, this is the end of the reading. If anyone has any comments to make...' Before Mr Westgarth had even finished his sentence, Edwina and Zak jumped up, bid goodbye to Mr Westgarth, and left abruptly.

Mr Westgarth said to Jamie, 'Would you mind leaving the room for a moment? My assistant will give you a cup of tea.' After Jamie had thanked Mr Westgarth for his time, he left the solicitor and Temp alone.

'Mrs Heslop and her brother did not seem too pleased with the outcome,' observed Mr Westgarth'.

'I suspected that would happen if it didn't go their way,' replied Temp. 'Yes, I can see that, but surely, Mr Heslop tried to provide for everyone.'

'I would like to think so, but tell me, God forbid it will not happen if Jamie died before he reaches twenty-one, who would inherit the Compton Manor and Heslop & son Shipping'

'Mrs Heslop, of course, but what is on your mind?'

'It is just an old man letting his mind wander. Forget I asked the question, Mr Westgarth.' Temp knew he had put questions into Mr Westgarth's mind in case anything happened to Jamie or himself. Temp shook hands with the solicitor and went to find Jamie. What did you talk about and why did you not tell me you are my godfather?'

'We talked about his account, and I didn't tell you about my being your godfather as, like most sailors, I am superstitious. The feeling is if you had been told, it may have harmed your true father.' Jamie did not quite understand his reply.

Temp suggested that they should make their way to the dock office and find out what Edwina and her brother intended to do about Jamie's future and that he would not now be going to India. He decided to keep his decision regarding retirement to himself for the time being. .Zak and Edwina had gone directly to the docks and although they had little time to discuss the will, they both agreed that if they were to inherit everything they had to get rid of Jamie. Realising they had to devise a plan, they felt it better to treat Jamie with respect until arrangements for his demise had been settled.

When Temp and Jamie arrived at the office, Zak smiled at them and asked them to take a seat whilst Edwina told one of the clerks to brew some tea. He told Jamie that he and Edwina were very grateful to Jim for providing for them in his will and that they would do their best for him. If they all worked as a team to run the shipping company, they could fulfil Jim's wishes, as he wouldof wanted them too. Jamie smiled and thanked them both for their consideration and assistance, but Temp just nodded his head. He could not believe what Zak was saying. Temp stood up and said, 'I have to tell you of my two concerns. Firstly, Jamie wants to know what you would like him to do within the company. Secondly, I am going to retire. I am too old to go gallivanting around the world.' Zak said to Temp that he was disappointed he would not be going to India but asked if he would consider taking over the running of the shipping business here because he was going to captain the Lady Dorothea to India. Temp said he would consider this and let him know the next day. Zak looked at Jamie and told him he would think about Jamie's future and let him know the following day. Meanwhile, he explained he had to find someone to captain the Earl and asked Temp if both ships would be ready to sail on the evening tide on Sunday.

'They will be, Zak. Are you and Edwina going to Jim's funeral service? It's at two Sunday afternoon and will be held at the village church. The vicar has arranged everything.' 'Of course, we will be going,' Zak and Edwina replied together.

Jamie and Temp left the office and made their way back to Temp's house. Jamie felt stronger than he had done for days now things had been sorted out a little.

'I think they both seem quite genuine,' Jamie remarked. 'No, Jamie, they were not! I must warn you. Be very careful. They are up to no good. I am sure they want all the Heslop'sholdings.'

'You have no proof, only suspicions.'

'I know, but what don't you notice the change in their behaviour and why? I am telling you, "Beware". I have to hurry back to work, so if you are going out, make sure you take your dog out first.'

'Yes, Godfather,' which brought a smile from Temp. Jamie did, as Temp said. Managed to get a ride in a coach to go and see Kate in the village to tell her about the day's events. Kate opened the door, and when she saw Jamie, she put her arms around him and gave him a hug. She was so pleased to see him, sit down and offered him tea and cakes.

He told her everything that had taken place, what was written in the will and what Zak and Edwina had said afterwards. Kate started to laugh, 'They are going to treat you as their son! Next, they will be licking your boots, doing this all the time until you reach twenty-one years of age. You are joking with me!'

'Temp said he thinks they are up to no good.'

'I agree with him. He could be right that you have to be careful.'

They talked of other things and as the evening drew close, Jamie took his leave of Kate to go and see Edwina. He knocked on the door. Mary opened it and gave him a big hug and a kiss, informing him that Edwina was waiting for him in the drawing room. Edwina greeted him warmly and suggested he sat down. She rang the bell for Mary to bring tea and cake. Jamie thought to himself, that he wouldn't want any dinner that night with all the cake he had eaten. They talked about different things for quite some time until he announced he had to go. 'I have to get back and feed my animals.'

'Why don't you move back here with the animals?'

'Thanks, but for now, until Uncle Zak decides on my job, I'll stay at Temp's, but thank you anyway. Could your coachman take me to Portsmouth please?'

'By all means.' Jamie rode back in Edwina coach to town. Pondered on how agreeable Edwina had been and begins to think that Temp and Kate could be right.

Chapter 9

Zak had ridden his horse hard to return to Edwina and tell her of his news. It was not long when Mary started serving dinner to them both, with Zak being impatient to relate his news. Soon, Mary had left the dining room after finishing serving them, but unbeknown to them, she remained just outside the door listening to their conversation. Zak was very eager to tell his sister his plans and whispered to her, 'I have a way to get rid of Jamie'. He went on to explain that with Temp not going to India, he could get Jamie to take his place as captain of the Earl. This will keep Jamie from wanting to go with him on the Lady Dorothea. 'I will make Popeye head boatswain on the Earl, second to the captain. Then Popeye can get rid of him too"

'That sounds a great idea, Zak'

'Yes I thought so too and we be well rid of Jamie'.

Taken another sip of tea, Zak then went on to say he made a lot of money for them both today. Mr Humphreys has got hold of some young black slave children that he bought cheaply from one of the slave ships that came in and needed to find work for them or he will send them to the silk mills. We made an agreement between us is to sell them in France when we sail this Sunday, I will have to keep them out of sight from everyone on the dock or we could all be in trouble.' Edwina considered this proposal, 'The main thing for me is getting rid of that interfering boy, but I agree with your idea. I hate being kind to that brat, so the sooner we dispose of him, the better I like it.'

'Quiet, you fool...I heard someone outside,' Zak whispered. He crept over to the door. Flinging it open, he caught a glimpse of Mary going into the kitchen. Turning back to Edwina, he said, 'That was Mary. You better find out if she heard anything.'

'I will get rid of that old goat of a woman even if it's the last thing I do. Brother it's my pleasure to get rid of her now'. She stormed off to the kitchen to find Mary. 'I know you been listening at the door spying on us and I have had enough of it...I want you out of this house right away you're dismissed".

'Yes, I did hear everything you both were saying,' Edwina screamed at her, 'If you mention a word about this to anyone, I will make sure you end up the same way as Jim…. She realised what she said at that moment...anyway no one will believe you….they will think you made it up because you were dismissed.' Mary went to her room infuriated over the way Edwina spoke to her, packed her bags and left, unsure of where to go. Struggling in the dark with her bags, and it was raining hard; she decided to go to Kate's house. Kate welcomed her in, taking her bags and wet coat, and then asked what had happened to her and why she was so upset and angry. Mary told her that she got into an argument with Edwina and she had dismissed her, but didn't say anything about the conversation she had overheard. She knew she had to speak to Temp as soon as possible as he would know what to do for the best.

'Can I get to Temp's house tonight?' She wanted to see him before he went to work in the morning. Kate's grandfather replied, 'It's too dangerous to go in the dark and it's raining too heavy'. He told her he will take her first thing in the morning and Kate, for now she is welcome to stay here for the night, she agreed and thanked them.

Early the next morning, Mary, Kate and her grandfather left in his buggy. It was still pouring with rain. , Kate's grandfather dropped them off at Temp's house then headed back. They knocked on the door, he was really surprised to see them so early and bid them. After taking off their wet coats and hanging them up, Jamie had rushed down the stairs and gave the two ladies a hug. Soon they were all sitting down to drinking hot tea, then after Mary began to tell them what she heard, her voice choked up trying not to cry.

'I am going to tell you something, and I want you all to promise not to tell a living soul. Sadly, my dear friends, today after I have told you what I overheard, I will have to leave you all, because of the threat that Edwina has made towards me. I am going to live with my sister in Lancaster.' They all agreed and promised not to say a word to anyone. She told them what she had heard between Edwina and Zak and the confrontation between Edwina afterwards. In addition, what Edwina said about his father? Mary looked at Jamie. 'My dear boy, you have been like a son to me, but you must get away from here as far as possible, as I am sure you will not be coming back from India if you sail with him, so get far away from here.' Jamie and Kate could hardly believe it. Temp stood up, lit his pipe, and said, 'This does not come as a surprise to me. Although we do not have any proof to go to the town constable with, because it is our word against theirs, we now know they did have something to do with the murder of your father.' Jamie jumped up because by now, it had sunk in, 'I will kill them.'

'Stop, Jamie! We have no proof. It would be Mary's word against both of them'.

Kate went towards Jamie and said firmly, 'Think about what your mother said to you. If you have a problem, there is always a way around it.' She was trying desperately to calm him down. He looked at her, smiled, and said, 'You're right again. I will think of something.' Mary got up and told them she was going to Lancaster to live with her sister. She hugged them all and repeated,

'Jamie, you must go from here. One day, when you are older and you have proof, I will come back to help you, then you will get your justice in the court.' Kate and Jamie helped her with her bags to the stagecoach. They were sad to see her go but realised it was the best thing for her now. After she had gone, Jamie sat down with Temp. 'Mary has given me an idea when she said about my returning when I get older and getting justice for my father.'

Jamie asked Kate if she would mind taking the dog for a walk. When she left, Jamie quickly told Temp of his plan. He had asked Kate to go out for a reason. He thought the fewer that knew of his plans, the safer it would be. Thinking about it, Temp thought it was a brilliant idea.

With his help, it would definitely work, even if it meant he probably would not see him again for many years. 'That's a bloody good idea you have devised. Now, let's make sure it works.'

Before Temp left to go to work, he said to Jamie, 'When you see Zak later for god's sake, do not mention or show signs that you know about being captain of the Earl.'

'You can rely on me not to give anything away.' Temp reminded Jamie that the plan they had would mean that he would miss his father's service on Sunday and said that he would take his place. Jamie was very upset, but in his heart, he knew his father would not mind. The rain was still coming down when poor Kate got back with the dog. Both she and the dog were soaking wet. 'Thanks for asking me to do that,' she said with sarcasm. He smiled at her fondly, 'Any time. That's what friends are for.' Temp went off to his work at the docks, so Jamie and Kate spent some time together. He told her part of his plans but asked her not to say a word to a living soul as it could backfire. Kate was amazed at what he had told her and thought it was a brilliant idea. She said to him, 'I am going back to the village to see my grandparents. I need to put a suggestion to you, but I must speak to them first. I will be back in a few hours to see you.' Jamie got her a coach back to the village. He then asked the coachman to fetch her back here that afternoon.

It was still raining heavily when he went to see Zak, 'I want you to be captain of the Earl, Jamie and your first mate will be a man called Popeye'. Jamie thanked him and told him he was delighted but asked who Popeye was. 'He was the one who helped to captain the Lady Dorothea when...Oh, sorry, he helped sail her back with the help of Mr Thompson, the boatswain'.

''Is he a short and stocky with a patch over one eye?' Jamie asked

'Yes, he has, but why do you ask? Do you know him?'

'No, I just noticed he sailed with my father. He always seems to have three other sailors with him.'

'Does he? I did not know that,' Zak replied. Jamie knew he was lying. Temp had already told him that Zak knew them all and that he had to be careful about them., Zak stood up, put his hand out, and said, 'We have a deal, young man?'

'Yes, Uncleand thanks again,' shaking Zak's hand. As he turned to go, 'Uncle, it's raining today so if it is fine, tomorrow, can I take some of the youngsters from the Orphanage to clean the ships? They must be in a hell of a mess, and I believe that on Sunday morning, some of your clients are coming to look at the two ships before they sail that night.'

'Damned good idea Jamie I will give you a letter addressed to Mr Humphreys, requesting that you take as many youngsters as you need to do the job, but there is one thing however, Zak raised his head from the letter and said the lower hold area on the Lady Dorothea? You or the youngster will not be allowed; to go down there is that clear? He returned to the letter I don't need to explain myself. Here is the letter.'

'No problem, Uncle. I have no reason to go down that far anyway.'

'Then don't'

'Thanks, Uncle. I won't let you down.'

'I know you won't'

Jamie left, feeling very pleased with himself as his plan worked, but curious as to why Zak didn't want him to go down to the lower hold. He went straight to see Temp and told him what had transpired. Temp was very pleased that all was going to plan.

'I am sure the weather will be fine tomorrow' Temp told him that he had loaded everything on board that he would need for the journey, and later he will load the live animals. In addition, the violin from the Earl and some clothes stow away for the youngsters. 'Oh, I nearly forgot, plus the potatoes, carrots, and seeds. There is a big surprise that might come in useful too, but make sure you read my letter first.'

With those words, Jamie thought of his father and thanked Temp with sadness.

'I also have to tell Zak that I have decided to take up his offer and look after the company while you are both away,' added Temp. Jamie was relieved to hear this, as he knew that the management of the company wouldn't be in safe hands then.

It hadn't stopped raining all day, but now it was easing up a little. That's when Jamie decided to go back to Temp's cottage, when he arrived he found Kate had returned and to his surprise, she had two large bags with her. 'I'm coming with you to India, my grandparents wished me well, and I'm not taking no for an answer.'

Jamie smiled. 'I would not like it any other way. Glad to have you on board.' He explained to Kate that she would have the chance to see the Orphanage children again as Zak agreed for them to clean the two ships tomorrow. I was just about to go there now to see Mr Humphreys with this letter, and tell him Zak wants the children to be ready early in the morning.

On arriving at the Orphanage, they rung the bell, they were once again directed to Mr Humphreys. Jamie gave him the letter and after reading it, he nodded in agreement. Everything was in order and that the children would be ready early in the morning and returned later in the evening. Kate stayed at Temp's cottage that night, Temp got up before them the next morning and made them a hearty breakfast. Jamie and Temp explained to Kate some of their plans, which were that they would not be going to India. She was not at all surprised, as she had known Jamie would come up with something, and she was very excited. Temp took out his map and along with it a sketch showing the direction to the Keeling Islands in the Indian Ocean and handed it to Jamie. He then put the map into his bag and asked Temp if he would ensure their bags went on board. 'I take it you are not coming with us, Temp,' said Kate.

'No, I am afraid not, I am too old for the sea and want my feet back on the ground. Don't worry I have a lot of friends here my own age to grow even older with.'

And he laughed, but he was sad to see them go. I will still be here when you come back,6 years is a long time but it will soon go,' replied Temp.

It was now early Saturday and they knew Zak would be at Compton Manor. The only problem would be his henchmen who were guarded the ships. The rest of the crew would have finished loading the cargo by lunchtime and would have left. Temp went to work as normal and loaded Jamie and Kate's bags, his dog and cats, along with other things he thought Jamie would need. Temp was a familiar face and no one would stop or question what he was doing not even the henchman.

On the way to the Orphanage, Jamie said to Kate, 'When we set sail this evening can you take charge of all the children when I get everyone on board our ship? The four girls who sailed with us previously will use the other boatswain's cabin next to you. All the other girls below deck will live and sleep on one side and the boys the other side.' Being excited Kate agreed without hesitation.

Much to their surprise, all the children were ready, waiting, and lined up for them when they reached the Orphanage. 'How many of these brats do you want to go with you?' Sid asked Jamie. 'All of them. Due to the rain yesterday, the two ships are in a filthy mess, so if it is all right with Mr Humphreys, I'll take them all.'

Sid scratched his head. 'All right, then. What time will you fetch them back?'

'It could be quite late. After they have finished the work, I shall make sure they have a good dinner before returning them back. At the worst, it would not be later than nine or ten tonight.' Sid did not like it but agreed to meet him here at the gate at ten o'clock; he thought that at least he did not have to bother to feed them. The children cheered when Jamie told them he was taking all of them. He lined them up in pairs. Leading the way, he asked Kate to count them as they passed by her and then follow up in the rear. Kate whispered, 'Why did you tell Sid we would be back around nine with them?'

'That is because the high tide is at eight tonight, and we will be long gone by then,' replied Jamie. Kate nodded her head and smiled to herself, as neither she nor Jamie wanted the children to have any suspicions regarding their plan. Kate started counting; she counted 106. She noticed two of them were not looking too good but decided to wait until they were on board the Lady Dorothea to have a look at them. They arrived by the office at the harbour and Jamie decided to ask the children the question now rather than later that night; he did not want some of them shouting to get off the ship. 'If you were given the chance to sail on a ship, like some of you have already done, who would say, "No, I would not go"?' There was silence for a moment and then a young boy put his hand up, saying 'Me, sir.'

'Why is that?' asked Kate. 'I might get eaten by a sea monster!'

Everyone laughed; Kate put her arm around him. 'What is your name, young man, and how old are you?' Sir I think I am nine, and my name is Tom.'

'Well, Tom, you look a lot older than nine, so if I promised to look after you, would you go then?' The boy thought for some seconds and said, 'Yes, "ma'am".' Kate gave him an encouraging hug before she took the girls off to sort out their jobs. Jamie went in the storeroom to get brooms, brushes, shovels, and mops.

There was not enough to go round, so he gave the rest of them a cloth each. Jamie got the children working on the Earl first so that when it got late, they would be all on his ship finishing the cleaning. Kate took some of the girls to cook the meals for everyone to eat during the day. She set four girls to work cleaning the captain and boatswain's quarters, one of the girls being Sam. She then put the two sickly children in the boatswain's cabin for the time being and had given them some herbal drinks to make them feel a little better.

The day passed quite quickly without a problem and all the crew had gone by midday, except Zak's henchmen, two on each ship. Temp informed Jamie that he had managed to disable the Earl, which would give him two days' start. Jamie was delighted with that news. Temp also told him that most of what he needed had been loaded onto the Lady Dorothea, also the surprise that was waiting for him when he got to the Island, but it was way down in the hold. He added that he did not know what else Zak had in the lower hold but thought it had been loaded on Friday night. Spider had told him that morning that late on Friday night, he heard some activity going on in the harbour as he was going home from the tavern. He thought he saw Popeye and his mates with Zak leaving the harbour at around 10.30. 'Well, Temp, whatever he has got down there is mine now,' Jamie said with a smile. 'We will have a problem later, Jamie, as Zak has left two of his henchmen down there guarding it. Somehow, we must find a way to get them out of there as there are only two hours left before you sail.' Jamie looked at Temp. 'I have thought of a way. Nearer to the time, when we set sail' He asked Temp to go and see them both and tell them that Popeye is waiting in the tavern and wants them to go and meet him there for a flagon of ale? Then tell them that you will take over guard duty until they get back. 'It might work, but I had better take my special walking stick, just in case, I have need of it.' Jamie did not quite understand what Temp was talking about 'A special walking stick'? He knew Temp needed a stick to walk with, but a special walking stick, what was so special about that one? With everything going to plan and with only one hour left before high tide, all the children were aboard the Dorothea in the galley, finishing their dinner; some of them were clearing the tables. Then Jamie announced he was going to take them for a trip on the ship before he took them back to the Orphanage but that it would only be to just outside the harbour. He insisted they stay below deck until they were told differently as they all seemed to be a bit puzzled but they did as they told. Jamie then went on to say except for the boys and girls who had sailed with him before, as they would have to help man the ship. He did not want any of the children to be screaming out with delight at the thought of leaving the Orphanage and sailing away to a new life of adventure and freedom. Jamie gathered all the boys who had sailed on ships before and took them on to the top deck, telling them that as soon as he shouted out 'man the yardarms', he wanted them to respond straight away. Although for now the only yardarm that had to be braced would be the main central mast as the ship had to move away from the moorings slowly, once they get further out from the harbour, the rest could be dropped.

The boys already knew the procedure, but Jamie just wanted to remind them. He looked at them, saying, 'I have missed you, lads as you seem to have become my friends'. The boy called Joe Ben approached Jamie with his cap in his hand. Looking to his feet, he mumbled, Sir, I think you should not call me your friend. I have not told you something very important.'

'Do not fret yourself, Joe. Nothing is that important as to damage our friendship, so let's all get this ship underway.' He asked Temp if he could release the last mooring rope, as he was not going with them unless he wanted to change his mind.

Temp gave a sad smile. 'If I were your age, I would love to go with you, but I know in my heart you will be fine without me' It was now the time to put their plan into action.

Temp went down to the hold where Zak's two men were keeping guard and told them Popeye was in the tavern wanting to see them. Only one of them agreed to go as they had been instructed to always keep at least one on guard. Fortunately, for Temp, the larger man left. Meanwhile, on deck, Jamie had noticed only one man had left and wondered if Temp might need assistance. He selected two of the bigger boys and went down to check on Temp. By the time they arrived, Temp had already whacked the remaining henchman on the head with his stick. He turned to Jamie and the boys, saying,'Help this man. He has fainted, and we need to get him off the ship into some fresh air.' Jamie could not help but grin as they all carried the man off the ship and on to the harbour quay. 'Quick, Jamie. You must get ready to sail now,' Temp said with some urgency. It was a clear night lit up by a full moon, and the other two henchmen on the Earl clearly saw what was happening. Jamie and his two biggest lads were carrying their other mate off the off the Lady Dorothea, and dumped on the quay. They jumped off the Earl and came running at full speed towards Jamie and the others. Jamie drew out his sword. Temp had his walking stick and pulled a sword out from inside it, now Jamie knew what was special about that walking stick, and the fighting began. They needed to deal with these two quickly as, by this time, Jamie should have set sail. Sam, the young girl who had sailed with Jamie on the last voyage, could see what was happening and rushed to the captain quarters and grabbed a sword. She hurried back on deck and sprinted down the gangplank to join the fight. Jamie could not believe how good she was. It was not long before they had overpowered the two men, who ran off nursing their wounds. They realised they had to move fast as the two men would soon reach the tavern and tell of Jamie's escape with the children. Temp shouted to Jamie and Sam to get going fast, they both rushed back up the gangplank as they waved goodbye to Temp. Jamie yelled out to the crew to man the yardarm. Temp had cast off all the mooring ropes except the one at the stern in order to allow the ship to face forwards, bad luck played its part as a gust of wind caught the main mast sail and tightened the last mooring rope so Temp could not lift it off. He took out his sword and started to cut into the rope. Kate could see that it could turn dangerous for poor old Temp as time was getting on. Jamie attention was distracted away from what was happening on the quay, by trying to control the ship. However, Kate was watching what was happening and was horrified to see Temp lashing at the rope. Suddenly the man he had knocked out woke up, saw what was happening and stuck his sword into Temp's stomach. As Temp lay there dying he found enough strength for one more lunge at the rope which cut straight through it.

Kate was shocked at what she had just seen and started to cry hysterically. Sam ran across to her comfort her, as she had also witnessed what had happened. 'We could not have helped him, Temp knew he was on his own, he was a very brave man.' Sam managed to quieten Kate down by giving her a drink of rum, They decided not to say a word to Jamie, as they needed him in the right frame of mind, to take us to a new life, he would be devastated if he knew what has happened to Temp and probably would give up on them all. Kate nodded desperately trying to keep her sobs under control, knowing that if Jamie saw her he would want to know what was wrong. Jamie had managed to get the ship out of the harbour, and the ship was in full sail. He instructed the boy called Mick to take the helm. He wanted to talk to Kate to find out if Temp had managed to get away all right. Jamie went in search of her and found Kate sitting in her cabin on the bunk, looking very distressed.

He asked her if she had seen Temp, and she replied hesitatingly that she had seen him get away. She burst into tears, trying hard to control her sobbing. Jamie gathered her in his arms. 'Kate, my love, I know you will miss your grandparents and friends, but you will have a new life, and everyone here will need your help.' If Jamie only knew what had just happened!

It was nearly midnight when Jamie went below deck and informed those children who were still awake that he would talk to them in the morning. For the remainder of that first night, he took turns with Mick at the helm.

Chapter 10

Back on shore the next morning, all hell had let loose when Zak was informed of the previous night events. He raged at his men, telling them to get back to the Earl and prepare to set sail on the morning tide the next day. He vowed to make Jamie pay for his actions, no matter the consequences. Over the next few hours, Zak was preparing the Earl for her ocean voyage given instruction from the quay.

When Mr Humphreys turned up seated firmly on a large Nag, he shouted out loud to Zak,

'Where the hells are my kids and our slaves you have not paid me for?' Zak shouted back even louder, 'I have more problems to worry about than your precious ruddy kids. What about my ship?'

'So if that's the way you want to play it, then I will go and see my lawyer. You will be hearing from him shortly.' With that, Mr Humphreys was in a fearful rage, turned his Nag and prepared to ride off. Zak was in a worse temper than Humphreys was. He ran over to him and whacked the poor Nag right up its rump; instantly, the Nag reared up took off with Humphreys, clinging on for dear life. The Old Nag headed down the jetty towards the sea. Then as it got to the end of the jetty, it stopped dead, catapulting Mr Humphreys straight into the sea. The water was cold, and he floundered about, shouting for assistance, as he could not swim. Several sailors ran down the jetty and held out a pole. He clung on, shivering. It took much pulling and shouting to get him up on the jetty. He was furious; as all the dock workers were laughing their heads off. Humphreys grabbed his Nags reins, and with as much dignity as he could muster, with the help of four men, he mounted his Nag and rode off.

It had only taken Zak's men just over a day to repair the ship even though Temp had disabled it as best as he could, but they had managed to set sail after Jamie. Later on that day, a stevedore found Temp's body floating in the sea and called the town constable. He questioned all those who had been on the quay that day, but nobody admitted to seeing anything. Constable Grimes, as with all town constables, they do not receive payment for his services, and although he knew, he had to determine whether Temp had been murdered or died in a fight, he was in no particular hurry. He noticed blood on the quay near to where the Earl and the Lady Dorothea had been moored. So decided he would have to wait until they returned to conclude his enquiries.

The children back on the Lady Dorothea woke early the next morning, and Kate brought them up on deck to wash and have something to eat. Jamie and Mitch had gone down to the lower hull to inspect the cargo Zak had stowed. As they descended the wooden ladder, they noticed a strong smell. The farther down they got, the worse the smell got. They reached the bottom, trying not to retch at the overpowering stench. In front of them was a locked door, and behind it, someone was crying. Unlocking the door, they stepped back in total surprise to see at least forty young black children huddled up in a corner. He held his hand out to them, wanting them to go with him. None of them moved.

He asked them if any of them spoke English, and a small, frightened girl with huge brown eyes and short black hair spoke out, saying she did a little. Jamie asked her to come forward. She nervously approached him, as she felt he had a kind face.

'What is your name?' he asked gently. 'Jada sir.'

'Jada, I will not harm any of you, all I want to do is to help you. Would you ask the children to follow me?' She turned to the other children, translating what Jamie had

said. They all got up; stretching their cramped limbs, they followed Jamie and Mitch up the ladder to the top deck. JB, Kate, and the other two girls were on deck. They stared at Jamie and his group of children in utter amazement. Kate's first thoughts were food and water. They had obviously been in the hold for some time and must be starving. Jada approached Kate. 'Miss, we have not had anything to eat or drink for two days. Please, could you spare some bread and water.'

'Tell them they can have a drink of water now but they have to wash's before they can eat. I will find them some clean clothes, and we will burn the ones they are wearing. In the meantime, the girls will prepare you some hot food. Hurry now.'

The children didn't need telling twice. They lined up at a barrel of water, taking it in turns to drink from the ladle. Some thought it tasted a little odd, but others recognised the faint taste of the rum, which was in the water to stop it from going rancid. Jamie instructed Sam to take the girls to wash at the stern of the ship and Joe Ben to do the same with the boys at the bow of the ship. They set about hauling up buckets of seawater while Kate organised clean clothing. Jada, explained to the other children what they had to do and that after they had washed and changed, they were going to the galley to get food. They immediately set about getting themselves clean, feeling more relaxed and happy now they were out of that cage in the filthy hold in which they had been locked in. While Sam and JB were overseeing the cleaning operations, Jamie took Kate to one side and asked her. 'Would you like to teach you're girls to help sail this ship?'. I would rather be a teacher to the youngsters. I would also like to try and teach those slave children to speak English and to read and write if possible.' Her reply was, If you don't mind'..

'I knew you would say that. I will ask Sam instead.' Jamie walked over to Sam. 'I would like you to be a crew member and take charge of the girls and show them how to man the ship.'

'Yes, I would like to be your boatswain's mate,' Sam replied with a cheeky smile.

Jamie blushed. He found Sam quite intimidating but liked her humour. He knew they were going to get on well together. Soon all the hungry slaves and children had gone down to the Galley tucking into all types of food that was marvellous, so different to what they all had been use to eating.

He waited until all the crew, including the slaves and the orphanage children, had finished eating. Addressing them, he said, 'I want you all to meet me in ten minutes on the amidships or top deck..

Whilst he was waiting for them, Jamie's thought was drawn to Temp wondering how he was and how thoughtful he had been.

Loading plenty of clothes on board for the orphanage children and they had certainly been put to good use.Not only the orphans but now by slave children as well. When everyone had gathered on deck, Jamie stood at the helm and, looked down to them, said, 'I want everyone to call me Skipper. As you are aware, we are now out on the open sea. I apologise for not informing you of my intentions before this, but we needed to be clear of land first.Every one of them now, had realised that they will not be going back to that horrible orphanage and the slaves are free.

There were almighty shouts of hooray and laughing. He put his hand up and told them to be quiet. He told them they were going to a beautiful island abundant with fruit and coconut trees. There would be a warm climate with blue skies and a crystal clear lagoon filled with fish. It was to be their home until they got older, and then maybe some of them would like to return to their country of birth, whether it was England or Africa.

Jamie took a deep breath, and with a new air of authority, he said in a stern voice, 'I can't promise our new life will be easy, but we must have teamwork and help each other by sharing the skills we have to make our new life on the island the best we can make it. In doing so, we must have order on this ship. Everyone must behave, as an adult and fooling around, will not be tolerated at any time because a ship can be a dangerous place if my orders are not obeyed. Everyone has a role on this ship and some of the crew that have sailed on a ship before how the ship operates, so they will be you guilds and will take charge and be known as "Shipmates", they will have a red scarf to wear around their necks so you will recognise them when they give the orders. A very important thing to remember is to make sure the lids are always secure on the water barrels. Otherwise, it will get algae in it and would then be undrinkable and we cannot survive without fresh water. Anyone needing to ask questions, then it will have to wait for a few more days as there is a lot to do'.

He requested that all shipmates report to his cabin in fifteen minutes. 'Jada, before you come to my cabin, please find out if your group need anything more.' He strode off, leaving the whole ship's complement to digest all he had said. Some were nervous, some excited, but all knew that their lives had changed dramatically and wondered what the future held for them. While Jamie checked his dog and cats in his cabin, his shipmates plus Kate, and Jada assembled outside his cabin. Kate knocked on the door, and he told them all to enter.

'What I am about to tell you is to be kept between ourselves. There is a man called Zak, who is my uncle. He is the reason we are all here because', Jamie cleared his throat trying not to show any emotion, 'This man arranged the murder of my father and wants to kill me as well'. He told them he will definitely come after us, and we must never underestimate him. As he was a very clever man, who by now would realise that the slaves have been found and he will try to stop us, taking them back to their own country? Therefore, we should anticipate that he would sail down the coast of Africa to try to find us, so we will keep away from the African coast.

'All of you keep an eye open for ships. I will know if it's one is his.' We are going to think of a way to stop him.'

'Let's give him a broadside. I am a good shot with the cannon,' said Mitch'.

'No, Mitch I have friends on that ship. Maybe, even Temp is on it, so it cannot be done that way.'

Kate and Sam glanced at one another, knowing Jamie did not yet know about Temp. Jamie then asked Jada, if she and her companions wanted to return to their native homeland. She said they have no home, as most of them would like to stay and make a new life. Jamie continued telling his shipmates that the drinking water would be rationed, as they might not see land for months at a time and he asked them to make the lightweight sails into a funnel to catch the rainwater if it rained. He instructed them to sort out three gangs, with each gang doing eight-hour shifts around the clock and that he wanted them to teach as many other youngsters how to sail this ship. Jamie knew that most of the children were young and undernourished, but with plenty of rations and fresh air, they would soon gain in strength and determination.

He then said.' Mick and I would select the two strongest boys and teach them to man the helm. Then everyone practices to rig and de-rig the yardarms. Some of you might know this, but for the rest of you, listen carefully. If a storm does occur, the ship's bell must be rung and everyone must make sure that all the ship's hatches are battened down, and only the shipmates, are allowed on deck during the storm. The remaining crew will be sent to their cabins.

Back in Portsmouth, it was 2 o'clock and the church bell is ringing hundreds of miles away in Kate's and Jamie's village. It was a very important memorial service to commemorate the life of a remarkable man. However, there was another important person not attending. The priest will be leading prayers at this memorial service for the late Captain Charles Heslop and now Captain Temp.

At that moment, Jamie on hisship asked all of his shipmates to join him in prayer in memory of his late father on board ship, asthey were all going to a better life because of him. They all bowed their heads as Jamie said a prayer, for not only Jim but also all of us to be kept safe on the journey ahead of them. After they had all gone, Jamie sat thinking of his father with sadness, looking around the cabin that was once his and then going through the heavy oak desk, he came across a key to the ships safe. On opening it, he found a lot of gold coins and knew that Temp would have put them there.

As the days went by, they were all enjoying their new freedom Kate remarked to Jamie. How the Orphans keep staring at the black children never seen none of them had never seen one, well made Jamie laugh. The wind stayed strong, and although some of the children suffered from the effects of the movement of the ship, they soon found their sea legs. After their chores in the evening, Dingle would start to play the violin, and they would dance and sing well into the night. Teresa, one of the orphanage girls, was originally from Ireland. Her parents had gone to London looking for work and died of diphtheria, so she had ended up in the orphanage.

She remembered her mother singing her Irish folk songs, which she now sang to the crew. She had a wonderful voice, and they all loved listening to her.

Jamie was pleased with the way everyone improved over the next few weeks. Some of the black slave children had learned a little English, but best of all was that everyone was learning how to sail his ship. He was on the lookout all the time for his uncle, Zak, whose ship could come into view. Jamie knew that for Zak, it would be like looking for a needle in a haystack. However, there was always a chance he would find them. With this in mind, he started to make a number of kites over the next few days, having an idea of how to use them against Zak. The first one he made, he tied a cloth at the tail end and poured a little water on it and up the tail. He managed to get it to fly without a problem and felt quite pleased with himself and when some of the children saw him flying the kite, they asked if he could show them how to do it. Jamie had a plan in mind with regard to the kites, so he readily agreed to show them. He kept this to himself so as not to frighten them, telling them to practice flying them every day. Sometimes, he would take the ship to starboard or port depending on which way the wind was blowing and every time putting a little water on the cloth and the tail. Some of them improved quickly, so Jamie told them he was going to soak their tails and cloths in lamp oil instead of water.

Now it was time for Jamie to tell them something else.

'The first thing to remember now is to work in pairs, one to start flying the kite, the other to hold the tail as far away from the ship as you can reach, then set the cloth alight and let it go. I will help you do it now. So remember we may have to do this all over again in the future.'

With that, they lit the cloths that were attached to the kites, and up in the sky, they flew. He demonstrated this, and the others tried it out. It went well and they soon got the hang of it. Up and up they flew until the whole kite disappeared in flames. Jamie was pleased it had worked so well and knew that when the time came, they would all be ready, kites and all.

Chapter 11

Winds remained steady, and they made good progress. It took them almost eight weeks to cross the equator. The orphanage children struggled with the heat and humidity, but the black children revelled in it, remembering the heat of their native birth. They had adapted to life on the ship, but some longed to be on dry land. To improve morale, Jamie decided they would adopt the usual equator crossing ceremony and have some fun. He approached Kate and made some suggestions; she was in full agreement. The day dawned hot and sticky, and Jamie gave orders for a stool and several barrels of seawater to be placed amidships. The boys were curious, and at midday, Jamie put them out of their misery. He told the boys to line up and for the first boy in the queue to sit on the stool. Kate and some of the girls appeared. She had a large pair of scissors in her hand, and the girls had an assortment of razors, soap, and scrubbing brushes. They proceeded to cut hair, shave, and scrub the line of boys. There was much laughter when little Tom asked for a shave, but Kate told him he would have to wait a few years first. The girls made a big show of scrubbing faces and heads, but at the end of the day, there were some very clean boys. 'No more lice!' shouted Kate. 'What about the girls?' called one of the boys? 'We are already clean, and we don't need a shave!' retorted Sam. The girls then brought food up on deck, and they ate and danced into the night. The following day, most admitted they felt better with less hair in the intense heat. They had been at sea for almost three months, and Jamie appreciated all the problems that Captain Cook had encountered on his voyages and was concerned with the provisions getting low. He decided they would sail to Saint Helena

Island run by East India Company. There, they could get fresh water and supplies. His problem was that they were all very young, and he knew he had to find a way to explain this to the Islanders.

Meanwhile, on the Earl, Zak had the same thought. He knew that Jamie would be running low on supplies with all the extra children he had on board the Lady Dorothea. He would only have had enough provisions for seventy crewmen, not for 146 children plus livestock. Therefore, he decided to leave the African coast and head across towards Saint Helena to try and find out whether Jamie had stopped there for provisions.

A couple of weeks passed when early one morning a shout saying 'land ahoy' Mitch shouted from the top of the main mast. Jamie looked through his telescope. 'It's Saint Helena Island,' a cheer went out. It looked like a huge rock jutting out from the sea, but the sea was calm. They dropped anchor just inside the harbour. Jamie said to Mick, 'When I leave the ship, I want you to keep an eye open on the horizon for any ship approaching. Send someone up the main mast. They will spot one from there easily. If there is one, then fire the cannon. I will take my telescope with me just in case it could be the Earl. We should just about have time to up anchor and run.'

Jamie then turned to Kate with instructions,

'Make sure the small youngsters stay down below deck. The rest must look like grown-ups. Tell them we don't want anyone on shore to see we are all so young. JB, I want ten of your biggest crewmen to come with me to go ashore. We will use the long boat.'

The ten crewmen and Jamie rowed to the dock. Jamie approached some men and asked,

'Where can I get provisions?'

One of them laughed, 'Ha- ha we have sold all our toys and baby clothes!'

There was loud laughter from all the other men. Jamie blushed. 'We are here because all the men on board our ship have got scurvy.'

The man felt sorry for them and pointed in the direction of the provision market. They managed to buy all they needed with some of the gold coins Temp had left. They even found fresh water, but it took a few days to row back and forwards to the ship to get everything on board. Jamie deduced that Zak had not been there because no one had said anything about a man looking for him. It had taken them four days of hard work to get everything on board and in order. They had seen a few sharks swimming about and had to avoid the sudden swells that came rolling in from the Atlantic Ocean, but soon, everything was loaded and the ship got underway. Jamie was pleased that all had gone well because if Zak had caught them in the harbour, he would have had no problem in boarding them and that would have been the end of the journey for them all.

They had been sailing for about three hours when there was an almighty yell from the crow's nest that there was a ship approaching. Jamie looked through his telescope and noticed straight away that it was the Earl of Cornwall coming after them. He breathed a sigh of relief that at least they were in open seas and not in the harbour. He quickly called the boys who manned the yardarms. 'Be ready on my command to climb up the main mast as fast as you can and roll up the sails. Get the kites on deck and everyone who has mastered flying them. Send the rest of the youngsters below deck at once.' The boys hurried to carry out Jamie's instructions, and when they were assembled on deck with their kites, he said to them, 'I want you to dip only a little water on to the long tails of the kites because I do not want that part to burn. The cloth at the end is to be dipped in lamp oil and a bit on the kite itself, but do not soak them with too much oil as they may not fly. We are going to fly these lighted kites into the Earl's sails. Keep repeating it until I give you orders to stop.' The boys could hardly wait to get going. 'Timing is very important. Wait for my command to light the cloth. Help each other by starting to get the kites into the air as we have practised before lighting them. It must be done quickly when the Earl begins to pass, but only on my command.' Luckily, there was a strong breeze for the kites. It would be a good hour before Zak's ship caught up with them, so it gave them plenty of time to prepare. Jamie knew that if this way did not work, he would not have time to devise another plan, other than try and outrun them in the dark. He knew Zak would not take a chance boarding them at sea, in case they collided and damaged both the ships. Zak would then follow them until they docked again for provisions and then board them. The Earl was the faster ship, so he could stay behind them for weeks.

Jamie's assumption was right. When Zak caught up with them, he just sailed behind them. He knew that if his plan was to work, the timing had to be exact. He went to Mick, who was at the helm. 'Mick when I put my hand up, steer the ship slightly over to port to allow the Earl to pass. Make sure we are only fifty yards apart more or less. Hold her at that. Is that understood?'

'Yes, Captain,' replied Mick. Jamie now had to put his plan into action. He made sure the boys had lit oil lamps and had put some oil on the kites. Now was the time to set his plan in motion. He shouted to the riggers to start to dismantle the mainsail. Ever so fast they climbed the mast and started to haul in the sail. At the same time, he put his hand up towards Mick. Within minutes, Jamie's ship had slowed down and slightly moved to port. As predicted the Earl was taken by surprise, it started to sail past about fifty yards away. The boys had got the kites ready, and Jamie ordered them to light the cloths at the end of the tails and get them airborne. The Earl began to pass. Jamie shouted to the boys to steer the kites into her sails. The kites were flying up and up with the tail cloths on fire straight into the Earl's sails. The canvas sails started to catch alight, and the kites themselves were now completely on fire. Jamie was overwhelmed with emotion, thinking to himself what an amazing group of boys he had. He quickly gave orders to rig the yardarms and told Mick to steer clear of the Earl. As the Dorothea sailed away, he could see Zak frantically shouting orders, making some of the crew go up the mast to release the burning sails, whilst other members of the crew were trying to put out the fires below. To Jamie's relief, the fire did not do much damage to the lower part of the Earl. What had been burnt would then take them at least four weeks to repair, and that would only be a temporary job enough to get them back to England. From now on, it would be the last time he would see Zak for a few good years. With the ship, sailing away from the Earl the last person

Jamie saw on it was Spider at the helm, who took a chance to raise his hand to Jamie as if to say goodbye. Jamie filled with emotion for his friend. He would have liked to have him on this long adventure, but he knew Spider would have chosen his family first.

Chapter 12

The Dorothea was pulling away fast now that it was in full sail. Everyone was relieved; the violin started playing, then the singing and dancing followed, with Jamie going around congratulating everyone for doing a good job. The following morning, Jamie assembled everyone on deck. 'Yesterday was a job well done, but next time, it could be a pirate ship, and we may not be so lucky'. He asks them all again to keep a lookout for ships and shout straight away if they saw one. Therefore, he could find out if they were friend or foe. As the weeks passed, Jamie made sure not only that the children learnt to read and write but also that some of the boys learned to be carpenters, farmers looking after all the animals on board, and furnisher makers. The girls were taught to make clothes, and cook. Jamie knew they would need these skills when they reached their paradise island. He had no illusions about pirates, knowing they would take the ship and cargo without hesitation, apart from the slaves, the rest of crew and himself would be thrown overboard. The Lady Dorothea was flying a merchant ship flag. Normally, merchant ships just tried to outrun pirates, so Jamie hoped they would not open fire if he came across them.

The weather was clear and warm with a stiff breeze pushing them through the ocean. All the crew were busy working, so Jamie went to find Kate and asked her how she was coping with teaching the children. She told him they were all learning well, especially the slave children. 'Jamie, you look worried,' observed Kate.

'We will have to think of a way to stop a pirate ship in case we are unfortunate enough to meet up with one.'

'Remember what your mother taught you: You'll find a way around the problem'.

'I will do just that,' he replied. Jamie spent several days pondering on the problem, but an idea started to form in his mind. He decided to give it a try, as he knew a pirate ship could appear at any time. Needing the strongest of his crew, he selected Skip, Bates, Curly, Hermit, ginger, and Rabbit. He motioned for them to follow him down to the hold, making them search amongst the cargo to see if they could find cotton sheets. Before long, they came across a trunk full of them. Jamie instructed two of the boys to take nine of the sheets up to the deck and the other four boys to find some empty barrels. He told them to take six to the deck, then Jamie found some fishnets and took them also. When they all arrived on deck, Jamie said, ' Right Lads I want you to tie three sheets together firmly, like making a rope, tie a fishnet around each barrel, and then secure a barrel to each end of the length of the sheet'. The six young lads wondered what the skipper had got in mind. When they had tied the barrels to the length of sheet, Jamie checked they were all secure and told the boys to take them to the stern of the ship. The boys worked in pairs, hauling the barrels up to the stern of the ship. Jamie told Skip to take one barrel across to the port side and Curly to take the barrel on the other end to the starboard side.

'Bates, I want you to hold the middle. Then on the count of three, all of you throw it into the sea. It needs to end up in the water in as straight a line as possible.'

Jamie counted to three, and the boys threw the long length of the sheets along with the barrels attached at either end as far as they could over the stern of the ship. They did quite well on the first attempt. Jamie told the other three boys to do the same with the next set of barrels and sheets. They did slightly better. The boys and Jamie watched as the barrels and sheets floated further away. Luckily, the barrels kept floating apart for quite some distance, which gave Jamie hope that his plan should work. He told them to make more and practise for a few days and that he wanted at least forty of them made and put to one side, just in case they needed them. The sheets and barrels Jamie had told them to make was an idea he had, hopefully, to use against the pirates, but so as not to alarm everyone, he kept this idea to himself.

Everyone on board was getting more professional each week doing their specific jobs. As each day went by, even the two extra boys on the helm had progressed steering the ship under Jamie's watchful eye. They were making good progress; the wind was in their favour, and the weather was hot, so Jamie decided to make for Cape Town in South Africa to replenish their supplies. He knew that the weather could change instantly and kept a watchful eye on the sky. This particular day the horizon seemed to darken, and he knew instantly they were in for a storm. The skipper told the crew to batten the hatches securely and sent all but the deckhands down below. Buckets were secured on deck to catch as much rainwater as possible to add to their depleting drinking water. The storm worsened. Jamie shouted to ring the bell and take down the sails except for the forestaysail, which they needed to help keep the ship on course. The decks were soon awash with rain and seawater as the wind battered the ship relentlessly. Most of the young crew were quite scared, as this was the first storm they had encountered, and the younger children and girls huddled together down below, praying for their lives. However, Jamie had been in a storm before with his father and he took the helm, guiding the ship through the storm, shouting orders to his deckhands. The storm blew all night, and next morning, as it started so quickly, died down the same way. Many said a thankful prayer, after an exhausted night. Jamie gave orders to raise the sails. He gathered all the ship's complement on deck, to do a head counts, then asking if everyone was accounted for. There was silence for a moment when Bates shouted out, 'I have not seen my friends, Curly and Hermit.' 'When did you last see them?' asked the skipper. 'Last night, up here on this deck I think they may have been washed overboard because their bunks haven't been slept in.'

'Are you all sure that nobody has seen them?' Everyone looked at each other, but nobody had seen them. Jamie was heartbroken to have lost two young boys overboard. He said to everyone, 'I want you all to pray for the deaths of these two brave young men now.' They all bowed their heads when the hatch door that led to the lower hold opened with a squeak and out came the two boys, stinking of rum and very drunk. With that, everybody started laughing. Jamie was furious and shouted at the top of his voice, 'This is not a laughing matter! They have disobeyed my orders and therefore must be disciplined when they have sobered up! Now, get them both out of my sight.'

Instantly, they all stopped laughing and hurried away to go silently about their chores, wondering what disciplinary action the captain would take against the two boys. Then Jamie went down to see Kate. Luckily, she was on her own, straight away Jamie, erupting with laughter, put his arm around her. 'Did you see their faces they were horrified at what I said.'

'Yes, I did and just hope you did not mean it, for those two boys, like the rest of them, have been through hell during their short lives, losing their parents and ending up in that dreadful orphanage.'

'Kate, I had to scare them. We have to depend on each other. We are not adults, and it takes two of us to do one man's job sometimes. So when I have disciplined the pair of them, with what I have in mind for them, you can guarantee no one else will step out of line again.'

During the evening, Curly and Hermit had been told, of all the different types of punishment that they could face by their laughing friends. They were petrified and hardly slept at all that night. The following morning, all those not on duties were assembled on the top deck, and the Captain told Curly and Hermit to come and stand beside him. Curly was trembling with fear and said to Jamie, 'we are very, very sorry, sir. We will never do anything like this again. We thought there would be no harm in having only one glass of rum each, but after I had drunk only half of it, I do not remember a thing'.

Jamie was trying very hard not to laugh. 'I hope you both mean that, but I still have to discipline you both. When you went down below to the lower deck, next to the rum barrels, was there a bad smell coming from the lower hold?'

'Yes, Skipper. I think it is coming from the livestock,' replied Curly. 'It might well be the livestock, but it is not that smell! I want you both to go down to where the slaves were locked up. That's the smell that I am referring to you are to scrub it out and throw all the rubbish into the sea. 'Aye, sir,' they both said with a sigh of relief. However, after a moment, having thought about it, they looked at each other and said, 'Oh, hell!' not them! As for the rest of the ship's complement, they were mightily relieved it was not any of them. They scattered quickly as no one wanted to incur Jamie's wrath, and be given duties like that. Jamie asked Kate to stay. 'Kate, the punishment I have given those boys was not that bad.'

'Quite right and that should be a lesson they will not forget,' smiled Kate.

As the day wore on, Jamie found Sam and asked her how the boys were getting on with their fencing lessons. 'They are coming on very well, especially the big black lad. When he is not with the crew learning how to sail this ship, he is back with me again, taking fencing lessons.'

'Yes Sam I had noticed this young man was working hard, learning as much as he could.'

AS Mitch was nearby, Jamie instructed him to fetch this big lad and Jada, to his cabin. Jamie went directly to his cabin, and almost immediately, there was a knock on the door. Peggy started to bark; Jamie picked her up to keep her quiet, opened the door telling them both to enter. He told Jada, to let the young man try to speak on his own and he would try to understand him.

'Skipper, I believe you want to see me?' He spoke in quite good English.

'I do, but please both of you sitdown,young man what is your name?'

'Rosen, Skipper,' he replied. Jamie noticed that although Rosen was only about fourteen years of age, he was nearly six feet tall, and the well-developed muscles rippled across his silky black skin.

'Rosen, I am very pleased with the way you are performing. From what I have seen, you must have been on a ship before.'

'Yes, my father was a fisherman, and he showed me how to handle a small sailing boat.'

'Tell me, Rosen, why you have not asked me to take you back home to see your family?'

'They were all taken into slavery, my two young sisters, my older brother, my mother and my father Skipper', He then told Jamie he wanted to be like him when he grows up, good at everything, and one day own his own ship so he would find them and then take them back home'.

'Looks like we both have a score to settle when we get older.' Jamie then went on to tell Rosen about his problems and that perhaps one day they could help each other. He stood up and offered his hand to Rosen. Rosen shook Jamie's hand, and they smiled at one another, knowing they had a common bond. As Rosen and Jada, were leaving, Jamie commented on how well Rosen spoke English.

As the days passed, everything was going to plan, they had only sighted two ships, and both of them were merchant ship. One of the sows had given birth to ten piglets. One of the girls called Anne who looks after the pigs acted as midwife and had been washing them every day, so the rest of the crew nicknamed her Pig Wash Anne.

Chapter 13

By now, the Earl of Cornwall had managed to limp back to Portsmouth docks. After she had docked the town, the constable was waiting to talk to Zak. He asked him what he knew about Temp's murder. Zak realised that this was his opportunity to lay the blame on Jamie.

'Jamie Heslop has stolen the ship called the Lady Dorothea, along with all customers' belongings on board. Captain Temp tried to stop him, but Jamie ran his sword through the poor old man. I have four witnesses who saw him kill Captain Temp. Fetch them here, and they will give you their statements of the event.'

After the constable had heard all the evidence from the four witnesses, he issued a warrant to the arrest of Jamie Heslop for the murder of Captain Temp Elliott. Spider knew this to be untrue, but he had to keep his mouth shut as he would lose his job or worse and his family could be put in danger. Zak returned to Compton Manor and told Edwina a story of how he nearly caught Jamie but he slipped through his fingers. He didn't want to go into too much detail, as he didn't want anyone to find out that a mere boy had got the better of him, but next time he wouldn't and he would have great pleasure in killing him himself. He also told her that he had framed Jamie for the murder of Temp. She was a bit concerned that when Jamie returned and told his side of the story, it would be his word against Zak's.

'Edwina, if he does return, I will make sure he will end up in a coffin. Once he steps off his ship, anyone can kill a murderer with no questions asked, and that keeps us all within the law.' Edwina felt much relieved by this, and they smiled at each other.

Now Lady Dorothea was now approaching Cape Town; with a strong north westerly wind behind them, it was not long before they entered the harbour. They all could see a huge mountain before them, and the orphanage children gasped in amazement. Most of them had never seen grass before, let alone mountains and beaches. They dropped anchor, and Jamie gathered and told them to abide by the same rules as they had in St Helena Port

I will remind you again in case you have forgotten because this is important. The very young must keep below deck and stay out of sight. The rest of you who helped before with the loading, remember to wear the clothes that make you look like adults.'

Rosen asked the skipper if he could go with him this time. Although Jamie would have liked to have Rosen with him, he explained that the only time English merchant ships had black people on board was as slaves helping them or locked up below deck. He could not take the chance of Rosen being seen as part of the crew. Then, as before, he instructed the same ten to lower the longboat and one of the pinnacle boats and load them with empty water butts, reminding them not to call him Skipper once they were off the ship.

Whilst they were getting the two boats ready, Jamie went to the safe in his cabin to collect some more of the gold coins. Ten of the strongest boys rowed the longboat, and Jamie took six boys with him in the pinnacle boat and used the sails to get them to the dock. When they reached the shore, Jamie repeated the same story about the older men having scurvy so as not to arouse suspicion. The manager of the warehouse was unperturbed. All he wanted to do was sell his goods. It took Jamie and the lads three days to load their provisions on to the ship. This time, they had to load a lot of cornmeal for the livestock. Jamie had been vigilance as ever taken notice of the other ships moored up in the harbour, fully aware that they could be slave ships or even pirates and that he must remember to recognise them in case he was to meet up with these ships in the future.

Everybody was working very hard, loading the boats and then unloading their stores on to the ship and taking it all down below deck. There was only one thing on each of their minds, that they were all determined to reach the sanctuary of this paradise island.

Whilst they had been loading the ship, unbeknown to them, a devious old scumbag who went by the name Hooknose had watched them from the shore. He was unable to get work on a ship now, so he had to beg for money. He looked a lot older than his fifty years and had earned his nickname due to the shape of his nose. Watching what Jamie and his crew were doing, he thought it odd that only young boys were taking cargo to the ship. Each day, he had looked through his battered telescope but never saw any older men, and a fisherman friend of his had mentioned that the ship's crews are only kids who were dressed to look older. Hooknose decided to mention this to his friend, One Arm Jacks. Jacks, was a old pirate, who had seen better days. He rarely washed, and his long black hair was filthy and matted. Somewhere in the past, he had lost an arm in battle. Hooknose thought he might be able to make himself a bit of money, hoping this old pirate might be interested, but after a few days he could not find him anywhere. Neither, One Arm Jacks nor his ship, so he decided to wait until Jacks returned.

Everything by now had been loaded aboard the Lady Dorothea Successfully, Jamie congratulated everyone as they had done a good job, and he was very pleased and said that they were to set sail in the morning so to get a night's sleep.

Jamie used this time to talk to Kate and Sam. 'Have there been any problems with any of the youngsters?'

Sam replied, 'Yes! All those who had stayed on board would like to go ashore if only for a few hours, just to stand on firm ground.'

'I understand this problem as I felt the same way the first time I sailed with my father. Once we get clear of Africa, I will stop at the first sighting of land, providing it looks safe. Now go and get a good night's sleep as we have a busy day tomorrow.'

They wished him goodnight and hurried away to their beds.

As dawn broke, all the crew are scurrying around the ship, preparing to set sail. It took a while, but they were all becoming more proficient with their tasks..

Soon, they were in full sail, blowing in a strong breeze. After they were underway, Jamie asked the main members of his crew to meet him in his cabin. He told them all of the dangers they would be encountering whilst sailing around the Cape, particularly the strong currents that occur when the cold Atlantic Ocean meets up with the warm Indian Ocean. Jamie indicated the position of these on the nautical map he found in his cabin. 'This can make the weather very unpredictable, so I was told by my friend Temp. He also told them. 'I am keeping well clear of the shore in case of a sudden gale that could blow us on to the rocks. 'We will encounter this weather within a few days. Temp also told me that to sail well beyond a place called Cape Point and not to mistake it for the southern tip of South Africa. If we started to turn north too soon, we would sail into a place called False Bay, and that is full of shallow rocks with two bigger ones. It is a graveyard for ships. I want everyone to keep an eye open for this bay. I might not be on watch at that time, so you must be on guard at all times until we have sailed clear of this place and reached the Indian Ocean.'

Jamie was satisfied that they understood as they all looked worried, and he knew they would all do their best. He told them to inform the rest of the crew to take care whilst sailing through these dangerous seas.

For now, everyone on board was relaxed as the ship sailed calmly towards Cape Point. Jamie figured that the steady breeze should take the ship to the Cape by morning. If there were to be bad weather, at least it would be during the day, so he decided to get some rest, leaving Mick at the helm. He woke up early the next morning just as they were sailing past Cape Point. The ship was at least four miles out to sea. Suddenly, within minutes, the weather changed. There was a crack of thunder, and the ship was heaving in turbulent water. Jamie rushed to the helm to help Mick and shouted out to JB to ring the ship's bell. The crew were already hauling in sails, and it was getting more dangerous by the minute. Again, they left the forestaysail up to help steer her. The wind was so strong the ship was slowly being blown towards the shore sideways. Jamie could hear the younger children screaming in the decks below and the cattle bellowing, as the ship was being tossed around like a cork.

Jamie was frightened. For the first time, he wondered if he had done the right thing by putting all these young lives at risk, as things were so bad. He did everything he could to stop the ship being blown towards the coast, but it was no good. It still kept drifting. After battling for what seemed like hours and near to exhaustion, one of the crew shouted out that there were rocks ahead.

The rain was coming down in torrents, and the decks were awash, but they could just see two enormous rocks jutting out of the sea along with some smaller ones on either side. They were only about half a mile away from them. As the ship drifted closer, they could see a gap between the two rocks that looked identical to the one at the entrance to False Bay. The ship was being blown straight towards them broadside on. Jamie knew if they continued on this course, they would then be crushed to pieces.

The ship was now within 300 yards from the rocks. Jamie tried not to panic as his mind was racing, trying to think of a way to save them all, hoping not to shout 'ABANDON SHIP'.

Then all of a sudden, he remembered what his father had said about the ship. He shouted to Mitch to try and raise another sail and to Joe to go down to the lower hull and find out if they had taken in water.

JB soon came back with a reply, 'Skipper, there is very little water down there.'

Thank God! Jamie thought as he was hoping this was because the ship was very new and it should be watertight. He shouted out to everyone to hold on tight, and he quickly turned the ship head on towards the two rocks. With the extra sail, it was heading towards the gap between them. He was hoping and praying it was big enough to get through. He had remembered his father had told him the ship had a flat-bottomed design to go in shallow waters. The ship was near enough now for Jamie to be able to see that the gap between the rocks was just big enough for the ship to sail through, hopefully without hitting the rocks on either side or any submerged ones.

Mick and the crew could not believe what the skipper was attempting to do as the ship was being tossed from side to side. Jamie battled with the wind to keep on course as he could see the rocks on either side of the hull now. The Dorothea stayed firm and sailed between the rocks and apart from a few scratches came out the other side undamaged. Everyone relaxed and cheered Jamie for his efforts. He was quick to remind them it was not over yet as they were now in False Bay and still in the storm. Just as he had said those words, the storm had begun to subside as quickly as it had begun. The crew asked Jamie how the hell he had thought of doing what he did.

'I think it was as if my father had put the thought into my head, telling me what to do. Perhaps he is looking over us,' he said with sadness, wishing his father were beside him.

By now, the storm had subsided enough for everyone to come back out on the deck. Some were feeling unwell or being sick, but happy to be alive.

Chapter 14

Once the weather calmed and the crew had rested, they sailed out of False Bay and continued on their journey. It had given Jamie time to go below deck to see Kate and check the rest of crew Pig Wash Anne waylaid into their Skipper, complaining to him that her pigs had been frightened during the storm. Wanted to know why he had not stopped the ship, from rolling from side to side.

Jamie had tried very hard not to laugh. 'Sorry, I will not let it happen again.' Everyone who had overheard her burst out laughing. When he got to Kate's cabin, the door was open. Some of the children were lying on beds and the floor all around her cabin. Kate was using it to look after the sick.

'Kate, why did you not tell me that some of them are not well?' 'I think you have enough worries with the storm without me adding to it' 'Where are you going to sleep tonight?'

'I am staying with Sam and the girls in their cabin.'

'You seem to have it all under control, so that's one less thing for me to be concerned about.'

With the weather and the wind in their favour, the ship sailed past the Port Elizabeth, which was the last point before sailing out into the Indian Ocean. The crew had cleared up after the storm, and things returned to a steady pace with everyone doing their normal duties. Jamie once again called everyone together, telling them that it could be some time before they sighted land and to use all food and water sparingly. He informed them that they were well over halfway and had now been at sea for over twenty weeks and that they had made good time and hoping they would reach an uninhabited island before long, which brought a big cheer from them all.

Jamie went to his cabin with Mitch to look at the ship's map to try and find any small island on the way to their Island but realised they would have to change course slightly to find an island to stop at. Jamie decided to do this and find an island to dock his ship, even though Temp had warned him of pirates in the Indian Ocean. With that in mind, he making sure everyone on board was on the lookout for them.

They had been sailing for about three more weeks when early one morning, the boy at the top of the mast shouted out 'Land Ahoy'. Sure enough, there was quite a large island. Jamie looked through his telescope and could see a number of volcanoes on the island. He summoned his crew and told them, he thought the island was called the Santa Apolonia So the Skipper told them. 'If my memory serves me right, the French could occupied this Island they trade in slaves, so we will have to be very careful. We will have to take a chance and find an uninhabited place to drop anchor, then go ashore in the small boats, as it is too dangerous to beach the ship. Everyone can relax on the beach, and everything should be fine for a few hours just in case we have to make a quick getaway'.

'Right, Skip, Bates, and Curly, you will be our scouts and I want you three to be the first ashore when we drop anchor.' He carried on telling them. 'You threespread out about 500 yards apart away from the beach, where everyone will be, and keep an eye open for any French. If you spot them, you must get back to me fast. I will signal the ship to fire the cannon, which will be the signal to start weighing anchor and get the hell out fast.'Rosen, I want you to use the pinnacle boat to ferry the youngsters there and back. I will use the yawl boat. Mitch, you and some of the other crew take the longboat first with my scouts and then help ferry the rest. Rosen,' I'll wager I can ferry more young ones than you.'

'Ha-Ha it's a bet, Skipper, my skill against yours,' Rosen said in some kind of English.

They both laughed, and then Jamie said to Joe, 'I want you and a couple of others to stay on board to look after the ship, especially you, Mitch, as you are a good shot with the cannon. Now, let's all get back to work.'

After scouting around for a couple of hours, it was about mid-morning when they came across a small lagoon. There was smoke coming from a volcano overlooking the beach. It was deserted with beautiful golden sand. As the ship dropped anchor, Rosen said, 'That volcano looks as if it may erupt at any moment, Skipper. Perhaps it is not wise to anchor here.'

'We will only be here for a few hours, so I am sure nothing will happen in that time.' The crew got underway, carrying out Jamie's instructions. Kate had made arrangements to look after the sick.

Sam had asked if she could take Peggy with her and Jamie readily agreed as he thought it would do Peggy good too, to stretch her legs, on dry land.

When everybody was shipped ashore, it gave them at least six hours to play, swim, and rest. Jamie took a few of them to pick fresh fruit and coconuts, as they were bored with eating sauerkraut and pickled vegetables. Peggy ran along behind them, excitedly sniffing the ground.

Sam noticed they were going off somewhere, taking a couple of the slave children to follow and pick fresh fruit.. Very soon, all of the gang came across some coconut trees. Some started to shake the trunk vigorously, but to no avail. The coconuts would not fall down. The slave children laughed, and then one of them shimmied up the tree and then dropped all the coconuts down to them. With having done this sort of thing before as young children. After an hour, they had enough coconuts to take back to the ship, as well as eating their fill and drinking the refreshing milk. They had also come across other fruits to take back, so they hauled it all back to the beach and enjoyed swimming with the others. The day was passing fast, and everyone was happy and relaxed when, all of a sudden, there was a loud bang and ash started falling from the sky. Rosen shouted, 'It's the volcano erupting. We must get back to the ship now.' Jada, was at hand to make sure everyone understood the danger. Jamie started waving a flag at the ship. Within two minutes, the cannon were fired from the ship, warning the three scouts to return at once.

Rosen told two of his men to cut some big leaves down and give them to everyone to put over their heads to protect them from the hot ash. There was no time to lose now as lava began to flow slowly down the hillside towards them. All but one of the three boys had returned from scouting around; Skip was missing. Jamie asked the others, 'Which way did Skip go'? They pointed towards some thick vegetation on the other side of the beach. Jamie told Mick to follow him and shouted at the rest of them on the beach to return quickly to the ship.

Jamie and Mick ran off in the direction they had been shown. It was not long before they found him. He was crawling slowly along as he had sprained his ankle, but by now, they could smell the trees burning and had to move fast. They had no choice but to carry him back to the beach. When they got there, everybody had left except Rosen, who had stayed behind with Jamie's boat. Rosen called out to them to hurry and get into the boat. There was not much time left. The lava was now coming down the beach, so they threw Skip in the boat and rowed quickly away from the shore.

When they were all aboard, they weighed anchor quickly and sailed away. Jamie was soon to say to Jada, that he should have listened to Rosen. She agreed with him, saying that perhaps he would listen next time. Feeling a little subdued, he went to his cabin, and there was Sam with his dog to greet him.

'My, that was close, Sam.'

'Yes, it was, Skipper. So let's have a small drink of coconut juice to celebrate, to a good job well done and along with lovely fresh fruit for a week or more.'.'

Sam had a jug ready, and they sat facing one another across Jamie's desk, drinking the sweet juice. They were soon relaxed and smiling, chatting about the events of the day and enjoying each other's company.

That day that Jamie's ship had set sailed from Cape Town Harbour, by now Hooknose found his friend One Arm Jack late in the evening in the tavern. He asked Jacks if he could sit down at his table to give him some information he had come across.

'Make it quick, you old scumbag. It better be good as I have had a bad week.'

'I have seen a ship that only had young lads on board. They loaded supplies from the stores here, but they were all youngsters.'

'Are you sure, your eyes are not seeing things in your old age, your old fool'? He replied back. 'No sir, for sure I saw the ship full of young lads.' Being interested 'Go on, tell me more' Jacks said in a stern voice.

'What's it worth to me?' Getting an answer back abruptly. 'At this moment, your life, so get on with it,' replied Jacks getting impatient with the old scumbag and he wasn't sure if he was been strung him along for gold pieces.

Shaking in his smelly, worn-out boots, Hooknose said, 'My fisherman friend told me he had sailed past this ship and had seen about forty white and black kids on board'. Hooknose went on to say, These youngsters were trying to hide that they were only kids.. However, they didn't fool me I could see that some of them were dressed up to look like full-grown men. Also I could hear cattle noises coming from inside the ship'. .He also went on to tell Jacks that the ship was very unique and that he had only ever seen one ship like it a few years back, captained by a James Cook.

'Yeah, I remember seeing that ship as well,' said Jacks.

'My friend also said that the ship seemed not well armed it only had a one pounder cannon and one swivel gun.'

Hooknose paused to sip his beer.'Get on with it you old bugger! I haven't got all day, what time did the ruddy ship sail and in what direction?' Jacks asked.

'It was heading south around the Cape towards the Indian Ocean, probably going to India as most English do now. They left about mid-morning today.

Jacks rose from his stool and hurried down the harbour to a different tavern. 'Jacks where is my reward'? But Jacks was long gone.

He went in search of his Dutch pirate friend called Captain Nancarrow, knowing he was around somewhere as he had seen his ship anchored in the harbour. This man, Nancarrow, was one of the fiercest pirates you could come across. He was a huge beast of a man standing well over six feet. Fighting was his life, which showed on his scarred face and hands. Everybody gave him a wide berth because with his long ginger hair and penetrating dark-green eyes, he looked extremely fearsome.

Jacks found him in the tavern as he thought he would and sat down at his table, calling for two jugs of ale. He repeated to Nancarrow exactly what Hooknose had told him but omitted to tell him which direction Jamie had sailed off to, hoping he would get away with that piece of information.

Hooknose said 'I have a problem with my old girl. A bad encounter with a Spanish ship and just made it back here. My ship is in need of repairs, could take three weeks or more. Your ship is fast, I'll borrow yours'. 'Like hell, you well!' exclaimed Nancarrow in a loud voice. He took a large gulp of his ale before continuing. 'You can tag along with me to capture the ship and we share the spoils. I'll have the black and white kids. Sell them to the Arabs for gold you can have the ship. I think that's a fair deal?. I'll need you to use at least half your crew as most of mine have left or been killed.'

'Deal' said Hooknose and they shook hands. 'Drink up you scallywag, times a wasting' Nancarrow said. Therefore, they downed their ale and hotfooted to the harbour to organise the crews and load supplies. Timing was important, and they knew they would have to set sail within the next day. The first thing Jacks did was to find Hooknose. He told him that if he wanted to be paid a reward, he had to sail with him to help recognise Jamie's ship.

Hooknose readily agreed. At the very least, he reasoned he would have somewhere to sleep and food to eat, however bad it might be. Nancarrow's ship was ready late the next day and set sail going south, heading for the Indian Ocean. They made sure they were flying the English flag, which would enable them to get up close to the Lady Dorothea, without them suspecting anything.

Meanwhile back on the Lady Dorothea, Kate, Sam, and a few of the girls had laid the table in the galley with fruit and some buns and a freshly made cake. It was Jamie's fifteenth birthday, and they wanted to mark the occasion. Kate had made sure he was at the helm and passed the word around and that they were all to keep the surprise quiet. Mick told Jamie he had to go to the galley quickly and he would take over the helm.

Jamie ran to the lower deck, thinking there was a problem, but when he opened the door, he found nearly all the crew crowded into the galley. Even Skip, standing on one leg, was there. They cheered and slapped him on the back, wishing him well. He was overwhelmed and struggled to maintain his composure, fighting to hold back his tears of emotion, but when he managed to talk, he said to them all, 'Thanks. I hope and pray I can get you all to our paradise island safely.'

The rest of the day is spent relaxing with Dingle playing the violin and Teresa singing, Except for the crew that where on watch as they kept the ship on course and were on the lookout for pirates.

The following day, it was back to the usual routine, with Jamie, inspecting everything to make sure it was shipshape and that everyone was doing their chores. It also gave Jamie time to talk to some of the youngsters. He wanted to know what trade they were learning on board ship because he knew they would have to build shelters to live in on the island for the next six years when they arrived there.

During the previous two weeks, after they had left the island Santa Apolonia, there had been sightings of four ships. When Jamie had looked through his telescope, he had told the crew they were merchant ships and were only passing by. However, today, they spotted a ship on the horizon. Looking through his telescope, he did not like what he saw, so being cautious, he ordered Mitch to ring the ship's bell whilst he kept an eye on the oncoming ship. Soon, he realised this ship that was sailing towards them was a thirty-gun cruiser and was the one that he had seen in the harbour back in Cape Town. Then it had been flying a French flag; now it was flying a British one, and the name of that ship he remembered was called the La Liberte, but the name was now been blanked out. Jamie knew in his heart that something was very amiss; he called urgently to his crew to be alert and for everyone else to go below decks. He yelled at Bates, 'get the same gang we used to make those sheets and barrels. Go to the stern and take the covers off them and get ready.'

Bates hurried to carry out Jamie's orders, and the boys threw the covers off the barrels and sheets. Just then, a hand grabbed Jamie's arm. He looked down and saw it was little Tom.

'Why are you not below in your cabin, young man?'

'Mr Skipper, they say we might be all going to die, so I wanted to say thank you for taking me away from that nasty Mr Sid, and I do not mind dying with you, sir,' replied Tom.

With a lump in his throat, Jamie said, 'No, little fella, we are definitely not going to die, so, Tom, I want you to be a man and go down to the cabins and help me by looking after the girls.'

Tom was delighted to help and, with a big grin on his face, said, 'Yes, Mr Captain.' He saluted, and off he went. Jamie turned his mind back to the problem at hand. The other ship was getting closer, and he estimated it could be within a quarter of a mile in about an hour. He quickly gathered a few of his crew. 'Get everything that floats that we do not need and to take it amidships. If need be, get some of the youngsters to help. Hurry! We do not have much time.'

They rushed off, and within a few minutes, there were chairs, tables, wooden boxes, even parts of carriages, and carts that they had broken up, stacking it all amidships. Jamie told Skip, Bates, Curly, Hermit, ginger, and Rabbit that it was now time to put into action what they practised with the sheets and barrels.

'Joe, Mitch, and I will hold each sheet in the middle. When I give the order on the count of three, go'! Janie told them it was very important that they throw the barrels and sheets into the sea at the same time. When the first one is thrown in, the next one must be ready, and must be thrown in straight after the first, then the next and the next and so on. It must go like clockwork as their lives may depend on it. The idea was that hopefully one or more of the two barrels will pass down each side of the ship and carry the sheets under the ship's keel and get entangled in the ship's rudder. The rest of them will be amidships with all the debris that they have piled up, and when Janie shouted, they must start throwing it all over the side. He told them to make sure they throw it out a bit at a time as far out into the sea as they could so that it didn't get caught up in the sheets as they were throwing the debris over the stern. We want them to think that along with the sheets and barrels, we are trying to lighten the load in order to outrun them.'

Jamie had decided not to use the kites this time as he had with Zak because he knew the pirates would not think twice about opening fire on them. They would undoubtedly use guns, not cannons, so as not to damage the ship that, as to them, it was worth a lot of money. A few dead youngsters would be no problem to them. He told everyone not to fight the pirates because it would be a waste of time, just surrender because he did not want anybody to get hurt or killed. Unfortunately, Sam had her own opinion. She was not going to let a dirty old pirate touch her. Jamie did all he could to make her see sense as she could endanger the others, but she only half-heartedly agreed. Jamie hoped and prayed that what he was doing would work, but having not practice on a real ship doing this, he knew they would also need a good bit of luck.

Back on board the La Liberte, Hooknose was the one who had spotted Jamie's ship.

Captain Nancarrow also looked through his telescope and called out to Jacks that he had been correct as he could only see kids on board the ship. Soon Nancarrow addressed his crew, 'There is no need to use guns or cannons. I will take this ship right up against her.

We will all go aboard, but I do not want any harm done to the kids because they are money to me alive, and you, Jacks, will be the new owner of a ship.' He laughed out loud, thinking this was easy prey.

The pirate ship had taken down the Union Jack and hoisted up the skull and crossbones. 'This flag should put the fear of God into them,' shouted Nancarrow.

When the pirate ship was only 300 yards away, Jamie yelled at his crew, 'One…two…three…go!' They started throwing the rubbish over each side; the barrels and sheets followed into the sea from the stern. On seeing this, Nancarrow and Jacks burst out laughing, saying, 'Look at them throwing stuff overboard. They are like scared rats, trying to lighten their ship to outrun us.'

Jamie feared his plan was not working. The pirate ship was getting closer and closer. He knew they would come close then turn starboard or port side at the last minute in order to board them. He could see the pirates' face quite clearly as their ship was now no more than a 100 yards away.

In a last desperate attempt, Jamie told the six boys to quickly tie the last of the fishnets on to the middle of the sheets with the barrels and let it go...

With his head down in despair, he went down to cabins, where most of the children had gathered. With a lump in his throat, he said to them all, 'I am very sorry my plan is not working. I am going to show the surrender flag.'

Leaving them somewhat petrified, he went back up on deck with his flag. Within a few more minutes, the pirates would be near enough ready to board them. Jamie thought like hell he would make it easy for them and shouted to Mick, 'quickly turn to starboard'. Mick obeyed, and the ship turned sharply. Then one minute, two, three, then four minutes passed, and the pirate ship did not follow them. They could now see clearly the pirate captain raising hell! Jamie and his crew then realised after all his plan had worked.

The ship's rudder was jammed. It could only steer straight ahead.

Then it was bedlam aboard the Lady Dorothea. Everyone on deck was jumping up and down, waving their arms, knowing they had stopped the pirate ship. The others came up from below and joined in the cheering, hardly daring to believe their narrow escape.

Captain Nancarrow with One Arm Jacks beside him shouted across to Jamie, 'If it takes the rest of my life, I will kill you, you son of a bitch, for making me look like an idiot.'

Jamie just shrugged his shoulders and thought to himself how close that had been and looking upwards towards the sky gave thanks to his mother and father as he felt they had been watching over him.

Very soon, they were well out of range from any cannon fire should the pirates decide to fire and were now sailing away from the distressed ship. Everyone on the Dorothea was overjoyed with the outcome, thanks Jamie for his efforts, but he was soon to say to them all, 'It is not over yet. There are still more pirates out there. We will only be safe when we get to our sanctuary island, but for now, just work hard and keep your eyes open.'

Chapter 15

Over the next few days, everything went back to normal, the skipper had dinner every evening with his crew, and this gave them all time to talk things over, including finding out how much food and water remained. Everyone on board was improving at the trades they were endeavouring to master. One particular evening, Mitch told Jamie that on the day the pirate ship had been after them, he had been down in the hold looking for things to throw overboard at them, and he had stumbled across a large trunk with writing on it and a big red cross. Jamie found this curious and wanted to find out what was inside it, so he made plans for them both to go down the next day to investigate.

The next morning, the weather had changed, the trade winds had stopped blowing, and all was calm. This was bad news for Jamie as he remembered his father saying that this could last for a number of weeks. He decided to launch the longboat straight away with a full rowing crew and tow the ship towards their goal, but he also knew it could be a problem as the rowers were only boys and had little experience. But he had to try. He reasoned the trunk in the hold would have to wait for another day. Right now, he had to try and use the sweeps that were huge oars about twenty-eight feet long. These were used inside the ship, and even with the biggest boys, it would be a problem for them to row.. Everyone involved tried their best, but it was all in vain. The boys rowed and rowed, but it was too much rowing, the longboat for two hours and was completely worn out. It was very hot, and everyone was drinking a lot of water. By the end of the day, Jamie had given up any hope of moving the ship this way. He knew he had to tell everyone to stay in the shade and not to rush around and to stop work, thinking this would help to save the water. When everything was in order, he returned to his cabin.

Kate saw the way Jamie was looking and went down to try to console him. She knocked on his door and walked in only to find him with his head in his hands.

'Come on, Jamie, you have no reason to be like this.'

He looked up at her and said, 'I can nearly always find a way out of situations, but against Mother Nature, I cannot do anything.'

'But it is not your fault. No one blames you,' she said.

'I know that, but you do not realise we will be out of fresh water in four to five weeks.'

He went on to tell her, 'You must not tell anyone what I am going to say to you. This island may have no water, that's if we make it there, and that would mean we would all die because…it would take us at least another two months to sail on to another island.'

Kate replied, 'What will be ,will be let's just hope there is water on this island. Anyway, we could live on coconut milk if we have to.'

This brought a smile to his face. She carried on, 'You have been bloody wonderful up to now, and hopefully, things will improve.'

Jamie stood up and said with a big broad smile, 'Kate, you swore!' With that, they both started to laugh. Even Peggy started barking, and both the cats ran off in fright.

'Before you go, Kate, I want to ask you one question.'

'What's that?'

'How did you know it was my birthday the other month?'

'I was told by your father and wrote it in my diary. I have always kept a diary since our first meeting, along with everything we have done together. Sailing from England to the West Indies right up until now…including those dreadful things Zak did to your poor father and Temp.'

To her horror, she realised what she had just said. Jamie was quick to ask, 'What do you mean? Poor Temp?'

Kate sat down again and looked up at him. 'I am sorry. I have never told you, but that lovely old man gave his life to us all. He was killed helping us.'

He fell into his chair with tears in his eyes. Glaring at Kate, he said angrily, 'Why Kate did you not tell me…I could have done something about it, like catching the scum that did it.'

'I did not tell you because' ,she stops to take a deep breath. 'Because Temp gave his life for us all so we could all get away for a better life. If I had told you what had happened, I knew you would go after them and we would have not escaped and Temp would have given his life in vain.'

Jamie hesitated and looked at Kate, 'Kate, you are right again, and I so-so very sorry that I spoke to you in that tone of voice.'

'It's understandable to feel that way. JB wanted to tell you something back in England but was too frightened. He would not say a word to me about it, Zak's henchmen properly threatened him, but I think he will tell you the truth now as he has properly found the courage to tell you. It was obviously something that occurred during the time this young lad was sailing back on the Lady Dorothea with your father. Do you remember that afterwards, he asked you not to call him a friend?'

'Yes, I remember that day. It was the night we left England,' said Jamie. 'Shall I will go and get JB and ask him to tell you what he saw?'

He nodded his approval, so Kate went to search for JB. Whilst she was gone, Jamie took the opportunity to calculate the navigation on his map to see if the ship had drifted with the currents. He was pleased to see that the ship had drifted slightly towards their paradise island. Shortly, there was a knock on his door. Peggy was barking and wagging her tail.

'Come in,' said Jamie. Kate ushered JB in, and Peggy started licking JB in greeting. 'She's taken a liking to you.'

'Yes, Skipper, we get on well together.'

Jamie offered them both a seat and then quietly and calmly addressed JB, 'Did you see anything the night my father fell overboard?'

'Yes, Skipper,' replied JB. He had his head down, looking intently at the floor, not wanting to look directly at Jamie.

Kate tried to reassure JB. 'Do not worry. Everything will be fine. Tell Jamie what happened that night. He will not be angry with you.'

Jamie smiled at him, 'All I need to know is did you see how my father died?'

JB cleared his throat. 'I was in my cabin early one morning, and there was quite a storm blowing. Peggy started barking, and she wouldn't stop. I thought there could be someone outside my cabin door. I opened it, and Peggy shot out and ran up the stairs to get out. I thought that maybe she needed to relieve herself. He went on to say that, 'I opened the hatch, he saw four men fighting a man. It was wet and dark, but it looked like your father. He was putting up a fight, but the four men overpowered him and threw him overboard. It all happened so quickly. He told Janie there was no time to get help and he was so sorry. 'Skipper, one of the men heard Peggy barking and then saw me. He came after me and chased Peggy and me down the stairs to the cabins. I tried to close the door, but he put his foot in it'. JB paused...than went on to say. ' This man threaten me, saying he would kill me if I said a word to anyone about what he had seen. The man then took his knife out and made a gesture of cutting my throat.

Luckily Peggy wouldn't stop barking and someone was coming, so the man pointed his finger his, wagging it menacingly, and left. 'Then my friend wanted to find out what the commotion was about and asked who the hell the man was. I told them he wanted me to stop the dog from barking. The stupid thing is if he had not come after me, I would never have recognised him as it was so dark'.

Jamie, was trying to control his anger, but not for JB, but the men that did this to his father. Said quietly to JB, 'Who were these men that murdered my father'?

'Skipper the man who threatened me had a scar running down the left side of his cheek. On that night we were getting ready to set sail from England, it was the same man down in the hold with Temp who said he had fainted and we all had to carry him off the ship and put him down by one of the moorings.'

'That's right. I remember that man,' said Jamie.

Kate stood up, remembering the night Temp died. 'He was the same man who killed Temp. He was lying on the ground quite near Temp, and then I saw him get up and go across to Temp and run his sword through him.'

None of them spoke for several minutes, trying to absorb all this. Jamie stood up, trying not to show any emotion. 'Thank you both for telling me what happened. I remember sailing with these four men to the West Indies. They kept looking at my father and me. I will never forget their faces. I remember the man with the scar, and one of the other three was called Popeye. He had a patch on one eye. I know that in a few years' time when I return to England, I will find these four henchmen along with Zak and Edwina, who killed my father and Temp, and I will hand them over to the constable. I will see justice for Temp and my father.'

Jamie was now feeling better knowing that when the time came, he must get back to England and seek justice for his dear lost father and Temp.

They all left and went their own ways. The weather hadn't changed. There was still not a breath of wind, and the sun was blazing down from a clear blue sky. Jamie asked JB to find the crew and meet him here in fifteen minutes. JB scampered off, pleased that he had lightened his burden by telling Jamie of his secret.

Jamie heard a noise coming from over the side of the ship, and leaning over the side, he saw Rosen in a small boat fishing. Jamie shouted out to him, 'I hope you got one for me!'

Rosen grinned up at him, saying in his not quite perfect English, 'I has.'

'Good. Now, get yourself up here, please. I want to talk to everyone.' It was not long before all the crew had assembled in the amidships, Jamie stood in front of them and determined to deal with the situation they had found themselves in, he began to say it had been ten weeks since they left the Port of Good Hope. He didn't know how long the weather was going to last, supplies were getting very low, especially their drinking water so they have to do something to get them themselves out of the situation. Food must be rationed as to their drinking water. Seawater will be used for washing themselves and their clothing. He then paused to let the gravity of the situation sink in. Then Jamie continued the decision to start towing the ship must begin tomorrow morning in earnest on a shift base that can be sorted out among themselves Rowing will begin when it gets light and while it is still cool until the sun gets hot. Crewmen, on the first shift, will assemble on the deck just before it gets light. Then again, in the evening for about three hours, Rosen and Sam will teach the ones that cannot row by putting two small boats on the deck and show them how to use the oars, they all replied aye-aye Skipper.

To Jamie's astonishment, Dingle said, 'Skipper, this will ruin my fingers. I will not be able to play the violin.' There was an almighty roar of laughter. 'That will be no problem. I will lend you my gloves,' retorted Jamie quickly. At that, they all laughed again.

When the laughter died down, Jamie continued, 'Some of you will have to get ready for tonight's rowing, so go and arrange yourselves into a crew.'

As they were all leaving, Jamie shouted to Mitch to remain for a moment. Turning to Kate, he said, 'I would like you and some of the girls to keep an eye on those rowing as they may get overcome with the heat.' She nodded to Jamie and went off to organise the girls she had been training to deal with the sick.

'Mitch, follow me down to the lower hold and show me where you found that big trunk.'

Mitch led Jamie down to the hold where the trunk was. Jamie was surprised to see the label on the outside of the crate "Army Use Only" made by The Portsmouth Works.

'I know of this steelworks. As the owner, Mr R Hill was a friend of Temp's.' Jamie wondered if this was the surprise Temp had told him about, he could not wait to see what was in it 'Come on then, Mitch, let's open it.'

To their amazement, there are one large and one small cannon in side. They had never seen anything like it before. The large one had a smooth twelve-inch bore with a flared muzzle, made from hardened Bronze. There were boxes of canisters filled with gunpowder but not as Jamie had seen before and had pointed brass heads that were attached to them and there were hundreds of boxes. Mitch gasped, 'What a beauty!'

'Mitch, we will call her just that—Black Beauty. Let' us put everything back for now until we get on dry land. Do you see it has wheels as well? Not a word to anyone.'

'Aye, Aye Skipper'

Just as they began to put everything back, Jamie found a letter addressed to him from Temp. He put it in his pocket, deciding to read it later when he was on his own. They would carry on searching to see if there was anything else they could find that maybe as useful and came across several barrels that also had "Army Use Only" written across them. They prised the top off one of them, and to their surprise, it was full of beer. Mitch chuckled, 'These could be a blessing to us. We can drink some every night before we go to bed. It will save water.'

Jamie had to think about that but after a few seconds agreed. 'It looks like we have no other option than to drink it.'

They went back on deck, and Jamie asked three of his crew to go with Mitch and fetch two of the barrels of beer up to the deck. He wanted to get them ready for that night, but when Jamie looked up, the crew they were all grinning. Jamie knew that he often made mistakes but felt sure this was certainly going to be one!

The rowing was going according to plan. As it became dusk and the heat started to die down, the first rowers started. They rowed for an hour and then a new crew started. This carried on until it was too dark to see. Jamie called to the last rowers to come aboard ship. He told everyone to assemble in amidships to have their pint of beer to quench their thirst before they went to bed. About an hour after everyone had drunk their beer, they heard a noisy commotion coming from below the deck.

Jamie asked Sam if she would go and find out if everything was all right. She stood up, her legs felt wobbly, and she shouted, 'Don't anyone touch my beer or else!'

She staggered back within a few minutes and could not stop laughing. 'What are you laughing about?' asked Jamie.

'You would not believe what I have just seen.' She stopped to wipe the tears from her eyes and tried to speak in between gulps of laughter.

'Well, get on with it,' shouted Jamie a little impatiently.

She managed to compose herself. 'It's Pig Wash Anne. She gave her pigs some beer, trying to save water, and the pigs have got out and are running all round like headless chickens. They are as drunk as hell, and now Pig Wash is trying to catch them.'

This brought storms of laughter from all on deck, and JB raised his glass and said, 'Let's toast Pig Wash Anne and her pigs and pray she catches them soon.'

They all toasted Anne and her pigs, and in less than an hour, they were all very merry, dancing and singing. Very soon, one by one, they fell asleep where they were, exhausted due to a hard day's rowing and the beer. Somehow, Jamie made it back to his cabin to sleep but woke early the next morning. His head was thumping, and he knew he had drunk too much beer the evening before. He could hear loud knocking noises. 'Who the hell is knocking on my door? Stop! It's giving me a headache.'

There was no reply, so he dragged himself out of bed. Throwing open the door, he saw nobody there. He went to the porthole and looked out to sea. To his delight, there was the longboat bumping against the hull. That could only mean the wind and waves were doing it. He jumped for joy. Forgetting his hangover, he ran up to the deck, shouting out as loud as he could. 'The wind is back. Everyone, get up, you lazy lot. There is work to be done!'

Those on deck woke with a start, most holding their hurting heads. More bodies appeared from below deck to find out what all the shouting was about.

Quickly, they started clearing up the mess from the previous night's revelry when the skipper called his crew together. He told them that it would be too dangerous to man the yardarms with them having hangovers, so he sent them off to rest and clear their heads before they set sail again. Jamie had known it was a bad idea to let them drink the beer when he noticed Kate looking at him. She was obviously upset and quite angry.

'What's wrong, Kate?'

'What's wrong!' she shouted. 'Half the youngsters were in my cabin being sick and drunk all night, and my girls were running around, catching pigs, and you ask me, what's wrong!'

'Steady on, Kate. I am very sorry. Don't stand there screaming at me like an old fishwife! I never realised how strong the beer was. I was only trying to save water.'

'Now you call me an old fishwife!' She stormed off.

Sam, who had been standing nearby and had overheard the conversation, said with a grin on her face, 'OH dear Skipper you did not handle that very well.'

'I will wait a while then I will go and see her better give her time to calm down.'

'Skipper you'd better make it a few months or years. She was very angry, and you were very rude.'

Jamie noticed that several of the crew had stopped what they were doing and giggling. He turned on them angrily, telling them to get lost or work harder. Sam leaned over towards him. 'Jamie, you have always got me.'

'No thanks, Sam. One headache and a telling me off are bad enough.' He stormed off, angry at himself for shouting at Kate and then his crew, angry at his thumping head, which was making him bad-tempered, and angry at the beer. He went to his cabin to work out exactly where they were in the Indian Ocean. He grabbed his sextant and went back on deck and pointed it towards the horizon. When he had collected his readings, he went back to his cabin and took out his maps. To his delight, he estimated they were only about two weeks' sailing time away from their island, weather permitting.

He was checking his calculations when there was a knock on his door. He called out for whoever it was to enter and was quite surprised to see Kate.

'I am sorry. I remonstrated with you over the beer. I realise your intentions were good,' said Kate apologetically.

'I am sorry too. It was a big mistake in letting them drink the beer, and by the way, I should not have compared you to an old fishwife, because you are a beautiful young woman.'

Kate blushed. 'We are still good friends then?'

'Of course, you will always be, Kate. By the way, I have some good news, we should reach our island within two weeks, wind prevailing.'

Kate moved forward to hug Jamie. He put his arms around her and slowly and gently kissed her. Kate was lost in the moment. She felt like she was floating. They moved apart, both of them feeling embarrassed and not sure what to say next. Kate took the lead, saying, 'That's really good news, Jamie. This makes it all worthwhile. I always believed you would get us there.'

'Don't say anything to the others just yet, in case we hit any problems. I wouldn't want to raise their hopes and then let them down.'

Kate took her to leave of Jamie, and he decided to rest for a while. His thoughts kept going to the dangers that lay ahead. He prayed he had made the right decision for these young people, hoping he had picked the right Island.

And prayed there Paradise Island would have water and also provide enough food to sustain them all, and the poor animals cramped in below in the ships Hold.

Later that afternoon, when everyone seemed to have recovered from their aching heads, Jamie gave orders to retrieve the boats and then to set sail. When they were underway and with a strong wind behind them, he went to each person on board asking them what type of work they would like to do. He made notes so that when they reached the island, he could put them to work almost straight away.

Luckily, the wind kept up for the next two weeks, so it was no surprise that early one morning, there was an almighty cry from the lad at the top of the mast. 'LAND AHOY! It's our island.'

Dawn was just breaking over the horizon. Some of the children were still asleep, but at that cry, they roused themselves and rushed on deck to join those already there. Some of them scrambled up on to the yardarms. They were all excited to see a string of small islands appearing over the horizon. As they got nearer to one of the larger islands, they could see the beautiful clear blue sea with soft waves moving slowly up and down glistening white sand. Beyond the shoreline was a lush plantation of trees and bushes. There were coral reefs jutting out from the sea surrounding islands. Even some of the smaller ones had vegetation. In the distance, they could see another small island with the same plantation on it. There was huge excitement on board the Lady Dorothea. They ran around hugging each other; some were overcome with emotion. A few of the crew slapped Jamie on the back, congratulating him for getting them there. Some wanted to swim to the island, but Jamie told them the waters could be dangerous as there could be sharks about. The girls all crowded around him, and he said to Kate, 'Seeing the happiness on those young kids' faces will stay with me for the rest of my life.'

Kate pointed out to Jamie that those wonderful kids were now a year older, having left England just over a year ago, they were growing up fast, and maybe one day, he would have to perform a marriage.

'I never thought about that,' replied Jamie. Turning his mind to the more serious matters in hand, he informed the crew that when they were closer to the largest of the islands, they would use the longboat to go ashore to find the best way of getting the ship on to the beach without running aground on the coral rocks.

When they were as near as they dared, they hauled in the sails and dropped anchor. The longboat was lowered into the water and Jamie told Rosen to take some of the lads and find a safe way through the reef.

He knew that if anyone could find a way, it would be Rosen as being a fisherman he understood what hazards to look out for. Rosen set off; after about an hour, he came back and shouted up at Jamie, 'Skipper, we are lucky it is high tide. I have found a way through. Tie this tow rope on, and we will do the rest.' It was not long before the Dorothea was slowly moving between the coral rocks towed by Rosen's crew. They entered a large lagoon with no rocks, just clear blue sea.

Jamie shouted to Rosen, 'I am letting go of the tow rope so I can hoist some of the smaller sails, and hopefully, the wind will blow the ship up on to the beach as far as possible. See you all ashore.' Jamie managed to do just that. The ship went a good way up the beach. The boys tied off some ropes and threw them over the side for Rosen and his crew to fasten to palm trees. The walkways were lowered over the side of the ship. Jamie told them to go ashore one at a time and assemble on the beach. They were overjoyed to be on dry land at last, although finding it difficult to stand up and not fall over after having been used to the movement of the boatBefore long, the last youngster was ashore with Jamie being the last, carrying Peggy. It had been decided to take the bigger animals off the boat in the morning and the rest can wait until their pens were built.

He asked Rosen to take charge, looking for water even though his English was not too good. Rosen took control easily. He told them to look for drinking water as that was obviously their priority. The girls were to go along the beach to see if there were any streams of running water flowing into the sea. Some of the boys were to go with him inland had been warned to watch out for snakes.

The gang searched everywhere there was no fresh water to be found anywhere, they had started digging for trapped water. Their supplies from the ship were running very low, and they knew that very soon, it would be coconut milk. Jamie was becoming increasingly concerned as he knew that without fresh water, they would not be able to stay on the island much longer. All the youngsters were getting more dejected every day. None of them wanted to get back on the ship and set sail again. Jamie instructed everyone to pick as many coconuts as they could as he thought that they could mix the milk with beer. At least, it would suffice until they found another island near with water, but the cattle would still have to drink fresh water not coconut milk or beer, knowing full well what the pigs did.

Early one morning, Rosen asked Jamie if he could go fishing just for an hour then back looking for water. Jamie thought that was a great idea but wanted to go as well. JB overheard and insisted that he and Peggy went along as well. After about an hour, they still hadn't had a bite, so Jamie and JB asked Rosen if he thought it was safe to swim in the sea. He took a good look around and said, 'It looks fine. No sharks, only you two on this boat.'

They all laughed, and the two plunged into the sea. All was fine for a while until Rosen spotted a shark fin in the distance coming towards Jamie and JB. Rosen shouted to them to quickly get back in the boat. They started swimming swiftly back towards the boat. Jamie was the better swimmer and reached the boat ahead of JB. Rosen helped him in, but as JB nearly got to the boat, they could see he was not going to make it as the shark was just about to pass the boat. They were just about to make a grab for JB when suddenly Peggy jumped off the boat into the shark's path. Rosen already had an oar in his hand to whack the shark, but it had got a hold of Peggy in its jaws. Rosen hit the shark with all his might on its head. It let Peggy go and swam off. Jamie reached out to get hold of JB, but he wanted Jamie to grab Peggy first. They hauled the dog in and then grabbed JB. He fell inside the little boat, shaking. It had scared him badly, but the others turned their attention to Peggy. She was bleeding very badly, so they rowed quickly back to shore. Kate was waiting for them as she had seen what had happened. JB carried Peggy to Kate and laid her gently on the sand. She looked at Peggy and then said sadly, 'I am very sorry, but she is dying. She has lost too much blood for me to help her.'

Within a few minutes, Peggy had stopped breathing. JB stood up and screamed out loud, 'Oh, no, no! This precious little thing gave her life for me. I would rather have died myself. At least, I would not have this pain that is now inside of me.' He took Peggy in his hands and cradled her with silent tears falling down his cheeks.

Almost everyone had their heads bowed and were weeping. Jamie walked away, wiping away the tears, wondering when all the dying in his life would stop. All those he loved, his mother, father, then Temp, and now Peggy. He suddenly felt so alone.

JB sat with her in his arms all through the long night, and the next morning, he asked Jamie if he could bury her. Jamie agreed without question and he would later make a cross for her, from the wood of one of the kites that Peggy had loved to chase. Nobody felt like eating anything that morning, so they gathered around the spot that JB had chosen to bury Peggy. It was under some coconut trees that overlooked the sea. JB and Jamie took turns to dig. When they had got about three feet down, JB looked up at Jamie and said, 'Look, Jamie, the sea water is coming up in the hole.'

Kate looked down into the hole. 'That doesn't look like salt water. It is too clear. Also, it is well above the sea level.'

'Pass me that coconut shell,' shouted Jamie to one of them. He bent down and scooped up some water and tasted it. To his delight, he found it was fresh drinking water. There was one almighty cheer from everyone, cuddling each other jumping up and down.

Temp was right there was water but they weren't looking in the right place. When the rains came, it had seeped through the soil to the water table below and was trapped. All anyone needed to do was dig down.

'Not only has this poor little dog given me my life, but she has also given us all a future. Now, we can live on these islands in peace,' said JB. Jamie was filled with emotion but managed to say, 'I believe my little Peggy found this water for us, so now, my little dog would rather be buried at sea. Let's build a small raft and let her drift a little way out to sea before we light it.'

They all helped build a small raft, stacking it with dry wood and grass. JB placed Peggy on it, and everyone joined in a prayer that Jamie was reciting. He then pushed the raft out to sea, where Rosen was waiting in a boat just outside the bay with a torch. He lit the raft as it passed, and it continued to drift into the great Indian Ocean.

Over the next few days, they dug many holes and found enough drinking water to sustain them for a long time, thanks to little Peggy.

Chapter 16

Early the next morning, Jamie rang the ship's bell and called for everyone to wake up. 'I want you all to assemble on the beach in one hour with or without breakfast.'

Within the hour, everyone was waiting on the beach to find out what the skipper had in store for them. Jamie stood on a high ridge and shouted, 'I am going to organise you all into working groups.' He pulled out his notebook and called out the first name,

'Buster' 'Yes, Skipper,' a young boy replied, walking towards him.

'I see you know all about farming. When some land has been ploughed, I want you to take the responsibility of sowing seeds and planting potatoes, and do not forget the carrots.'

Buster beamed with pleasure at being given the duty of providing food and fresh food at that.

'Rosen, you and some of your countrymen can clear the trees and bushes to make way for the plough, but I want you to save some of the timbers for building materials. The rest of your boys can help with the building. The next name on my list is Malley. Step forward.' Another boy stepped forward, eager to find out what Jamie had in store for him.

'Malley, let's see if you are as good as you say at building huts.'

'I am, and I won't let you down, Skipper. They will withstand a cyclone.' Jamie smiled to himself. They all seemed so keen to do what he asked.

'They had better be Malley because there could be one in this area soon.' He then addressed them all, 'When Malley finishes these huts, they will be for the boys to sleep in. The girls will sleep on the ship.' The girls clapped. They were pleased with this arrangement, and with the boys off the ship, they would have more room and some privacy.

Sam was grinning from ear to ear and shouted out, 'I suppose this means, Skipper, you will be the only man to look after us on the ship?' Everyone started laughing. Jamie smiled and replied, 'No! I will be sleeping in a hut. Now, listen, it is not a laughing matter. To survive here, we must all work as a team' Silence descended as they realised that what was before them was a serious situation. They had already struggled so hard to get to here, and they did not want to leave this lovely island.

Looking again at his notes, Jamie called out to Pig Wash Anne, 'Gather together all those who helped you on board the ship. They will help you again here to look after chickens and ducks as well as the pigs. Malley will build you huts for them.' She was delighted. She loved the pigs, and now, they would have proper pig-sty's, which would be easier to keep clean. 'The donkeys will be looked after by Hermit and Rabbit, and you will have to use them to plough the land Rosen clears.' Jamie then looked across to Kate. 'You will carry on teaching and providing the medical care we need as well as looking after everyone's well-being.

Take as many of the girls you need to help you.' Taking a drink of the fresh water they had found in plentiful supply, he continued, 'I believe we all owe Kate a big thanks for the good job she has done so far aboard the ship.'

The others all agreed and added their thanks. Kate blushed; she did not expect any praise as she loved doing what she was doing.

Jamie thought he would get his own back on Sam and shouted out, 'Sam, I want you to be in charge of training in the art of fighting.' Sam was pleased and started to walk away.

'Hold on a minute, Sam. I have not finished with you yet. I also want you to look after the sanitation and sewage.' Sam was not amused.

'Sewer and sanitation, never in your life!' she was very humiliated

Everybody fell about laughing, but Sam could just not see the funny side of it. Jamie cried with laughter as he watched the sheer horror on Sam's face. .When they all calmed down, Jamie walked over to her and smiled. Putting his arm around her, he said,

'I was only joking. The look on your face! Oh, I am so sorry, Sam still didn't see the funny side of it, but as he was grinning at her as she swiped at him. He ducked, and she began to relax and join in the merriment.

Jamie composed himself, coughed, and said, 'Smithy?' From the back of the group, a boy came forward. 'I want you to be our head blacksmith. Can you manage that, Smithy?' Again there was much laughter. Smithy replied that he would do his best to live up to his name.

With that, Kate said to Jamie, 'I think you had better call it a day. We all have work to do.'

'I think I will.' Then he shouted. 'That's all for now. You lot, get to work now!'

They scattered quickly, and those whom Jamie had allocated work to began selecting their teams, They were all keen to start working as they knew they needed food and shelter. Kate started organising some of the girls to prepare food for everyone. The rest of the girls would have to help with washing, repairing clothes, cleaning, and other necessary chores.

Having organised the youngsters into work groups, Jamie decided to go to his cabin and read the letter Temp had left with the cannon. He sat down and began to read in amazement.

Dear Jamie

By now, you will have found two cannons in crates marked Army Use Only. There is a big cannon and a smaller one. The smaller one looks like a swivel gun. These cannons are only prototypes, and the small one has only been fired a few times but with excellent success.

I only discovered the trunks this week when I was loading your ship, and some army chaps delivered them and helped me load them. The young sergeant told me exactly where they came from and the history of them. A young student invented them in his spare time.

He was a young French lad called Jean Paixhans, and he hoped his brother Henri in the French army would be able to use them.

Due to the Portsmouth foundry cutting back their workforce and moving most of the plant and men to Merthyr Tydfil, the manager Mr Hopkins instructed his workers to scrap the cannons. The foundry in Merthyr Tydfil was only interested in making pig iron, not experimental guns. The army asked Mr Hopkins if they could buy them. Mr Hopkins was only too pleased to be rid of them.

I found out that the large cannon is a twelve-pounder and is cast in a hardened bronze and has a flared muzzle swell. As you will see, it is six feet long and weighs just over half a ton. It can fire a brass shell or ball or a canister. In the crates, there is also gunpowder incorporated with a sabot wedge on the shells that gives it a longer range.

These two cannons were supposed to be delivered to the army in India, but I think they might be more useful to you. Captain Jamie Heslop!

Jamie smiled remembering Temp with great affection, wishing he were here with them now but vowing to make Temp's death worthwhile by giving the children their freedom.

The letter continued. Jamie you will find instructions in the crates on how to fire them both, also what to use to support them when firing them and how to transport the large one. Temp made it clear to be careful when he used them for the first time. The army chap had told him that the big cannon should have a range of at least a mile with no problem, and if you used the pointed shell, which has a timing device inside, it sets off a high explosive when it hits the target. Temp finished the letter telling Jamie he loved him like a son and to be careful and return safely.

Jamie felt very emotional, saying over and over in his mind why everyone he loved back in England ended up dead. He managed to pull himself together, heaved a sigh, and knew that he now had to prepare these cannons as their safety may depend upon them.

The day wore on, and everyone was busy cutting wood, clearing some of the land, collecting anything edible. The day was warm with a slight breeze, and they felt relaxed and very pleased to be on dry land.

That afternoon, Jamie found Mitch and JB and told them about the cannons in Temp's letter. They could not wait to get started. Over the next few weeks, they began arranging everything that they needed to assemble the big cannon. They used the ship's davit to hoist the large cannon on deck. Smithy made a metal stand to enable them to swivel it. A couple of the boys reinforced the deck to make it strong enough to withstand the pressure from the big cannon's firepower. When all this was completed, they assembled the big cannon to a swivel and fixed it in position at the stern of the ship. They dragged the smaller cannon to a high place over looking their camp, so as not to put anyone or anything in the line of fire. When everything was in place to Jamie's satisfaction, they were anxious to start practising. They realised that when firing the two cannons, all they had to do was use a hammer and hit a hex head bolt on the base of the guns as it had a flint inside that ignited the gunpowder.

This was far quicker than their old type of cannons. Jamie and some lads had made a raft to use for target practice, and they towed it about half a mile out to sea. Some of the youngsters followed them across the island to watch them practise.

Mitch and JB were ready to fire the small cannon upon the highest point near the camp, the skipper made them use the ball shot only. He gave the order. 'Fire!'

There was a huge bang and a hiss as the small ball shot rang through the air towards the target. It missed by a mile, and everyone fell about laughing.

'Well, my two gunners, I hope you do better than that next time. It was totally off the target. I thought it was going to hit us instead,' Jamie called out at them. Laughter broke out again, and the two boys had very red faces. They kept practising all week, improving until they had sunk the raft. Several of the children had been watching and clapped and cheered. Jamie was delighted. He turned to the two boys. 'Are you ready to fire the big one now on our ship? Have you read the instructions carefully? But you can only use the ball shots for now.'

'Oh, yes, Skipper. We have read the instructions time and time again no problem. It will be as easy as throwing a stone.'

Jamie led them back to the ship across and took them to the cannon. Kate and Sam came up to watch them but stood well back, smiling and wondering what to expect.

All the children had got bored watching them practise with the small cannon, so they started to go about their various jobs. Mitch and JB told Jamie they were ready to fire, and he again said on the count of three to fire. Then an almighty BANG.

The entire ship seemed to jump six feet in the air. The blast threw the three of them across the ship followed by a cloud of smoke and soot. Even Kate and Sam were overcome by smoke and soot. The girls struggled to their feet, asking everyone if they were all right. Although shaken and covered in soot, from head to foot, otherwise they were all fine. Those on the beach were petrified in case someone was killed, but luckily no one was hurt.

Rosen and his gang came running after hearing the bang from a mile away, thinking that maybe the ship had blown up, or under attack.

All the animals' including sheep, donkeys, had scattered across the island. Pig Wash Anne was hysterical, and her gang of helpers were trying to catch her pigs, especially Anne's favourite pig with the unlikely name of Rose Bud.

Jamie was covered in black soot, and then looked at the two boys, also covered with soot. 'What in the hell did you do wrong? Did you not read the instructions?'

'Yes, Skipper, right down to the bottom of the page where it said PTO,' replied Mitch, trembling in his boots. Jamie grabbed hold of the instructions. 'What do you think PTO means?'

'I think it means, practise to operate, Captain Sir.'

Jamie was exasperated. 'No! You dumb heads, it means, please turn over. There are more instructions written on the back. Now read it!'

Jamie thrust the instructions back to the boys, who were looking very shamefaced. They read the other side, and it said that because no one had fired this gun, they should only use half the usual quantity of gunpowder and should keep adding more powder until the required amount is reached for the cannon to find its target. Katealso was furious she went across to them and shouted, 'You idiots, did you not learn anything at the lessons I gave you?'

When the smoke cleared, Jamie started to see the funny side of it. When he looked at Sam's and Kate's faces, he could not stop laughing. 'You both look blacker than Rosen!' Then he looked at all the commotion going on below. Everyone was running around trying to catch animals; by now, they were all crying with laughter. It took them the remainder of the day to catch all the animals and for things to get back to normal. Even though some chickens and ducks were lost forever may be they had heart attacks.. Later, when Jamie went off to bed, he still could not stop smiling to himself.

Chapter 17

The weeks flew by, and everything was almost finished. Mitch and JB had become quite proficient at firing the big cannon with no further mishaps. The fields they had ploughed and planted had young shoots growing tall and straight.

Rosen told Jamie that a few weeks earlier when he was clearing the last of the bigger islands of bushes, he had come across a few bushes with green berries. One of the pigs had eaten some, and it went into a trance. It lay down as if it was asleep for about an hour. He was getting worried as he had felt he had to go and tell Pig Wash Anne that one of her pigs was dying. Luckily for me, it woke up and appeared to have no after-effects. Jamie was interested in this bush and asked Rosen to show him where they were. Rosen said he had burned them all as he had been afraid the animals might eat them but he had saved some for Jamie to see but that there were more of the bushes on the other smaller islands. He also told Jamie that he made a shelter with the branches and bushes as he thought it might come in handy one day for some of the younger ones to hide in the event of a visit from pirates or Zak.

Kate reminded Jamie that it would be Christmas the following week and asked, did he want her to do a special meal for them all? Jamie replied as long as it wasn't fish! Kate laughed and assured him it would not be fish but a pig and chickens if Anne would let them have a pig. They could make a fire and roast them on the beach.

Jamie thought that was a grand idea. 'But you can ask Anne,' he smiled. 'Kate, I nearly forgot. I have some berries that you can make into a juice because apparently when you drink the juice, it will send you to sleep. If you have to operate on someone, this would be of great use to you.' Sarcastically Kate told him. 'You might be right. I might have some myself as I may not know what I am doing.' Jamie smiled back at her as she wandered off to find Rosen for him to ask Anne if they could kill one of her pigs to eat on Christmas.

Before they knew it, Christmas had arrived. Everything went to plan, cooking the pig, even if Anne did shed a few tears. The only problem before cooking the pig was finding someone to kill it, but one of Rosen's gang offered and was obviously experienced in such matters. That day, everyone exchanged gifts of fruit and shells, and some of the girls had made beautiful chains of flowers. Kate thought it was wonderful to see everyone enjoying themselves. Some of the African girls had made dresses from leaves and flowers and did their traditional dancing. Even some of the orphanage girls were persuaded to wear the same attire and dance to music from Dingle's violin. The girls danced with the flowers swirling around them. They felt free and unfettered, growing into young women with the boys clapping and laughing. The boys felt stirrings in their loins as they too were growing into healthy young men. Jamie relented and allowed them to have some of the beer but only half a pint each.

Later in the evening, when all the festivities had calmed down and everyone was sat around the dying embers of their fire, Jamie started to ask some of them about their past. First, he asked Jada how she had become a slave and where she had learned to speak English.

'I lived with my English mother and African father on a ship called the Mayfly. My mother worked as a cook, and father worked as a senior sailor, and they both taught me to speak their native languages. After a year, my father had been made to first mate on a ship that was transporting cargo from England to India for the East India Company. Whilst sailing back to England, we ran into a cyclone and were lucky to have survived, but it had blown us off course. The ship needed many repairs after this storm, so we anchored near a small fishing village in Tanzania. The village people helped us to repair it, but it took a few weeks to do. During that time, I often left the ship and would row to the village to see some friends I had made along with Rosen and his family.

'Then one day, when I was in the village, all of a sudden, I heard a lot of yelling and shouting. A large number of men with guns and swords came running down to the village. These were pirate slavers. Rosen, his family, and I were taken, prisoner. My poor mother and father could only look on at us from their ship. I hope one day, Rosen and I will find our families.'

Jada felt sad remembering her parents as she wiped away tears from the corner of her eyes. She wondered where they were and what they were doing now and if they missed and thought about her.

Jamie was struck with emotion. 'Jada, I promise you I will find yours and Rosen's family.'

'It was terrible. Skipper we were chained together. One chain was attached to a ring around our leg, and another chain was attached to a steel collar around our necks. Then we all had to march with the other slaves they had captured to a place called Dar-es-Salaam. We were taken to this small harbour where three ships anchored. One of these ships had about 300 slaves, all crammed into a small part of it. I was told by some of them that they had been taken captive some months earlier and that most of them had lived in villages scattered around Tanzania. Several of them had lived over a few hundred miles inland and had been made to walk all the way there carrying ivory on their backs. Some of them were in a bad way; most of the elderly had either died on the journey or on our ship, and their bodies were thrown overboard. We were taken to a place called Stone Town in Zanzibar, and there, we were sold as slaves still in our chains. Before the auction started, everyone was separated into age groups then again into male and female and then sold like cattle.'

Rosen interrupted Jada, with tears in his eyes, 'This was the last time I saw my two sisters. They had been sold along with two other girls and were taken away and made to walk behind a horse-drawn carriage.' Rosen could not continue so Jada carried on the conversation. 'Luckily, I overheard someone mention the buyer who had bought Rosen's sisters. They said it was a rich Sultan's son called Bin Said buying young girls again. Hopefully, they were going to put them both to work as maids in his mansion on Zanzibar.'

Rosen took up the sad tale. 'My mother, father, had been sold earlier. I last saw them being loaded like cattle on to a ship.'

Kate spoke gently to Jada, 'However did you end up in England?'

'All I can tell you, Kate, is that we were bought by some man who was English and ended up there. It was hell sailing to England during those months on the ship. I would rather not talk about it. Sorry.'

'I understand. I apologise. I should not have asked,' Kate said, struggling with her emotions.

The other slave children had similar stories to tell, and the orphange children, although they had been treated badly, realised it was nothing compared to what the others had been subjected to. Jamie was very upset as he listened to all these stories and said to Jada and Rosen, 'I am sorry for all that you have been through, but I must ask, did any of you recognise the ship you were on that took you to Zanzibar first?'

'Yes, I remember the name. It was called Sea Eagle. It had an eagle's head carved on the beak head, I will never forget.' Jadareplied.

'Well, that's good news, Jada. One day, we might come across it and do something about it as they were the ones who helped to capture and enslave you in the first instance. What about the ship that took you to England. Would any of you recognise it again?'

'I might, but I did not see the name of it.'

'That's fine, but, Jada, did you recognise the name of the ship that took Rosen's family?'

'Sorry, Jamie, I did not see it. The only thing I do remember is the name of the man who brought Rosen's family because when the hammer went down, the man selling them asked for the name of the buyer. This man was French, and his name was Louis Bourbonnais. He had long grey hair and was very fat and ugly. He also looked vicious.'

'At least with your description of this man and his name, we have a chance of finding Rosen's family. Thank goodness, you know English. Now to you, Sam, where did you learn to be so good with the sword and armed combat?'

'Well, Skipper, I had a lovely mother and father. Unfortunately, they both died when I was twelve. They were killed when their horse and carriage overturned. My father was in the army, so we never had a house of our own but moved from one barracks to another. Because of this, when they died, I was put in anorphanage as I had no other relatives.

'My father was a lieutenant in the army, and I think he would have preferred it if I had been a boy. Whenever he had some spare time, he taught me to fight with a sword. I started to learn this with him when I was only six.'

'I am sorry, Sam, to have reminded you of their early death.

'It is not a problem because I now have the memories of our adventures and have loved every second I have spent with you.' Sam blushed and continued correcting herself saying, 'Sorry, I mean having enjoyed being with you all.'

To help Sam over her obvious discomfort, Kate roused everyone to agree that they had all enjoyed their journey with Jamie so far and for giving them all their freedom.

Jamie stood up to address them all. 'I hope my questions did not upset you too much. I am sorry. If we are to find your families, I need to know where you all come from. But for now, it is getting late, and we have much work to do tomorrow, so off to our beds!'

Jamie damped down the last of the embers from the fire, and they all went off to their separate sleeping quarters. going down the beach to their hut, Rosen remarked, 'I don't like the look of this night sky.'

'Why is that?' Mick said. 'It's the same as always—black!'

'If you look carefully, it is different. The last time I saw a sky like this, the following day, we had a cyclone, and all hell broke loose in our village. Some of our people died.'

'I only hope you're wrong, Rosen,' said Jamie, looking up at the night sky, thinking it had been a wise thing to dampen down the fire and make sure all the animals were safely bedded down and penned in.

Chapter 18

Rosen was proved right the following morning when all hell let loose. The cyclone had arrived; the wind was swirling, but luckily the torrential rain damped down the sand to stop it from getting in everyone's eyes. Jamie shouted to all the boys to get into the ship for shelter as there was a lot of dangerous debris flying about. He looked around and spotted Malley. 'This storm will test your huts, young man.'

'They will withstand this as long as it gets no worse,' replied Malley as he ran towards the ship.

They spent the next twenty-four hours on the ship, thrown around by the heaving seas. The younger ones were frightened, and Jamie and the older boys tried to calm them down by making them laugh.

'I hope my crew moored this ship up well?' Jamie shouted to be heard over the creaking timbers of the ship and the lashing of the rain on the deck.

Someone shouted back, 'Aye, yep, we did so, Captain, so we did, with bits of string,' making them all laugh.

They had little sleep that night with hammocks rocking and anything not secured correctly rolling around and the sound of the wind and rain. By morning, the storm had abated, and they went on deck to survey the damage. What a mess! Half of the huts Malley had built were strewn across the beach, palm trees were uprooted, canvas sheets had been ripped apart, and branches and bushes were lying everywhere. Jamie climbed to the quarterdeck and took out his telescope to survey the debris and search for the animals. He could not find any, but as he was about to close the telescope, something caught his eye. He looked again in the distance to the furthermost island due north about a mile away and, to his amazement, saw a shipwreck. Assuming this ship had blown on to the rocks in the previous night's storm, he rang the bell and shouted to his crew to man the boats as there might be lives to save. It did not take them long to get ready and to stow a few things they might need.

Jamie asked Kate to go with them in case anyone was hurt. She climbed into the boat with her bag stuffed with bandages and ointments, and when all three boats were ready, they cast off. Jamie went in the yawl sailing boat with some of his crew. He knew he would get there first using the strong breeze, hoping to find survivors. Jamie was also aware it could be a pirate ship and wanted to make sure it was safe first, so he continually looked through his telescope.

Jamie's boat was well ahead of the other two, with JB operating the sails and Rabbit helping him.

'Can you make out her name?' asked Kate.

'I do think it is an English ship. Yes, it's the Kitty Moth. I have seen her a few times in Portsmouth harbour, and by the look of it, she has hit some submerged rocks. Her bow is half underwater. Yes, it is her,' exclaimed Jamie.

When they were within shouting distance, Jamie stood up in the boat. Cupping his hands to his mouth, he called out.

'Ahoy! Ahoy! Is anyone there?' There was no response, so he shouted again, but still, there was no answer.

They prepared to board the ship. Jamie went first, followed by Kate, then JB, and Rabbit. Jamie turned to JB and Rabbit, pointing to below deck and telling them to see if anyone was alive down there.

'Kate, we will go to the captain's quarters and have a look there.'

Just as they got to the captain's cabin, they heard JB give almighty shout. 'Skipper, come here quickly!'

Jamie asked Kate to search for the ship's log and then dashed off to see what the problem was. Kate started to search the cabin. She saw the desk and realised this was the obvious place to look. She started to move papers and charts about when she looked up in amazement. Nailed to the wall was a large sheet of paper with Jamie's name on it.

Kate was speechless. It was all she could do, not to shout out to Jamie to see it for himself. She realised it would be better to wait until they got back on the island.

Meanwhile, Jamie was with JB, who had found two young heifers that appeared to be in calf and were standing in seawater that was getting worse by the minute. They also managed to rescue some goats, rabbits, and ducks, but unfortunately, everything else further down in the hold towards the bow had drowned. The remainder of the cargo that was edible had been ruined by seawater.

Kate had left the captain's cabin and gone in search of Jamie. The rest of the crew were searching for anyone who may be alive when Rosen caught up with Jamie.

'Skipper, did you notice there are a lot of sharks swimming around the boat?'

'Yes, I did. I also noticed on the beach the wreckage of some small boats.'

'I did as well, Skipper. I think the crew thought the ship was going to sink and took to the boats only to get crushed on those rocks.' Rosen pointed towards the rocks, which were only about 500 yards away from the island. 'I assume they would not have seen the rocks as it was so dark during the storm, but there is no sign of bodies, so the sharks must have got them.'

'I agree, Rosen. What a terrible way to end.'

Jamie instructed JB and Rabbit to be careful and take the small boat to the island and have a good look round just in case anyone had survived. They set off, and the rest of the crew began to load the two boats with the animals and anything else they had found that could be useful.

Kate approached Jamie and said sternly, 'What are you doing about those poor cows?' Jamie had to think quickly. 'Err, err, we are taking them with us.'

'I should hope so,' answered Kate.

Jamie had actually been prepared to leave them because he realised that as soon as they got into the sea, the sharks would get them. The boats were too small to carry them. Sam had overheard their conversation, and as Kate left, she walked up to Jamie and said with a grin, 'Oh, Kate. Yes, Kate. Whatever you say, Kate! You are like an old married man. You may as well be locked up in a cage.'

Suddenly, Jamie threw his arms around Sam and gave her a resounding kiss on her lips. 'You are a darling. I know precisely what to do now.'

Sam staggered back in amazement, not entirely sure what Jamie was talking about and lost for words by his emotional outburst.

Jamie then turned to his crew. 'Take down the metal fences around the cattle pens and bring them all up on deck.' Just then there was the sound of breaking timbers coming from down below in the hold. He shouted for them to hurry as the ship was becoming unstable. He shouted to Rosen, 'Those berries you gave me the other day. Kate should have them in her bag. Get them and give a few to each of the cows to calm them.'

Rosen hurried off, wondering what Jamie was up to now.

They were soon all to find out when Jamie started giving orders for them to tie the metal fences together to make two box-shaped cages without a lid. Then he told them to tie the large empty watertight barrels they had found all around each cage about halfway up.

'Rosen, get the cows up on the deck.'

Rosen laughed. He had no idea how he was going to get them out of the hold. By now, the berries had just started taking effect, so he wedged a plank of wood from the deck down into the hold and led them up.

Very soon, the cages were ready, and Jamie gave further instructions. 'Get four more watertight barrels and tie one on each side of both the cows. This will act like floats. Then use the ship's davit to lift the cage into the sea carefully place these sheets around the stomachs of each of the cows. Then lift them one at a time into each cage. I hope these cages will stop the sharks from attacking them.'

Kate had been watching whilst all this activity had been going on. 'You are marvellous, Jamie. I knew you would not leave them behind. I should have known you had this on your mind before I even spoke about it.'

Jamie looked around at Sam, who was making a gesture at him by putting her hand across her mouth and smiling at him. Making the cages had taken them at least four hours, and Jamie hoped they could now transport everything back to the island before dark.

Whilst all this had been going on, JB and Rabbit had been searching the beach. They had found no human footprints, but they had noticed dog prints. They had searched and searched, calling for the animal until their mouths went dry, but to no avail. Just as they were about to leave, they heard a bark, and a large light-brown dog with long fur came running over to them. It kept licking them and wagging its tail. They were pleased with themselves for finding the dog, realising that somehow it had managed to swim from the ship. They rowed back with it to the ship to help with the loading.

Everyone on the wreck wanted to make a fuss of the dog, but time was running short, and they knew they had to get back to the island. Jamie told JB to tie his boat to the cages, and Jamie tied his boat to JB's, and the longboat towed Jamie's boat.

Just before they left the wreck, Jamie asked the crew to join him in a short prayer in remembrance of the dead crew of the Kitty Moth. They then clambered aboard their boats and set off for the island, towing the two cages with the cows in. The cows were oblivious of all that was going on as they were still feeling the effects of the berries.

The rowing proved very strenuous, but they did not mind. They all loved it and sang as they rowed in a line, pulling the cows behind them.

Chapter 19

They arrived back safely to the island quite late in the evening. They had a little difficulty getting the cows on to the beach whilst keeping a couple of sharks at bay. Everybody loved the new additions from the wreck especially, the dog which they named McKay . Moreover, in a few weeks' time, they knew they would have fresh milk and cheese.. The only problem was that no one knew how to milk a cow. Early the next morning, Kate found Jamie and told him she had something important for him to see in his cabin. Jamie asked what it was as they walked into his cabin, but she would not say. She suggested he sat down first.

'I found this in the captain's cabin on the Kitty Moth,' said Kate,

She handed Jamie a sheet of paper. Jamie read it silently. Then feeling the anger arising in him, he shouted, 'I'll kill that Zak and all the lying buggers that helped him.'

Several of the crew heard him shouting and came running, wondering what the matter was. They found out what the Portsmouth Constabulary had accused Jamie of. Word went around the ship quickly, and they gathered on the quarterdeck.

Mitch asked their captain if he would come to the quarterdeck. When Jamie arrived on deck along with Kate, he was wondering what else is going to happen.

Mitch stood on the capstan, looking at everyone. 'Jamie, our captain and friend, I say to you, everybody here thanks you for giving us the chance of a new life, and we will all give our lives to protect you. In England or any other country that we go to, we will prove your innocence and fight anyone who has made these false accusations brought on you.'

Jamie was completely overwhelmed. He too climbed up on to the capstan and addressed his crew. 'You have given me a new life as well. I will not let anyone die for me. If we have to die, it will be for what we believe in—Freedom!'

They all cheered and slapped each other's backs. They knew without Jamie and his strength, they would be back in the orphanage or slaves to someone unknown.

The next day, Jamie sat in his cabin to look at the Kitty Moth logbook. He read she had been sailing from India to a new colony called New South Wales in Australia, taking tea, silks, spices, and animals working for the East Indian Company before she ran aground. The log also said that the ship's crew had to keep a vigilant watch twenty-four hours a day for French corsairs, especially during the next sailing to England after they left Australia.

Jamie had decided to call his leading crew together right away to his cabin for an important meeting. They all arrived, and when they were all seated, he said, 'I have decided that in the next couple of weeks, we set sail and find Rosen's family and free as many slaves as we can.' Rosen was surprised, and one of the crew asked, 'Why now?'

'I have been wrongly accused back in England of murder. If or when I went back, they would probably shoot me first and ask questions afterwards. We talked about fighting for freedom yesterday, so that is what we are going to do. It is time to do something about it. I have been watching you all, and over the past six months, you have improved so much with your fighting skills and sailing abilities. Anyone of you would be a match for anyone, except me, of course.'

This made everybody laugh, but knowing it was true. Jamie was an excellent swordsman, and his shot was perfect. 'I would even say you're all the best bunch of fighters in the world.'

They all started talking and discussing this at once. Jamie held his hand up for silence.

'Please sit down. I have a lot more to say. The first thing I want to be done is to change the name of our ship. My mother would not approve of us, killing others and using her name. If you all agree, I like to call this ship Swordfish. I have chosen this because you are all exceptional and. You all are amongst the best swordsmen and women

I have seen, better even than my fencing instructors back in England, and certainly the best sailors.'

They all started talking together again and finally agreed that the name was good as well for their exceptional Skipper. Jamie was overcome with emotion, and quickly had to get back his composure.

'Right lads the other thing is I will only take a crew of seventy. The rest will have to stay and look after our island and the younger ones. The crew I will be taking will be mostly boys and a few good fighting girls.' Apologising with a grin, he said 'I mean young ladies.'

Several of the boys grinned at this remark, but Sam wasn't impressed. She never wanted to be classed as a lady!

'I will let you know tomorrow whom I decide to take. Over the next two weeks, we must ensure that everything we need to take with us is placed on the beach, ready to be loaded. Once we have pushed the ship out into deeper water, we can then load her as I don't want to risk her getting stuck in shallow water with the extra weight.'

Jamie called the meeting to a close, and they wandered off contemplating who would be chosen to go. Rosen and Sam were confident they would be included. Jamie sat in his cabin for the remainder of the day and decided whom to take. He wrote a long list, striking out names and adding others until he finally decided on who was to go and who was to stay. Early the following morning, Jamie called Kate to his cabin.

'Can you recommend one of your girls to look after everyone I leave behind and would be competent enough to take over from you?'

Kate told him of a young girl called Cindy, who not only did a lot of cooking on the campfire, hence her nickname, but was also a good nurse. Jamie was happy with Kate's recommendation of this girl, trusting her judgment. His biggest problem was who to select to take charge of the remaining youngsters, to take control and protect them in his absence.

The only two he felt would be capable of this was either JB or Mitch. He decided to wait a few days as there were other important things to do before he made his final decision.

'Kate, I need your help on something else.'

'What is it you want me to do?' Kate smiled, knowing she would do anything within her power to help Jamie. Her feelings for him ran deep, although she knew she would not speak of this until she knew if he felt the same way.

' I want to make two of the ship sails larger so that she catches more wind and would sail faster. Is it possible for your girls to stitch an extra canvas to each side of two sails?'

'That is no problem, Jamie. Just get me the extra canvas laid out on the main deck and leave it to my girls.'

'Thanks, Kate. You are wonderful. I will have the canvas on deck ready for you tomorrow morning.' He took her hand and pressed it to his lips. Kate blushed and, with her heart pounding, turned and left his cabin, not wanting him to see how flustered she was.

Jamie followed her out and went to instruct his crew to find some spare canvas. They also needed to extend the yardarms on the main topsail and fore topsail in order to accommodate the extra canvas and to strengthen the mainmast and foremast. In addition, he told the blacksmith to adjust the slave chain clamp's locking mechanism, telling him how he wanted them altered.

Over those next two weeks, Jamie made his decision as to who would go with him to rescue Rosen's family. He had been observing everyone's abilities in every aspect but mostly their aptitude with the sword. Although there would be a few girls, most would have to be the older boys for this mission.

By the end of June, the weather had cooled slightly and there was a light breeze although the humidity was very high and some of the orphanage children were finding it difficult to motivate themselves. They anticipated sailing in two days, and everyone was helping to move the ship off the beach into deeper waters. They waited for high, and the ship floated off into the deeper waters of the lagoon. They started to load the ship with everything they needed, including swords, rifles, and ammunition, especially for the big cannon. Using the small boats, back and forth they went until everything they had stored on the beach was loaded. He told Rosen to collect as many of the green berries as he could find and stow them on the ship.

By the time evening came, they were exhausted, but Jamie called them together to announce his decision as to who would go and who would stay.

Before he had a chance to make his announcement, JB stepped forward. 'Skipper, I would like to volunteer to stay behind to take care of those left here.'

Poor JB, he wanted so much to go with him, but Kate had told him that Jamie did not know whom to choose, him or Mitch. Before Jamie had a chance to say anything, JB continued, 'It is so that I will have more time with my dog, McKay.

Also, your carrots and potatoes need tending.' Some of them smiled at this, knowing the true reason for JB volunteering to stay behind. 'I will be very honoured to do this, but the next sailing I want to be picked Skipper sir even if it might be in six or eight months' time when you return.'

'Jamie accepted JB's terms, glad that his problem had been solved.

The evening before they were due to set sail, Jamie and all his crew were eating on the beach, when Jamie said to JB, 'You are an excellent shot with that small swivel gun, so I would like you to teach someone else how to fire it while we are away, and can you continue the things Sam has been teaching them? You have learned so much from her and make the young ones work at it as well. Make sure you take good care of our new dog, McKay, and the cats, Molly and Spike.'

JB looked at him and said, 'Ay, ay, Skipper, I will.'

'JB, my trusted friend, I will miss you, but I know you will do a fantastic job. I am leaving the small boat for you to get around the smaller islands and for fishing.'

JB nodded his thanks but wishing he was going with them.

Chapter 20

The day had arrived, and everyone was busy loading the last of the cargo, checking sails and provisions. Those sailing with Jamie clambered aboard, shouting and waving their goodbyes to those left on the beach. They hoisted the sails and set off through the reef barrier into the open sea. Jamie shouted at his crew, to man the yardarms and set full sail. Those on shore watched until the ship disappeared over the horizon.

The Swordfish was now on a course to Zanzibar, and over the next two months, all was fine with no sighting of any other ships, friend or foe. Over dinner, one evening with the main members of his crew seated, including Kate, Jada and Sam, Jamie told them of his plans to find Rosen's sisters, so they would first call at Zanzibar.

'I'm sorry, Rosen, but you cannot go on to the island when we get there as you might be arrested for being an escaped slave. I cannot take that chance. Jada has lighter skin and would be seen as an Asian or Arab, so she will come with me to walk around the slave market unhindered.'

Rosen desperately wanted to search for his sisters but agreed with Jamie that it was the safest plan.

'Jada and I will go ashore first and find out who this Sultan Bin Said is and where he lives. Jada knows you're two sisters. If we are lucky and find them, we can make arrangements to free them. What are their names, Jada?'

'Minnie the other sister is calledMo, skipper.'

'That's good. So let's hope all goes well and we don't have to use force to free them. We will fly a neutral flag, and if anyone asks who we are when we dock in Zanzibar, we say we are being paid by an Asian princess from India who is buying a few slaves for her plantation and using us to ship them there. That should be good enough excuse.'

'My word, Jamie, how do you think up all these things?' asked Jada.

'It's probably my mother making me think of getting over things. However, another thing, when Jada and I are in the slave market, we will inquire about this Frenchman who brought Rosen's mother, father, and brother.'

Jada said smilingly, 'Yes, Skipper, don't forget his name is Louis Bourbonnais.'

'Jada, you spoke just like a Frenchwoman,' observed Jamie.

'I should be able to. My mother taught me to speak French.'

Jamie thought that would be very useful whilst looking for the Frenchman. He was glad he had Jada with him.

As they finished dinner and were about to go on deck to watch the sunset, someone on deck shouted out, 'Ship ahoy.' They rushed up to the deck to see what ship it was. Kate paused and put her hand on Sam's shoulder. 'Sam, could you stay for a little while? I have something to ask you now that we are alone for once?'

'What is the matter, Kate? What's wrong?'

'Nothing wrong I just want to ask you a question.' She felt embarrassed having to ask her, but needed to find out. 'What feelings do you have for Jamie? You can tell me to mind my own business if you like.'

'Kate, that's fine. My feelings, for him, are of friendship. He always wants you with him, not me. It's you he is interested in.'

'I do not think so, Sam, my good friend. Jamie is a very special friend, and I love him in that way, but I want a husband and a family when I get older. Jamie is too adventurous to be a family man. He would be sailing halfway around the world all the time. That's not the sort of man I want to marry even though he is a wonderful, caring young man. You would be ideal for him.'

'Kate, let us both wait and see. It is far too early for us to talk about lovers and marriage.'

Kate knew in her heart it was Jamie she loved but was prepared to let him go and give him the freedom he needed. They went in search of the others only to find the ship the crew spotted was only a merchant one.

Meanwhile back in England in a small village near Lancaster town called Aldcliffe, where Mary is living with her sister. She often thought of Jamie, the young boy she had helped to raise and wondered where he was now. This particular day, she had gone to the Lancaster port to buy fresh fish and met an old friend called Rose, whose husband was a captain.

Rose greeted Mary warmly and told her that her husband's ship was being loaded and would be leaving the next day to return to Portsmouth. Rose then told Mary all about what had happened to Jamie and that he was wanted in connection with Temp's murder. Mary was horrified at Rose's tale, knowing Jamie could never kill poor Temp. She could not bear the thought of her poor Jamie being accused of murder, knowing full well that Zak and Edwina had got away with murder. She realised that she had to return to Portsmouth to tell the local constabulary what she knew. She asked Rose if she could sail back with her. Rose readily agreed as it would be nice to have the company.

They sailed early the next morning from Lancaster Port and by the end of the week had arrived in Portsmouth. Mary bid Rose farewell and went ashore, careful to cover her face with her scarf for fear of any of Zak's friends recognising her. She was making her way to the constabulary when she met Spider and told him what she knew.

Spider was furious and offered to help her as he knew someone who might help with the truth. He told Mary to go to the constabulary and that he would meet her there with Mr Thompson, the boatswain from Jim's ship. By the time Spider arrived with Mr Thompson, Mary had already informed the constabulary of the conversation she had overheard between Zak and Edwina. Spider also told the man leading the inquiry about the four men who had sailed with Jim. That these men were spending a lot of money the night after the Lady Dorothea had docked without Jim. Spider also told him the names of two, one called Popeye and another called Scarface, but he didn't know the names of the other two, but all four of them frequented The Crow's Nest Inn.

Mr Thompson then gave his account of events. 'I was Jim's boatswain. The night of that storm, I had just got back in my cabin when I heard someone shout, 'man overboard. I rushed up and threw into the sea whatever I could find that floated, even a bundle of round glass fishing floats. Someone shouted it was the captain. He had been hit on the head by the tack, the corner of the spinnaker sail pole, and fallen overboard, but as far as I know, there were no problems with the sails. I had inspected them only half an hour before the storm started. I recognised one of the men that Spider has just mentioned he was on deck at the same time Jim had fallen overboard. I later heard that one of these men went down to the deck below and frightened the life out of a boy called JB. I was told also this man has a scar running down the left side of his cheek, but the poor boy would not tell me what this man had said to him.'

The constable thanked them all for coming forward with this information and told them he would question all the four men and Zak and Edwina. They would all go before the High Court, and if they are guilty, they will hang. He said he would also need to question the boy called JB just to confirm the story, but meanwhile as far as he was concerned they would stop looking for Jamie. They left the constable's office, very pleased with the outcome. Outside, Mary looked a little lost, and Spider asked her what was wrong. She explained she had nowhere to stay, so Spider kindly offered her a bed at his house. They said goodbye to Mr Thompson, who remarked that it was about time justice was done.

The constable went in search of the four men and took them in for questioning. They continued to maintain their innocence that Jim had fallen overboard during the storm. He told them separately that if they admitted to killing Mr Heslop and Temp before the boy JB returned, who obviously witnessed everything, they would not be hanged but exiled to Australia instead. Having no solid evidence, the constable was obliged to release them. He hoped that Jamie would get to know that he was not now a wanted person no more and return with JB.

His next step, he felt, was to question Zak and Edwina separately and hope they might let something slip. The first thing the four men did after leaving the constabulary was to hurry to see Zak, telling him what had happened and that he would be the next to be questioned.

Zak was furious. 'Why did you not kill this JB, you numbskulls, when you had the chance?'

'Sir, we let him live because he told me he hadn't seen anything.'

'What! you idiot, you believed him!'

'Yes, sir,' replied the man, shaking in his boots.

Zak shouted even louder, 'Scarface, you are a damned idiot! Get out of here, all of you!'

Edwina had arrived during this altercation and shouted at Zak, 'I thought you had everything under control?'

'I thought I had, but I did not allow for these stupid numbskulls. We must leave England straight away, in case one of these idiots lets it slip to the police and tells what really did happen or if this JB comes to testify.'

The next day, the constable called Zak and Edwina in. They both denied any knowledge of the event leading up to Jim's death, but when they left, they went in search of his henchmen and told them to prepare the Earl for sailing with enough provisions for eight months but not to say a word to anyone.

It took them two days to prepare the ship for sailing. The only problem was that Edwina wanted to fill the ship with her belongings from Compton Manor. However, Zak had other ideas and told her to leave everything, only fetch all the money, jewellery, and gold. He said they would sell all the cargo the merchants had stowed in the hold to be shipped to India plus keep hold of all the shipping money they paid. Then they would get out of England and search for Jamie and JB and kill them. That way, there would be no witnesses. She agreed it seemed the best course of action and liked the idea of stealing the merchants' money.

'I am going to take you to a place where we will make a living by capturing black people and selling them as slaves. I have been told that we can make a lot of money in a place called South Africa. It's a well-known place for the slave trade. Then we will be able to buy our own mansion.'

Upon hearing these words, Edwina could not get packed up to leave fast enough. They left on the next tide, heading for South Africa. When the constabulary found out they had fled the country, they knew the six were guilty of murder and quickly issued pamphlets offering a reward. Spider also heard the news and hurried to find Mary and told her.

'Let's go and see Jamie's solicitor, Mr Westgarth. Temp told me about him, and we can ask him for permission to look after the mansion and the shipping company, what's left of it.'

'That's an excellent idea, Young Spider. At least the workers will still have a job, and I can get Jamie's home ready for when he returns.'

They set off to see the solicitor. When they arrived in his office, Mr Westgarth took them into his office and offered them a seat. They explained the situation and that they had been to see the constable who had now dropped the charges against Jamie. Spider said to him, 'This morning, Edwina, Zak, and all his henchmen sailed on the Earl, so would it be all right if Mary and I ran the business and looked after Compton Manor until Jamie comes back?'

Mr Westgarth pondered for a moment, scratching his chin. 'I never did like that Zak and his sister, and I think it's an excellent idea to keep things going until Jamie's return. I have some money belonging to Jamie. His late father told me to give it to him in emergencies, and I think that time has now come. I will meet you tomorrow and avail you of some of it in order to get you started.'

They shook his hand and thanked him very much for time and consideration. They left Mr Westgarth, very pleased with the turn of events, and couldn't wait to get started.

Chapter 21

The Swordfish sighted Zanzibar on a bright sunny day in November 1792 after making good time from the island. They had sailed south and then picked up the easterly trade winds. The larger sails had seemed to have helped the ship along. Jamie rang the ship's bell, calling for everyone to assemble on deck. When they had all arrived, he said, 'I am only taking four of you with me ashore for now. That will be Jada, Sam, Rabbit, and Curly. Jada, I want you to dress like an Indian princess. Sam, you will have to wear a dress like you are he Lady-in-waiting.'

'DRESS a woman's Dress, a Lady-in-Waiting! Whatever next, I don't even own a dress!'

'Kate will help you with that, and no swords or knives under your dress Sam. We will also call you Sarah as that will be more appropriate to your position.'

Sam looked decidedly unhappy with both the name and the dress.

'All those remaining on board will wear a red scarf as this is the correct wear for a princess's crew. As for myself, you will have noticed I have neither shaved nor cut my hair for a while. This is in case anyone should recognise me. Rabbit and Curly, you need to smarten yourselves up before we go ashore. The rest of you can spend your time cleaning the ship.'

There were groans all round. Scrubbing decks were not their favourite task. At high tide, the following day, they sailed into the harbour near Stone Town and dropped anchor. Jamie called the girls, telling them it was time to leave. He could not believe his eyes. They both looked beautiful, especially Sam. He had never seen her look so stunning. However, he soon pulled himself together and got on with the mission in hand.

The five of them disembarked. The two young boys walked behind the girls. They looked just like Jamie had intended Bodyguards for the princess. They soon attracted a lot of attention; people were staring. Jada asked someone the way to the slave market, and they pointed to the east side of the town. They followed the directions they were given and soon found their way down a dry and dusty road. Jada told them to go to the back of the crowd when they got there. As they approached the market, all but Jada looked in disbelief. There were poor black people being whipped, molested, and sold like animals. It was all Jamie could do, not to shout out in anger. Jada was looking for someone who might be buying slaves. Noticing a man who was bidding for slaves but who looked quite pleasant, she asked, 'Excuse me, sir, do you know where Bin Said lives?'

Looking down at her and seeing her guards, said, 'Who the hell would you be, miss?'

'I am Princess Adie Sing from India. My father is an emperor there,' she replied in a haughty voice.

'Well, that's different, Your Highness. Yes, I know where he lives. Ask that man over there with the horse and carriage to take you to Bin Said's plantation. Also, say Magnus sent you.'

She thanked him kindly, and he gave her a sweeping bow. Jada approached the man in the carriage, who agreed to take them all. They arrived at the plantation' to see this lovely big mansion surrounded by flowing fruit trees and a massive court yard. Jamie had already decided for Jada to go first and the rest of them would stay in the coach. Jada had previously been told what to say to the owner. She was very nervous. When she tugged at the bell by the main door, a servant opened the door and asked her what her business was. He stood back from the door and gestured for her to enter. To her amazement, she was greeted by one of Bin Said's wives called Vie, who seemed very hospitable. She led Jada into a study filled with exquisite furnishings and offered her a seat. Refreshments were laid out on a small side table, and politely Jada accepted these. When the formalities were over, Jada said, 'I believe the Sultan's son bought two young girls as slaves called Minnie and Mo. I am here to ask you may I purchase them from you.'

Vie stood up and smiled, 'I am sure you could, but you will have to talk to the girls first. I will go and get them.'

Within a few minutes, Vie returned with Minnie and Mo, who greeted Jada warmly. Jada told them the reason for her being there but was very surprised at their response.

Minnie said, 'Jada, my good friend, we love it here. We have so much to thank Bin Said for. We even get a small wage for working. We will never leave here. The only thing is we miss our mother and father and brothers very much.'

After Jada recovered from the shock of their reply, she said, 'Rosen is with my friends on board our ship outside the harbour. We thought it safer for him to stay on the ship.'

'You have a ship, Jada? If only you could rescue my family and fetch them back here, we were told that it would not be any problem for them all to live here and work on the land or catch him fresh fish.'

'Why has this Bin Said not tried to rescue them himself?'

'Because the island occupied by the French. They have called this island Isle de France. It is well fortified, and Bin Said does not have an army or a ship Jada.'

'I will try my best to free them with my friends and fetch them here, but I need something to allow us to come here again to Zanzibar if we manage to rescue them.'

'That is not a problem. I will get you a signed letter allowing you all free permission to go anywhere in Zanzibar.'

Jada realised there was nothing more she could do for them and, after an emotional farewell, joined Jamie and the others in the coach. On their way back to the harbour she told Jamie everything the two sisters had said to her.

Jamie was astounded and asked Jada howhe is going to tell Rosen that they wanted to stay where they were. Jada reassured Jamie that she felt Rosen would be happy enough with the outcome as long as his sisters were content.

When they arrived back at the ship the first thing Sam said 'What a dam waste of time me putting on address and us going with you'. Jamie smiled and told her. 'Sam it was just a precaution in case we had to fight, any way everyone on board wanted to see you in a dress.' That remark was followed by loud cheers. Jada by now had explained everything to Rosen who was obviously very upset but knew it was for the best. He also knew that when they returned from Isle de France hopefully with his mum and father, he would be able to go this time with his parent's to meet his sisters.

They set a course for the Isle de France, and Jamie gave the order to watch out for French corsairs because they did not want to get involved in a fight with them. Jamie spent a lot of time making plans with some of his crew, finally coming up with what they felt was the best idea, but unfortunately, none of them knew anything about this island. However, part of the plan was for two of them to go ashore and find out the whereabouts of this man Louis Bourbonnais. Once again, it would be Jada going with him as she could speak perfect French.

This yearChristmas came and went because everyone was so engrossed in what they were doing no one had remembered, or was it the hot weather?

They had been busy stocking up on supplies in Zanzibar but needed to preserve what they had. The reason they did not know where the next provisions would be coming from.

One evening,after eating dinner with Jada, Kate and Rosen he told them. 'This time I have decided that it would be only beJada and mewould go ashore, I want you Jada to take thesame part again but this time as a Arabian princess and I will be your bodyguard. But this time you are trading in buying andselling slaves and you have some to sell here when the slave market is open.It's going to be more difficult finding Rosen's family.'Jada and Rosen understood everything, the two girls left to find the right dress, leaving the two men to finalise the plan.

Early next morning it was not long before someone shouted 'LAND AHOY' it was the Isle de France. Both Rosen and Jamie had been checking on the skipper's entries in the Kitty Moth's log his ship had docked here a few times before. They had read that the main port was Port Louis, soon after arriving in the harbour; the skipper moored the ship. He made it clear to all the crew to stay on board even though he could be away for a few hours. Everything went according to plan as they went ashore and answered the questions put to them by the French port soldiers agreeingto let them both through. It was quite a long walk to get to the centre of the town, once they arrived Jada asked Jamie if she could have something to eat and drink. He readily agreed as the heat was making him thirsty and hungry they spotted a tavern and decided to try there. It looked very dirty, but it seemed to be the only place. They had just begun to take a bite of the hard bread when Jada noticed a man sitting in a corner of the tavern.

She pointed him out to Jamie, saying, 'That man is definitely the one who brought Rosen's family.' Sure enough, a local wench, who was touching his long hair, had just said his name, Mr Bourbonnais'. He had a vicious look about him and Jamie had to think quickly of a way to find out where this man's plantation was. He decided Jada would approach the man when he leaves and ask him if he wanted to buy some cheap slaves. They had to keep buying drinks in the harsh sunlight for about an hour when they noticed the man had got up and was going to his carriage. They both got up as Jamie walked behind being her bodyguard Jada approached him, trying desperately to keep her dislike hidden.

'Sir, could I have a word with you? Am I correct in believing you are Mr Bourbonnais a native here recommended you might like to have a deal with slaves I have for sale.'

He looked her up and down with a leery grin. .'I see but firstly young lady is there anything I can get you to drink also please call me Louis and your name is.'

Jada shuddered with distaste. 'I am Princess Jada and this is my bodyguard, Mr Louis on my ship I have twenty strong young slaves for sale at a good price.'

'To whom a good price, you or me Princess.' Ashe chuckled to himself, thinking he would be able to get a lot lower price and her into the bargain.

Jada suggested a low price knowing he would be tempted. He was eager to do the deal but did not want to appear too keen. He suggested an even lower price, and to his surprise, she agreed.

'If they are in as good a condition as you say they are Madam then we have a deal. Fetch them all to my plantation tomorrow at midday.' He pointed to the man at his side and introduced him as his chief overseer, telling Jada to meet this man here at eleven tomorrow morning, and he would show her with your slaves the way to his plantation. Jada played her part and looked at him coyly from under her fluttering eyelashes. 'Louis, could you give me authority in writing so we can all pass unhindered?'

'I will, of course, give you a letter of authorisation right away, and don't forget beautiful lady my chief overseer will meet you here in the morning.'

After giving her the letter, he took her hand and brought it to his lips and bid her farewell. Jada clenched her teeth, squirming inside at his touch. He climbed into his carriage and told his driver to go, giving Jada a final wave. she returned Louis's wave. Jamie was delighted with her and congratulated on such a wonderful performance.

'You even had me believing the story for a moment.'

'Jamie, let's just get back to the ship. I need to scrub my hands. The touch of that man makes me ill.'

'I am sorry to put you through this, Jada, but there is no one else suitable. Let's go now. I need to think of a strategy for tomorrow.'

Now both back on the ship, Jamie had for now formulated a plan in his head. He called twenty young black men, including Rosen, to the quarterdeck. He explained he would have to take them with him in chains. They disliked the idea but knew that to act the part of slaves, they had to be chained together.

'I am very sorry, Rosen, about the chains, but are you sure your lads know how to use the release catch?'

'Yes, Skip, they all do. It's just the thought of being in chains again brings back bad memories. But they will do it if it means rescuing my family and the other poor slaves.'

Another part of the Skippers plan was to use the green berries. He told Rosen to make them into a juice and to bring up two full barrels of the best wine and two larger empty ones. When Rosen returned, they poured the juice into the wine barrels, mixing them together. The others filled the larger barrels with the swords, the Skipper telling them all.

'We will give this wine to Louis and his overseer, which should keep them quiet for a while and sorry, no red scarves.'

Jamie had already selected ten of his crew as guards and Kate will be Jada's Lady in Waiting and three black girls to act as slave maids. He explained to the guards with genuine regret that they would have to wipe the twenty chained black boys acting as slaves now and then, especially in front of the French soldiers, just to make it look genuine. Rosen was to say jokingly, 'It better not be too hard a slap, because I will make sure the one who slaps me gets one back when we return.' Those selected smiled at Rosen's joke but felt nervous about Jamie's plan and Rosen's remark. The slavesalso thinking they had found their freedom once and did not want anything to go wrong and end up being made slaves again. Jamie turned to Sam. 'I like you to go as well, but you will have to look like a boy.' No one dare to say a word to her.'Sam make sure your long hair is hidden, and no swords please.' That remark made the boys laugh. Sam thought to herself she would make sure she had at least pair of pistols handy just in case.

The next morning, they all set off to meet up with Louis's overseer. Having the letter of authorisation, they had walked past the French soldiers in the harbour without any problems. When they got to the tavern,the overseer was waiting, he told Jada and Kate to get into thecarriage,she insisted he put the barrels of winein the back and securely tied down. Jamie knew he had to think of a way quickly,because going was not a problem, but coming back would definitely be a big problem with a lot more slaves,They walked and walkedin the midday sun it seemed like several hours before arriving at the plantation.Thisbeautiful massive white house enclosed by a high stone wall.Withseveral wooden shacks built off to the side, surrounded by a high wire fence patrolled byguards. Jamie assumed this was where the slaves were housed to keep them in secured area. The guard opened the massive entrance iron gates the overseer took them all into a big courtyard they all got out of the carriage and in amazement looked around. Ivywas growing up the walls; also in the centre of the yard was this big pound with a water fountain in the middle. There are different coloured Carp fish swimming around among the lovely flowing water Lilly's.

Louis was waiting to greet Jada, she walked across towards him with Jamie and Mitch following behind her, carrying the kegs of wine.

'Sir good day to you I give you these two barrels of my best wine for yourself and your menas a gesture of our new friendship and business agreement.' He thanked her warmly with a large grin on his ugly face, and then asked. 'What about the other two wine barrels?' She replied. 'Louis just see if you like the wine first, then after our deal is complete, you may have these two.' He agreed.

Taking her arm, they both started to inspect her slaves and appeared very happy with them, thinking to himself what a bargain he had got. He shouted orders to his overseer. 'Put our new slaves with the others for now and you can give some of this wine to your men, but only one glass each. I am feeling generous today! Jada your maids and Lady in Waiting along with your men can wait outside, whilst we go inside and sample your wine before I pay you.'

Jamie felt everything was going according to plan at the moment but was now very concerned when Louis suggested Jada join him in a glass of wine on her own. He need not have worried as Jada had already thought of an excuse not to drink it. 'I am sorry I do not like wine. May I ask for a cup of your tea instead?' He led her into a beautifully furnished room with many antiques and sumptuous sofas. It was light and airy compared to the heat outside, but Jada was unable to relax as he sat down very close to her on one of the sofas. A slave brought her a cup of tea, and as she sipped it, she watched Louis take a gulped down all the glass of wine then said.

'This is an excellent wine. It tastes very strong and so different.'

'I have been told it is, but let us get down to the business of payment before you drink too much.'

Louis smiled then leaned over the arm of the sofa put the empty glass down and produced a bag full of gold coins. As he pulled the bag up from the floor, he leaned in towards Jada. His other arm went around her shoulders, and she backed away. Just as he was about to make a lunge for her, he went limp. Jada breathed a sigh of relief as she pushed him to the floor, grabbed the bag of coins, and fled.

Running into the courtyard, to see Louis's overseers and guard were also in a trance. 'Thank God you are safe.' both Kate and Jamie saidtogether.

'It was a close thing,' holding up the bag of coins andlaughing out loud.,

Whilst Jada had been acting her part in this daring plan, Rosen had gone to the slaves' quarters and released them all. He hurried quickly to the courtyard with his arms around his mother, followed by his father and brother and about twenty slaves. They were all very emotional and a little scared knowing the fate that would befall them if they were caught escaping. Some of the slaves had decided to stay; mostly the servant's some thinking what would happen to them if they got caught.

Floggings amputated Limbs left in the burning sun with no water, all too terrible to think about. The good thing was it appeared Rosen's family was none the worse for their enslavement, only undernourished. Rosen told the other slaves they were free, but in order to get back to the ship safely, they would have to appear to be chained slaves along with his men. This has to be done when they were near to the town. They had to move quickly, not knowing when the guards would wake up. It was a long way back to the harbour, and progress would be slow. Jamie's men saddled up a few of Louis's horses and carriages and told the weakest ones to get in. .

It was early evening when they reached the outskirts of the town, as they had to chain the slaves together, explaining again the quick release mechanism. After dumping the carriages they started to walk through the town with barely a glance from anyone. All was going well until they reached the harbour. There the French soldiers are blocking the way. Jada whispered to Jamie that the officer in charge was going to stop them. Jamie passed the word around his crew to be prepared to fight. The French captain put his hand up and called them to a halt. 'Where have this lot come from?' Jada flowed by Kate, quickly gave him the letter.

'Princess, this note gives you all permission to enter the island with slaves not to leave with three times as many.'

Jada knew they were in trouble and whispered to Jamie what the officer had said. Jamie made a gesture to Rosen to get ready. The officer walked along the line of slaves and spoke to one of the boys acting as overseer.

'Do you speak French?'

Before the boy could gather his wits, he replied, 'I do not understand.' The officer drew his sword and shouted to his men, 'Arrest them all.

They are bloody English!'

The French are about to find out what two years of training have done for Sam's young cadets. Jamie shouted out, 'Defensive order!'

His crew reacted so quickly the French were thrown into disarray. The slaves released their chains, and Sam broke open the barrels containing the swords and threw them to Rosen and his men. It all happened in an instant. Jamie's men surrounded the new slaves in order to protect them, not allowing the French soldiers anywhere near them. The crew on board the ship had seen what was happening and ran ashore to help, but they were not to be needed. Jamie and his men were outnumbered two to one, but they fought with ferocity that unnerved the French. Kate in betweenwhiles watched the fight stood on a large rock with amazement. Jamie's men had been taught so well they were beating the French. Sam was magnificent, taking on three men and winning.

Jamie had beaten one soldier and had taken on the French captain. He lunged at the captain and knocked his sword from his hand. The captain fell to the ground and instantly pulled two pistols from his belt, aiming them directly at Jamie.

Sam could see what, was going to happenas she was standing near Kat she lifted her dress up to reveal her lovely legs and her red frilly underwear with two pistols tucked inside. There was a pause in the fighting, and every man stared at Kate's red frilly underwear. Without hesitation, Sam drew the pistols and shot the captain in the shoulders as he was looking at Kate as well. The captain writhing in agony called for his men to drop their swords as he knew they were beaten. After the crew picked up all the French weapons, Jamie stood over the captain, saying, 'Sorry, we can't stay to help you. A word of advice, just stop your countrymen selling slaves.' Jamie turned and called for his crew and the newly released slaves to run for the ship. They quickly unmoored the ship and hoisted sails, setting a course back to Zanzibar. When everything had settled down and the newly freed slaves had been shown to their living quarters, Jamie called his crew on deck. He praised their loyalty and fighting spirit, especially Sam for taking the initiative. The crew complimented Kate on her legs, at which she blushed furiously. The skipper thanked all his crew, especially Sam, giving her a kiss, which fetched a "Woo!" from the crew and left Sam blushing. He then said, 'Kate, you have a lovely pair of legs and beautiful underwear.' Mitch shouted out, with all the boys shouting, Yippee, leaving her also blushing more. They set a course due west in case the French gave chase. If they didn't sight them by dark, they intended to turn the ship and head for Zanzibar. The last thing they wanted was to be caught in Zanzibar's harbour by the French. Unfortunately, they underestimated the tenacity of the French, who had already set sail in pursuit.

Chapter 22

The next morning, a boy in the crow's nest called out the sighting of another ship.. He looked through his telescope and realised it was a French frigate with at least thirty guns and probably a crew of up to 200 men. He thought perhaps he could outrun them with his larger sails but was not willing to take that chance, so he decided to scare them off instead. Beforehand he ordered everyone except the crew manning the ship to go below right away.

He shouted to Mitch, 'Now is the time to see how good you are at firing that cannon. Use only ball shot on the French. I do not want to kill them. Just disable the ship. Aim for the masts if you can. I will let you know when we are in range, so be ready to fire when I shout.'

'I'll take Curly and Rabbit to help me load and reload her Skipper.'

'That's fine. You have a bit of time because the ship should be in range in about an hour. Then we will see what our Black Beauty can do.'

Jamie could feel the tension rising amongst his crew and knew he had to stay calm although he was very nervous as this was the first time they had used the cannon in combat. He was relying on Mitch to save them from being killed or taken prisoner. Therefore, he decided to get the surrender flag ready just in case but hoped and prayed it would not come to that.

The captain of the French frigate had ordered his men to prepare to board the Swordfish, believing its young crew would surrender having very little gun power to fight his large ship. He knew they were excellent swordsmen, but as he had over a hundred highly trained soldiers ready, he felt it would be easy to overpower the Swordfish but thought they would surrender first.

On the Swordfish, Jamie was watching the frigate intensely through his telescope, preparing to tell Mitch to start firing as the French were almost in range. He gave the order to fire. The French captain and his crew laughed seeing a puff of smoke from a cannon, thinking how stupid the English were as his ship was well out of range. Before they knew it, there was a loud hissing sound, and as they looked up, they saw a hole in the bottom sails. The captain looked in disbelief. Then another hissing! This time, the shot hit the foremast, and it came crashing down, narrowly missing the crew, who scrambled for cover. The captain ordered his crew clean the foremast off deck and called off the pursuit, knowing he could just about limp back to port before dark. To the amazement of those on the Swordfish, they saw the French turn and flee.

They had only fired two shots. Jamie breathed a huge sigh of relief and ordered the helmsman to turn north and head for Zanzibar. He went to Mitch and shook his hand vigorously. 'Mitch, you are a bloody marvellous marksman with that cannon.'

Everyone was relieved and relaxed enough to celebrate well into the evening, playing music and singing. Rosen took his family to one side and told them about Minnie and Mo and about how happy and settled they were. He said that the owner's wife would welcome them and the other slaves, but his parents decided to wait and see when they got there.

Over the next few weeks, the slaves talked about their horrific punishments. Even the slaves given control over their own would give out harsh punishments. There were frequent floggings and punishments. On hearing these stories, Jamie became more determined than ever to do something about the slave trade using his elite gang of fighters. He had some time now to put his mind to the problem of getting into Zanzibar as he had noticed on their last visit there had been several ships anchored and some of them had probably been pirates. Maybe even the La Liberte was there by now. He decided to drop anchor just north of Stone Town harbour in a place called Bububu. Most of the ships, including the Sea Eagle and La Liberte, would sail up from the South of Africa and would not sail past Bububu. It was late afternoon in March 1793 when they sailed down Zanzibar channel and arrived at Bububu. The sun was already starting to sink below the horizon, and it was hot and sticky, so Jamie decided to go ashore the next morning. Jamie gathered together Jada, Kate, Rosen, and some of his crew along with the slaves from the Isle de France. He also took his letter of permission to travel freely to Bin Said's mansion. Jamie decided to bypass Stone Town. This meant a long and weary walk with giant vegetation everywhere. They came across lizards, snakes and all kinds of insects biting ants allscurrying back into the undergrowth. Rosen was the one chopping vegetation down to lead the way, also he was singing all the time. It took about three hours to reach their destination. On arrivingVie was greeting them warmly, 'I am going to get Minnie and Mo and my husband, Bin Said'. She returned almost instantly followed by the two sisters. They screamed and cried in delight when they saw their parents and brother, rushing into their arms.

Bin Said told Jada to say that if any of the slaves wished to stay and work for him, he could gladly find room for them and stated his conditions. Everyone readily agreed, except Rosen, who was torn between staying with his family or continuing to help his friend Jamie try to abolish slavery. Vie had arranged for all the slaves to be fed in what would be their new homes. While the others inside the house had food and drink to be put out on tables, all enjoyed a few hours relaxing. As the day started to wear on, Jamie stood up and announced that they had to leave as they had a long walk back to the ship.. He thanked Bin Said and Vie for their hospitality and said goodbye to the now freed slaves. Rosen hugged his mother and sisters but was very sad to be leaving them. His father put his arm across Rosen's shoulders and wished him luck and courage to continue the fight against slavery, saying how proud he was of him. Rosen turned away not wanting anyone see his tears, as he led the crew back down the track towards their ship. Jamie caught up with him and said.'My friend, do not worry too much you will be able to come back to see them from time to time'. Rosen nodded saying. 'We became a family again for only an hour after being apart for years my sisters now being young ladies. As you say, I will be able to come back again,' He wiped the tears quickly from his eyes before anyone noticed.

Being a quicker way they decided to walk back through Stone Town. But to avoid the slave market on the east side they decided to walk well past the harbour and along the beach towards Bububu and their anchored ship. When they were passing the harbour, Jamie stopped in his tracks and let out a yell. 'Lookit's the Earl!'

He wondered why the Earl was docked there but came to the conclusion that either they were searching for him to claim the reward money or they were there to buy slaves at the market. Although the Earl was anchored just inside the harbour, it was possible that Zak's henchmen were wandering around on the quay, so they hurried past so as not to be spotted. Jamie was now deep in thought and assumed the Earl would not leave today as it was Sunday and there was no slave market. Ideas were forming in Jamie's mind, and he said to Rosen, 'How would you like to command your own ship?' Rosen looked at him questioningly, Jamie grinning told him to wait until they returned to the Swordfish and he would explain. It was late when they arrived back on board their ship; Jamie decided to tell Rosenthat he would think more about his plan of him being a captain and discuss it in the morning.

The next morning after the Skipper explained part of his plan to all the crew, it was now mid-morning. Jamie gave orders to pull up the anchor as they were going to sail around to the harbour. He had no way of knowing where the crew were or whether Zak and Edwina were on board. Assuming that at this time of day, they would either be at the slave market or in the tavern but hoping there were only a few crewmen left on board the Earl. They anchored just outside the harbour and could see the Earl from the crow's nest in the distance. The plan was for some of the black girls to go in the rowing boat dressed in their traditional costumes taking fruit to give to the crew on the Earl. The girls' boat would go to one side of the Earl and distract the crew by giving them fruit and fluttering their eyes, whilst Jamie together with Rosen and Sam and his crew in the larger boat would row to the other side of the ship, climb aboard, and overpower them when they were least expecting it.

Everything now was going according to plan, with the girls doing their part throwing fruit plus flowers and kisses up to Zak's crew. Jamie had been correct in thinking there would only be a few crewmen left on the Earl. They quickly climbed aboard and overpowered the few crewmen left on the Earl. The girls meanwhile had climbed aboard from their side, and Sam was enjoying herself fighting the Earl's crewman. It took only a few minutes, and before long, they had thrown the Earl's crew overboard while some had decided to jump.

By now the Swordfish had sailed gently alongside, and half of the crew scrambled on to the Earl to help Rosen sail her. They hauled in the two boats and got them on board. Jamie shouted to them to hurry and set sail. He turned to Rosen. 'Well, Captain, have a safe journey and Godspeed.' They shook hands hurriedly. And to you Sam Take care of them, and we will see you back on our island.' With that, he kissed her then grabbed a rope thrown from the Swordfish, climbed up a few feet, and then swung over to his ship shouting, Yippee. Rosen shouted back. 'Do not worry about us, Skipper. We will be fine and will beat you back home.'

'Like hell, you will Captain Rosen,' grinning from ear to ear.

The Swordfish raised its anchor when Jamie noticed a ship that was anchored in the harbour that he recognised. It was the La Liberte, which they had encountered over a year ago. By now, the Earl was a good way ahead of them, but they kept up a steady pace and knew hopefully they would wait for him to catch up. At lunch that afternoon, in the galley, Jamie addressed his crew, 'Having two ships will be a great advantage for us to ambush slave ships anchored up before they had time to load them. That's the time we will attack them.'

He had become relentless in his quest to stop slavery. After they had finished their meal, the young crewmen went back to their posts, and Jamie took the helm. Kate helped the girls clear the tables and went to her cabin. She lay on her bunk, mulling over Jamie's words. Sadly, she came to the conclusion that Jamie was changing from a shy, quiet young man and becoming aggressive with a thirst for killing those in his way. She did not like it, but part of her understood why.

Zak's crew from the Earl had swum back to the shore and told Zak what had happened. He was furious. He ranted and swore, threatening to kill them all. They ran off in fright, having no loyalty to Zak, whatsoever, and disappeared into Stone Town. Zak went down to the quay and got out his telescope, searching for the Earl. He saw not only the Earl but scudding along behind was the Lady Dorothea. He hurried back to the town to tell Edwina, and when she found out it was Jamie who had taken the Earl, all hell let loose. Zak tried to quieten his sister down and managed to say, 'I will find a pirate ship and pay the captain to help us hunt down Jamie and kill him.'

'Oh, you will-will you then? How in hell are we going to pay them to do this?' 'Sis we have all that gold and the money we saved and took from those Merchantmen for their goods we should have taken to India.' 'You stupid fool, it's on the Earl!' 'Edwina We'll pay the pirates when we capture the ships.'

'OH will we that's if we manage to capture them, and by the time we paid those greedy pirates, we would have nothing left.'

'There you are wrong! We would have two ships, so we could sell one.'

'So brother it appears there is no option. Go and find some kind mercenary pirate to help us if there is such a thing. Now!'

Zak hurried off, fearful of his sister's temper, and went in search of a pirate with an available ship. Eventually, he came across a tavern and was pointed in the direction to a pirate called Nancarrow. After introducing himself he asked him could he help find his stolen ship and quickly told him what had happened offering a reward. Nancarrow was not very interested. 'How long ago did she set sail?'

'She sailed about two hours ago sir. She was being followed by my other ship they call The Lady Dorothea.'

Nancarrow jumped up, knocking over the table and drinks then throwing back his chair 'What ship did you say?'

'The. Lady Dorothea, captain.'

'Ahu. That's what I thought you said. Well I have a score to settle with that young man. I'll take you for no reimbursement. I want him for myself to kill him.'

Zak had no idea what the pirate captain meant or was saying but was happy to go along with it, even if it means he did not need to catch the brat himself. 'Sir we had better hurry, as they have a good head start.'

'Sit down and have a beer Zak. There is no need to hurry yet. I will get my ship ready in two days because you see my friend; I know exactly where they are going. I spotted a boat fishing near some small islands, and the name on that small boat was Lady Dorothea, so I left a calling card for him to find.' He laughed heartily.

Again Zak had no idea what he was talking about but made his apologies and went to find Edwina and to gather what was left of his crew and tell them to be ready to leave on the early morning tide. Nancarrow was reluctant to take Zak, Edwina, and his crew with him as he wanted Jamie and the ships for himself but reasoned extra manpower would be useful. However thinking he would send Zak and his crew can row them ashore first to capture Jamie so that if there was heavy fighting, it would not only put Zak out of the picture but also save the lives of his crew.

He would make sure Zak did not survive, also any of Zak's crew left alive he knew they would gladly join him. The extra hands would also help to sail the two captured ships. Nancarrow called for another mug of ale and sat, grinning to himself.

By now, Jamie's ship had caught up with the Earl, and they were sailing together. It would take a few weeks to reach the island, but they had set course south-east to pick up the trade winds. Rosen and Sam have been too busy organising everyone the last few hours, now they have the chance to explore the ship. He and Sam checked the hold and found nothing of great importance, just some livestock and some barrels of pickled food. Sam was searching the forward part of the hold at the stern when she noticed huge piles of canvas sheeting. On pulling them back, she was amazed to find priceless works of art, beautifully carved furniture, and numerous trunks stuffed with silk and brocade curtains. Sam knew Jamie would be pleased with his find and went to tell Rosen he was surprised as well. 'Zak could be buying slaves with it all.' Rosen agreed with her and suggested they go and have a drink in the captain's cabin. They toasted Jamie's good fortune with a glass of very good wine they had found and started to look around. Sam came across a large locked trunk. Nothing ever deterred Sam as she pulled her revolver out and fired at the lock on the old trunk.

Rosen was taken by surprise and stood up hastily, hitting his head on the low oak wooden beams running across the ceiling. 'What in hell are you doing, Sam?

You might have warned me first,' rubbing his head. Sam collapsed with laughter. Rosen should have known by now that she acted first and explained afterwards. She opened it and gasped. To her amazement, it was filled with gold coins and precious jewellery.

Rosen came over to her to find out what had made Sam speechless for a change. 'Where the hell did Zak get this lot from?' Sam had recovered from the shock and looked at Rosen. 'Most likely stole it from someone, probably to buy more slaves.' They continued to search but found nothing more of interest, so they decided to search the boatswain's cabin. Rosen searched a chest but found it full of the boatswain's personal effects whilst Sam searched the desk. On opening a hidden drawer, she found a note book and started to browse through it. She called Rosen over to listen as she read aloud to what was written last in it.

We had to leave England in a hurry as the Parish Constabulary of Portsmouth has been questioning Zak and Edwina and four other accomplices about the suspicious circumstances of the deaths of Captain Charles Heslop and Captain Temp Elliott. I am certain Jamie is not guilty, but my loyalty is to Zak.

Rosen was delighted and couldn't wait to tell Jamie the news. 'Unfortunately, Sam, we have to wait until we get to our island before we can tell Jamie about this.'

Sam agreed as there was no way to inform Jamie of the good news whilst they were sailing. They continued their search in another cabin, rummaging in cupboards and more trunks. They were full of well-made clothes for both men and women. They realised the clothes must have belonged to Zak and Edwina. They found it very amusing that Zak and Edwina would now only have the clothes they stood up in and no money in their pockets. 'Well, Rosen, Kate's girls are going to love making new clothes with this lot.'

'I can look forward to having a new pair of breeches, can I?' 'And me,' laughed Sam.

By the end of June, mid-day they sighted their Island all of them were excited at being back to their adopted homeland. The incessant heat of the island had passed its height, now there was frequent rainfall, which kept the underground water chambers full. As they sailed nearer the young lad up the mast called down to Jamie. 'There's something wrong, Skipper.' 'What's wrong?' Jamie shouted up to the boy.

'It looks like most of the huts have been burned out, and I can't see many animals around. But wait, I can see some of our people running down to meet us.'

The skipper shouted back 'Let's wait until we dock to find out what's happened.' 'Aye-aye captain.'

Luckily, before leaving Zanzibar, Jamie had advised Rosen to drop the Earls anchor away from the reef. He decided to do the same until he had found out what had been going on. The two ships lowered both their longboats and rowed ashore. As they beached, JB came running over and appeared to be very distressed. 'I am so sorry, Skipper. I have let you down.'

'I am sure you haven't. Just tell me what the hell has been going on. It looks like a war zone.'

'It was the pirate ship the La Liberte. It caught us off guard and opened fire. I am sorry to tell you this; Jamie…' he choked on his words, fighting to control his sobbing 'Pig Wash Anne was killed along with her helper, Jasmine. They were trying to save Anne's favourite pig, Rose Bud. There was no time to use our small cannon on them. They took us by surprise. I managed to get everyone into Rosen's shelter, but the animals had to fend for themselves.

A lot of the sheep and pigs and chickens are dead, but the blessing is we have not lost our two cows and the two donkeys, but our Dog run off wounded and has not come back.'

Jamie listened in astonishment, angry, furious, and filled with remorse for having left them to fend for themselves.

'Skipper, we gave Pig Wash Anne and Jasmine, a seaman's burial. We did it the same way you showed us with Peggy.'

Jamie thanked him and went to check on everyone whilst his crew started to make some semblance of order out of the chaos. Rosen and Sam plus most of their crew had come ashore helping, and were all upset not believing what had taken place. Everyone had helped to rebuild the remaining huts and have got everything organised by late evening most of them just wanted to sleep.

Chapter 23

Sam had decided to wait until this morning to show Jamie the note book contents.

Early next morning after finding him she asked him to sit down because she has something important things to tell him, but firstly she said. 'I believe this will tell you are not a wanted man anymore.'

'What makes you think that Sam?'

'It's a note book I found in the Boatswain cabin abroad the Earl, I wondered why it was there, take it and read Skipper.'

Jamie read it and was delighted, saying to Sam. 'I think it could be one of Zak's men, covering his self if he needed too'. Jamie was over the moon and thanked Sam, thinking at least something good had occurred for once. Sam noticed that Jamie had a smile back on his face at last.

'Skipper it would seem that it is your uncle, Zak, and Edwina and the other four men the Parish Constabulary are after.' 'Yes you are right Sam'

Sam also told him of the valuables they found on the Earl. Jamie was feeling better all the time. 'Sam later on I will take a look in the Earl after once the crew have unloaded all the animals and what we need'

I will tell Kate the good news, and meet you back here later Sam. 'Aye-aye Skipper.'

When he found Kate he told her the good news and what Zak and Edwina had stolen from his house. Telling her they will see what was taken shortly once his crew have unloaded. In betweenwhiles they both decided to go for a walk. Kate saw he was still holding his head down, she clearly had noticed that his facial expression changes. Over the last few months he was becoming tense again even with the good news he got this morning. She thought to try and calm him down.

'Jamie, do you remember the first time I spoke to you on your way to the churchyard? Do you know that was well over two years ago?'

'It seems like only yesterday' He looked up at her. 'Has that much time passed already?'

'Yes, it was that long ago. The good thing is, Jamie, that we can go back home any time we like now.'

'Kate, apart from a few friends there, I would rather be with my wonderful crew, either here or sailing around the world.'

Kate's heart stopped and she thought it would break but she knew without a doubt now that Jamie would never settle back in Portsmouth but would want to continue sailing his ships. He loved the sea like his father did. She loved him deeply but wouldn't be the life for her. She wanted a settled life on dry land.

'Come on, Kate, let's get back'.

He took her hand and started to lead her back to the beach, when they heard a dog bark it was poor McKay he was so frightened and wounded, he had a splinter in his side. Jamie picked him up they carried him back luckily Cindy was on hand to try to help him. Kate and Jamie helped to pull the splinter out Cindy told them both she will take care of him,. They both knew McKay is in good hands and left.

When JB found Jamie he took him aside. He had hesitated before he told Jamie

'Sorry Skipper being late to tell you, I just remembered something the captain of the pirate ship had said when he started to sail away, he shouted out, Remember my name—Captain Nancarrow!'"

Yes Jamie was upset not being told earlier, but relished the thought and couldn't wait to come face to face with this man. Jamie knew full well that this man, Nancarrow, will definitely come back again sooner rather than later, especially if he met up with Zak, of which he thought there was a strong possibility.

'JB he will return to finish all of us off, I have to think of a plan to be ready for this Nancarrow and maybe even Zak will be with him. I must get ready for him by this evening..'

'Do you think Zak may come as well?'

'Yes, for sure JB, he won't give up.'

He told JB, 'firstly to find Rosen and we will go aboard the Earl to investigate what Rosen and Sam had found and told Kate to come as well.

Soon the four of them rowed out to the Earl and clambered aboard. Jamie was shocked.

'Some of these things come from my house. They must have taken it. Knowing they could not return to England.'

Jamie was incensed that his stepmother and her brother had taken furniture and valuables from his home. He was even more determined that they stood trial for murder in England. Kate could see how angry Jamie was getting, and her heart went out to him. They rowed back to shore, and Jamie called all everyone together.

Jamie knew that both Nancarrow and Zak wanted him dead and that they would stop at nothing. He also knew they wanted their two ships and valuable cargo, not wanting todamage them. Jamie could use his far-reaching canon on Nancarrow who then could turn tail, but then they may come back another day with more ships and men.

This was not what Jamie wanted .just wanting all this to end here and now without further threats to the young men and women he had taken responsibility for. Everyone had been preparing, working hard since dawn had broken, and by midday, they were tired and hungry. Some of the girls brought fruit and water as they all gathered together to take a rest. Jamie took this opportunity to stand up amongst them and tell them of his strategy.

'I am almost sure, my friends, that we will have visitors very soon, certainly within the next couple of days, if not before'.. 'There was no doubt in my mind that they wanted me dead, and take the two ships, they will have no compunction in killing any of you as well'. 'They will take the ships, which would be easy pickings with no one to defend them.

So we must stop that from happening, the ships will be purposely move them into the bay as close to the shore as possible and anchor them close together. Then, they will not use their cannons against us for fear of hitting the ships. So when their ship approaches, we will pretend not to have seen them. That would hopefully, make them think that they are catching us off guard and come ashore. That my friends will be their biggest mistake, they will soon realise that each and every one of us will fight as if we are ten men, and we will pay them back for their wrongdoings'. A cheer went up AYE-AYE Skipper.

'I purposely hide thirty of you in the bushes. Then they will think we are only fifty strong. Those fifty will fight alongside me. When and if this fight starts at the right moment, I will signal the Swordfish by waving a red flag. Mitch, with, Curly and Rabbit will operate Black Beauty and open fire on Nancarrow's ship. Then JB and Hermit will take the swivel cannon and place it just out of sight on the Earl. The red flag signal will apply to him as well to open fire on their ship and their long boats. Then both of them will use live shell ammunition on them. I hope the delayed fuse will work. If not, we then revert to the ball shot. JB will take Hermit with him.

'JB nodded and asked 'Why haven't we gone after them at sea? After all, we have this new canon.'

'I did consider it JB, but I was taught never to rely on the sea wind. It could subside at any time, and remember our ships are merchant ones, not like a thirty-gun cruiser. However, they have their cannon positioned on the port and starboard where our one is at the stern, but if they sailed either side of us, we would have no defence. If the wind dropped and we had fired a couple of shots, they could turn around and would know the strength of our cannon. Then this would give them the advantage to plan a different assault. They also have more sails than us, so we wouldn't be able to catch them. I think it is better it goes the way we planned.

JB understood the reasoning for this but asked Jamie if he could fight alongside him as he could recognise the men who had killed Jamie's father and Temp. He explained that he had taught Smithy to use the gun, and he was very proficient and that both he and Hermit were now excellent shots.

'I would be honoured to have you fight alongside me JB,' said Jamie, agreeing to let Hermit and Smithy take charge of the gun.

He told Kate, that when the pirate ship is spotted, her job was to take the younger ones to Rosen's shelter and Buster you make sure to send the animals off into the undergrowth out of harm's way. 'Now the rest of you, the beer barrels are to be placed behind each of our ships on the beach with some of them jutting out either side, so the pirate ship can see them. Then we'll build a fire alongside the barrels and have it ready to light. I want it to look like we are celebrating. Those with me are to hide their swords but have them near to hand for when I give the order to fight. Sam, you are to lead those hiding in the bushes. When I give the signal, come out fighting wearing your red scarves.'

Jamie had worked out there were 146 of them, including himself and Kate. With his fifty and Sam's thirty. He wanted to hide sixteen on each of the ships plus Hermit and Smithy to stay and use the Swivel cannons Mitch and Curly to man Black Beauty.

That would leave thirty to go with Kate and Jada with the smaller children to the shelter.

Including Rosen, it would leave him with 114 to fight against the 200 well-seasoned pirates and perhaps Zak's men as well.. He hoped the odds wouldn't be against them.

Now any question?' They all looked at each other and shook their heads. ' I'll take that as a no then.', They all laughed.

Jamie shouted, 'Go and get everything ready leave repairing and tidying up. This is more important. The chances are they could even reach us sometime today.'

He called Kate to one side as the others went off to make their preparations. 'Kate, if this battle goes well and we live through it, I would like to talk about our relationship.'

Kate blushed furiously, 'Do not say, If! We will win through. I know we will.'

Throughout the afternoon they hurriedly put Jamie's plan into action. They managed to move the ships and anchored them as near to the shore as possible. The two lookouts had climbed up into the two ships crow's nest. Sam chose her thirty young men and women and Jamie picked the sixteen out for each ship to come out fighting on his signal. They started to pile up firewood ready to be set on fire, they placed jugs on tables near the beer barrels. Then they went off doing other things. They were all nervous but filled with anticipation and excitement, waiting and waiting until later that day. There was a shout from the two ships crow's nest rung out, SHIP-AHOUY it was time to put in action all there plans.

'Now Dingle, when the time comes you can play your violin all of our group of fighters will dance and sing but keep close to our ships. I want Nancarrow to have the impression he has gone unnoticed and that we are drunk' 'Ok Shipper'

Back on the La Liberte, Nancarrow was telling his crew, they are going to attack later that day, and then he took Zak to one side and telling him his plan of attack.

'Zak when we approach there island, we will drop anchor just outside the reef. Then we will lower the four longboats, and you and your men together with mine rowing you will go ashore to attack them. The boats will then return to collect more of my crew, if necessary.'

Zak was soon to reply, 'Why can't we give them a few rounds of cannon fire first?'

'What's the problem, Zak? Are you scared of a few kids? I thought you wanted to kill this Jamie yourself, not blow him to pieces with cannon fire.'

'I just think it would be better to reduce their numbers by a few before we attack them face to face. The odds are in our favour anyway, but this would make it even easier.'

'Maybe a couple of shots wouldn't hurt. Just to please you, we'll do it your way then Zak.'

It had been mid-afternoon when Janie's lookouts in the crow's nest had sighted the La Liberte. It would be a while before Nancarrow lookouts would be able to see anyone on There Island.

Sam had gone to find the Skipper, then to ask him, 'How much time have we got before he sees us here on the beach Skip?'

'Their ship will be in full sail, so will be probably less than an hour Sara.'

They both looked at each other laughing, and agreeing to call each other by their appropriate names

'We'll be ready for them,' shouted Sam as she ran off to organise her troops. While all the rest set the Skippers plan in motion. Kate and Cindy had taken the youngest and the dog to Rosen's shelter.

In less than an hour the La Liberte was approaching the reef, Nancarrow is constantly looking through his telescope when he shouted,

'Hold everything lads forget about the canons!'

He turned to Zak and his master's mate. 'Look what they have done. They have moored the two ships alongside each other just inside the bay. They appear to be celebrating, probably the capture of your ship, Zak. We will drop anchor outside the bay. Hopefully, they will not see us. If I open fire on them, we'll hit the ships. We'll just have to use the boats now.'

'Yes, Captain you would certainly hit the ships, so better be safe than sorry. Surprising them will be the best option.' Said Nancarrow master's mate

Zak was in totalagreement; they started lowering the four long boats with Nancarrow's men rowing Zak's crew towards the island. All had been given orders, as not to make a sound, hoping for a surprise attack. Zak before disembarking had already told the four men who had killed Jim and Temp to find JB first and to kill him and leave Jamie to him. But Jamie was fully aware that Zak would go for him and have JB killed first, so to draw them out, so he made them both very visible.

As the long boats approached the beach, they could still see the youngsters drinking and enjoying themselves, and they appeared not to have not noticed the approaching boats. Edwina asked Nancarrow if she could have a telescope to observe the fighting and keep sight of her brother.

Edwina looked through the telescope to her horror, she then saw all the youngsters picking up swords and tying red scarves around their waists.

Jamie's men began charging down the beach together with the ones from the two ships to fight off the scum getting out of the long boats. Looking through his telescope Nancarrow shouted, 'Those dam kids have sprung a trap. They knew we were here. Let's hope your brother, and his men can beat a few kids.' Zak's men soon realised they were fighting a losing battle. In the heat of the battle, JB called out to Jamie and waved his sword in the direction of four men.

'Over there. They're the men who killed your father.'

Jamie let out a wild yell and ran towards them. 'You sons of bitches will pay with your lives for what you did.' Jamie took on two of them and fought furiously, spurred on by his anger. By the time JB reached him, Jamie had run both of them through. JB took on Scarface as Jamie killed the fourth man. JB let out a bloodcurdling scream. 'What were you going to do to me the last time we met, Scarface?' He swung his sword, but Scarface was a better swordsman than his mates. Finally, JB got the advantage as Scarface tripped and fell. Without hesitation, JB thrust his sword through his opponent's heart. Jamie had been watching JB ready to step in and help if needed.

'You're getting slow, JB. That took all of three seconds ha ha.'

The fight was in full swing, and before long, Jamie's young men had killed half of Zak's men. The second wave being Nancarrow's men arrived on shore. Jamie waved his hand to Sam, who had been waiting impatiently to join the fray. She and Rosen led the fighters down the beach, yelling as they ran. Zak saw them coming and made a dash for the bushes to hide. Jamie spotted him and took off after him.

'Stop and fight you coward. You are the one who gets other people to do your dirty work.'

'No, Jamie, it was my sister. She was the one who gave the orders to these men. She is the one you want, not me. Have mercy, young man, please.'

He knelt in front of Jamie, waiting for him to get closer. Suddenly, Zak jumped up, throwing sand in Jamie's face. Momentarily blinded, Jamie staggered back as Zak raised his sword. At that moment, Kate came running from the bushes and hit Zak from behind with a lump of wood. Zak staggered, but it gave Jamie the moment he needed to wipe the sand from his eyes. They faced each other again as Kate stood back to watch. One of Zak's men ran towards Kate with the intention of killing her. Sam spotted the danger and spun around from the pirate she had just run through and ran between Kate and the pirate. 'How about killing me? I am better-looking than her.'

He raised his sword to strike her instead, then as quick as lighting, Sam thrust her sword through him, killing him instantly. Zak had started to tire, and Jamie was getting the better of him. Zak fell and pleaded with Jamie for mercy again. 'What mercy did you show my father or Temp?' Jamie raised his sword, but Kate shouted at him, 'Don't kill him, Jamie. Take him back home to stand trial as your father would have done.'

Jamie hesitated; Zak quickly pulled a dagger from his belt. As quick as a flash, Sam threw her sword at Zak, killing him instantly.

'Thanks, Sam, for saving our lives. I owe you one'.

Nancarrow and Edwina had been watching through their telescopes. Nancarrow had never in his life seen young men and girls fought so brilliantly. His men were rapidly diminishing in numbers. He gave orders to raise the anchor and sail slowly towards the two ships anchored in the bay and blow them to pieces. He hoped his men left on shore would see his ship moving and get in the long boats and row back to the ship.

Edwina was hysterical. She was screaming and crying. 'That brat Jamie and some girl have killed my brother.'

'Be quiet, you stupid old hag,' shouted Nancarrow as he gave orders to prepare to fire the cannon at the two ships.

Edwina grabbed his arm, 'No, no! You cannot do that.'

'Why not, may I ask?' he shook off her hand and looked at her with contempt.

'There is gold and valuables on board the Earl.'

He pushed her to the deck. Knowing he did not have now enough crew left to sail two extra ships and filled with a vengeance to kill Jamie and all those with him, he repeated his order to prepare to fire Edwina was still lying on the deck clutching at his leg, screaming at him.

'Get this screaming banshee off me and off my boat.'

Two men pulled her off and threw her overboard. She screamed as she was falling.

'I cannot swim!'

They were her last words as the hovering sharks snatched and grabbed at her, pulling her deep below the surface of the clear blue water. Jamie noticed that Nancarrow was raising his anchor. He signalled to his ships to open fire. Within a second, there was a loud bang, followed by a smaller one from the two cannons, then again and again. Nothing happened; there was no blast from the shells. Nancarrow looked over the side of his ship with his men, and they all start laughing. Protruding from the oak timbers on the side of the ship were metal shells. 'What sort of cannons guns are they using against us?' questioned one of Nancarrow's men. Nancarrow laughed heartily. 'They must belong to the black guys. They are throwing metal spears at us.'

They had no idea that those innocent-looking metal spears had a delayed fuse, and were still laughing when there was an almighty explosion, followed by another and another. The entire ship was ablaze and, within seconds, had disappeared beneath the sea. A few of the pirates had managed to escape on boats, but the gunners on the Earl soon finished them off.

It was all over; for a few minutes, there was silence. Then they erupted into shouting and cheering. Cindy brought the young ones out of the shelter and the dog to join the others.

The first thing Jamie did was to give Kate a kiss. 'That's for saving my life.' Then he kissed Sam. 'Thanks again for saving Kate's life and mine.'

Everyone was congratulating each other, but Kate and her girls hurriedly tended the wounded. There were three quite badly wounded, especially one of the girls, but Kate knew they would all recover. Jamie told his men to put the dead into the longboats, which included Zak and his cronies and all the pirates. Out of respect, Jamie led them in a short prayer. They set light to the boats and pushed them out to sea. When Kate had bandaged the wounded, she went in search of Sam.

'Thank you for saving my life.'

'You would have done the same for me,' replied Sam.

Kate smiled. 'Yes, my friend, I would have done the same. But I wouldn't have said you are better-looking than me!'

They burst out laughing. Kate went to inspect the wounded, and Sam continued collecting dropped swords, daggers and guns. One girl was bleeding badly and in terrible pain from a gunshot wound. Kate instructed some men to carry her gently into the shelter and to make a small fire. She opened her bag and got out a small bottle of berry juice, making the girl drink some. In a short space of time, the girl was in a trance. Kate held her knife over the open flame of the fire to cauterise it and dug out the bullet. She poured some alcohol over the wound and watched while the girl fell into a deep sleep. That evening, they sat around a fire on the beach, discussing the day's events. They congratulated Jamie on his strategy and the girls for fighting beside the young men. Sam was particularly praised for the training she had given them. Jamie thanked Kate again for her swift action against Zak and for looking after the injured so efficiently.

'I am glad to have been able to do something for you for once. The wounded I will always look after. Tell me, Jamie, why didn't you take some of the pirates, prisoners?'

'They only know how to fight or die. That's the life they live. But if it makes you feel better, if I had taken some prisoners, I was going to put them on North Island to fend for themselves.'

Kate felt better knowing this. She had become increasingly worried that Jamie was losing his compassion for not only his friends but also his adversaries.

Chapter 24

Over the next few weeks, it had rained at times, and the temperature had cooled, although the days were warm and clear. They completed tidying up the island, harvesting the crops, cleaning and caulking the ships, and doing other general repair jobs. One evening, when most of them were sitting around the fires on the beach, Jamie remarked that the pirate ship had been a lovely ship. He said how he would love to have one like it and it was a shame it had gone to the bottom of the sea. Rosen turned to Jamie. 'I know where there is another one like it called Sea Eagle.' Jamie could feel the excitement growing. 'Where would that be, Rosen?'

'It was in Zanzibar main harbour by Stone Town.'

Jada joined in the conversation as she too had seen one in Zanzibar. 'Yes, I remember now. Come to think of it, I am sure it was that same slave ship, the one that brought us to Zanzibar from Dar-es-Salaam. She did look the same as Nancarrow's ship.'

Jamie smiled and asked them all not to mention that pirate's name again. They laughed and agreed. 'You lot have given me an idea about that pirate's ship, and hopefully, it is in Dar-es-Salaam harbour now.' There was a loud groan from everyone. 'Not again, skipper!'

The skipper laughed out loud. 'Time to call it a day I will think about that ship while I am in my bunk, good night to you all.'

A lot of things went through his mind over the next couple of days. For quite some time, he had noticed the older youngsters had matured. They were now young men and women, especially as some of them had paired off and were forming close relationships. Jamie decided to call everyone around the campfire on the beach that evening. They waited eagerly, wondering what their skipper had to say to them. He stood up and looked around at them all. 'My loyal shipmates, I have three different questions to ask each of you. I want you to go away and think about them and tell me your answers tomorrow. All of you under the age of thirteen will not do this as I will decide what to do with you all afterwards. Firstly, do you want to stay here and live on this island? Secondly, do you want to return to England and live there? Or thirdly, do you want to join me on a ship that will be fighting and freeing slaves?

Kate and Sam, this includes you. Tomorrow morning, we will meet here so that you can each tell me of your decision. Talk amongst yourselves until then and group yourselves together with others who have made the same choice. It does not matter what you choose to do. I have been honoured to be with you all, so let your hearts make the decision, not your loyalty to me.'

Jamie walked away, deep in thought, trying to sort out in his mind how to deal with each group. The others who had made up theirminds went to sleep,the rest talked well into the night. Next morning Rosen took the lead and made sure everyone was making his own decision and was not being swayed by anyone else.

By ten o'clock the next morning, Jamie with Rosen arrived on the beach to find three groups. One of the groups was very small, and he was praying it was not the group that wanted to sail with him, although he noticed that Kate was in this group. Jamie motioned for the smallest group to come forward first. There were four of them, three young ones and Kate. They explained they would like to go back to England. Jamie was amazed that Kate fell into this group but thought it more appropriate to question Kate in private but asked the other three why they had made this decision. They all had the same reason, because they all had been abducted at a very young age from their parents Some were taken by press gangs to be sold to the orphanage s and hired out for work or on ships. All they wanted to do now was to go back to England and to try to find their parents. Jamie was very sad for them, knowing what it was like losing your parents.

He called the next group forward. There were sixteen of them, this group represented the ones who wanted to stay and live on the island. To his surprise, this included Mick. 'Why do you want to stay, Mick?'

'Skipper, I would love to go with you, but this young woman called Eva standing next to me, we have sort of formed an attachment. We both adore it here and each other, plus we like farming, fishing, and the weather. I am very sorry, Skipper.' Mick put his arm lovingly around Eva and pulled her towards him.' That's fine, Mick. I wish you and Eva the best.'

He asked the others why they wanted to stay. It seemed that it was for the same reasons as Mick and Eva. Buster, the young man who had taken charge of the farming, wanted to stay, and Cindy, the young girl Kate had been instructing in medicine, also wanted to stay.

This gave Jamie peace of mind, knowing those staying would be cared for. Finally, he asked the last group to come forward. This consisted of 125. When Jamie had finished counting, he scratched his head and counted again. 'What is this?! Where are the younger ones? It seems to me you are all in this group of over-thirteens.' He noticed that even young Tom was trying to pass as a thirteen-year-old, along with about twenty to thirty others. Feeling very sorry for them, he said, 'I need help from the under-thirteen's. It is a very important job. I will tell you in a moment what I need you to do, but first, I see how many of you there are.'

There was a lot of pushing and shoving and muttering, and then about twenty-eight under-thirteen's walked away from the group. Doing a quick calculation, Jamie reckoned that left him about ninety-seven fighters plus himself. Kate and her three youngsters would have to sail with him as well. He told them all to get on with their work and to the younger group instructed them to return in two hours. He went to Kate and took her hand and asked her to take a walk along the beach with him. The waves were running up the golden sand, splashing their feet as they wandered along the shore, even McKay had recovered and was running with them.

'Kate, why do you want to live in England? Have I upset you in any way?'

'No, not at all it is because I really would like to be a teacher and study medicine and one day I want to get married and have a family. I cannot accomplish this sailing on a ship.'

'I understand your reasons, but surely you love doing this. We are having a great time, and you are wonderful with everyone.'

'Jamie, my love, this cannot go on much longer. We are well on the way being 3 years older than when we first left England. They can manage without me now.'

'I shall miss you very much, but if that is your decision, I shall respect your wishes. After we find the Sea Eagle and sink her along with her crew, we will be sailing back to England. That's my decision so I hope when we get there, you change your mind. Let's get back. I have things to sort out. I will beat you there.'

They took off, running through the sand in their bare feet, the light breeze ruffling their hair. Jamie got there first; breathing heavily, he told the younger children to sit down next to the dog as he wanted to talk to them and put their minds to rest 'Right, you lot, listen to what I have to say and then you can tell me what you want to do.'

There were murmurings amongst the group; they were wondering if he was going to make them stay. 'I am only going to take those of you who are over twelve on this next voyage.' There were shouts of glee from eight of them and glum looks from the rest.

'You have to understand this I am going on a dangerous mission. You will be safe here. I am truly sorry, and I will come back for you all one day.' One of the boys stood up and looked around at the others.'When you return, Skipper, we will be better crew members than that we are now. We will work hard and practise our swordsmanship and to be good seamen whilst you are gone. We will make you proud of us.'

Jamie swallowed hard. 'I think you will be, my young friends. When we hopefully complete what we set out to do, we will sail back to England, and you know how dangerous it was sailing coming here. We had to contend with pirates, unpredictable storms, and a shortage of rations, just to name a few. Those of you over twelve need to think hard. Is this what you want to go through again? Think carefully before you make your decisions. Then come and let me know tomorrow.' The children went off into little groups, but Kate, who had been beside Jamie during this discussion, questioned him, 'What is this dangerous mission?'

'All in good time, Miss Kate, you will find out tonight. I have called a meeting of those who are sailing with me,' he replied sharply.

'Jamie, you are upset with me, aren't you?'

'No not at all. Just sad, that's all.'

That evening all the ones sailing with him had gathered on the beach, Jamie started to explain what he intends to do. . 'Lads and ladies we are going to head for England but before that, we are going to Tanzania to the harbour of Dar-es-Salaam to hopefully find and sink slave ships and perhaps the Sea Eagle. It will be very dangerous. Some of us could get killed.'

Rosen felt he needed to speak. 'I am sure I speak on behalf of us all. You are our skipper and dear friend. You have proved yourself a capable and fair captain. We will come with you, no matter what happens to us as long as we have you by our side.'

Jamie was overwhelmed with emotion, 'Thank you all my devoted friends, I will send for some of you may be tomorrow when I have worked out a plan,so good night to you all.'

Kate and Jada were about to say goodnight to Jamie, when he asked them to stay and said'Jada, I want to talk about your parents. I have not forgotten about them. Everywhere we have sailed, I am watching for the Mayfly. On our way back to England, we will also look for it and put the word out that you are safe and well. If I still have my father's house, you can live there or Kate's until your parents return to dock at Portsmouth.'

Jada was overwhelmed and flung her arms around him. 'Jamie you are the most caring and kind, cleverest man in the world. I will remember you always.' She started to cry as Kate walked over to comfort her, putting her arm around her. Telling her she is more than welcome to stay at her nans when back in England. Jada still in tears they both said good night. Jamie said goodnight to them both and went back to his ship to sleep.But started to work out a plan to capture or sink the Sea Eagle. He hardly slept that night as ideas whirled around in his mind. He arose early and sent one of the young boys to find Rosen. The boy returned with Rosen, fetching the Skippers breakfast of flatbread, slices of meat, and a jug of fruit juice. Jamie thanked him and asked Rosen. 'I need your help in making these plans because you know the area around Bagamoyo. It's near where you used to live.' Rosen was delighted to help him. They spent several hours looking at maps, and Rosen had made some sketches of the area in case they needed to ambush the slavers inland. They were interrupted by the boy bringing more food. They hadn't realised the morning had almost gone. They ate silently, both pondering over the morning's discussion. Then all of a sudden he jumped up, telling Rosen to get all the crew together on the beach and that he would see them shortly. He then went to find the eight, twelve-year-old boys. He didn't have to search far; they were waiting for him to tell him they would work hard on his ship.

'I expect nothing less,' smiled Jamie. 'Over the next few weeks, learn as much as possible about sailing a ship. I will get Mick to teach you.' He was walking back towards Rosen and thecrew when someone shouted. Sam was running along the beach to catch up with him. Jamie stopped. 'Skipper I have been instructed to meet with you and some of the others, but is it alright if Kate comes along?'

'Of course, she can. I need her there. Why did she not ask me herself?'

'She thinks you might be upset with her for wanting to live in England,'

'No not at all. I will speak to her and put her mind at rest after the meeting later.'

Sam run off to get Kate, once everyone arrived they all sat down on the beach to find out the Skippers . Jamie told them of his plan, which would undoubtedly involve fighting in which some of them might die. He told them the men they would fight were no better fighters than Nancarrow's men.

'Damn, you made me mention that man's name again!'

They all laughed, but it had lightened the atmosphere a little then he went on to say, 'The problem we have is by not knowing the whereabouts of the ship or her crew, so we cannot make a final plan until we find out where they are. They could have gone inland, looking for more black slaves, or they may have already taken some to Zanzibar. This could take a long time, which we do not have, so let's hope luck is on our side. Do any of you want to ask Rosen or me any questions?'

JB said he did. 'Rosen, how many of these pirate slavers were there when they captured your countrymen?'

'There were at least thirty to forty heavily armed men and perhaps another ten keeping guard on the slaver's they had captured a few months earlier. They had taken them from somewhere near a big lake.'

A tall black lad stood up. 'I was one of those captured. I lived in one of those villages, and the lake is called Lake Tanganyika, and there were about ten slavers, waiting just outside my village with captured people.'

JB laughed. 'Forty or fifty pirate slavers! That will be no problem. It's what we can find to do for the rest of the day. That will definitely be a problem.'

The others laughed along with him. Even Jamie saw the funny side. It took him a few minutes to get them under control again. He cleared his throat.

'Right, you lot, let's start getting ready to sail in three weeks' time. This time, we take more drinking water, no beer.' Rosen led them all away to start preparing, Jamie put Kates mind to rest telling her she will be needed more than ever to treat the injured. She was not happy but new what Jamie was doing was his father's wish.

Jamie's Birthday had passed a while ago, and it went without notice. They had lost track of days and months. Everyone was so busy preparing for their next voyage. Buster was gathering crops for them to take on board including potatoes and carrots.. Cindy was helping Kate get a good stock of herbs and plants for medicines, and they were selecting which animals to take with them for fresh meat. The water barrels were left to dry in the sun, so they will be ready to be filled at the last moment. Jamie was continually inspecting everything, wandering from place to place, and advising where he could. Jamie came across JB, and pointing to a small island and asked.

'What is that loud noise coming from over there, JB?' 'It is your blacksmith blowing up coconut.' 'What in the hell is he doing that for?' 'You'll have to go over there and ask him, Skipper.' 'I'll do just that.'

Jamie strode off and headed towards the small island. He waded across to the small outcrop of rock. He had just set foot on dry land when Smithy came running across and pushed him down. There was a loud bang.

'What in the hell are you doing, Smithy using gunpowder to pick coconuts?'

Smithy grinded and helped Jamie up and grinned.

'I have invented a delayed hand-held shell explosion Skipper.'

'Have you, tell me more as it sounds interesting.'

'I have found a way of using coconuts as a shell by making a small hole straight through the eye of the husk then the shell of the coconut, drain the milk, letting it dry out. Then I mix the gunpowder and corn seed together, fill the shells very carefully by pushing the gunpowder mix into the shell. Then I get a cannon fuse and plug it into the same hole, then seal it. Depending on how long a fuse I use, that times the explosion. If say, you are on a ship being boarded by pirates, you could throw these at them, and it would explode killing many of them, but you must make sure you duck down'.

Jamie thought this was a joke. 'Yes, it is a good idea, but corn would not hurt anyone.'

'Sorry, Skipper I forgot to tell you. When you want to kill someone, you use very small metal balls instead of corn. Those small bits will keep the weight down, so one can throw them farther.'

'All right then, let me see how good this invention of yours is, Smithy.'

Smithy showed Jamie what to do using only gunpowder and the fuse. He told Jamie that the fuse would give them about twenty seconds after he had lit it to lie down to keep away from the blast. He lit the fuse, waited a couple of seconds, and threw it as far as he could. Smithy shouted, 'Get down!'

They threw themselves down, waited...and then bang! They were showered with sand and corn. Jamie jumped up to inspect the damage and found a big hole in the ground. He slapped Smithy on the back. 'Smithy, you are a ruddy genius. This will be amazing to use against the slavers and their ships 'I will send some of our crew over, and you can teach them how to use them and to help make more over the next two weeks.'

Smithy puffed out his chest, feeling important after Jamie's praise. 'Glad you like this idea. Leave it to me. I will make sure the hand shells are ready by the time you sail.'

'I nearly forgot Smithy. Could you make sure those quick release chains are loaded on our ship together with a few sets of master keys? They may come in handy.

'Aye Skip'

'Thanks again, Smithy.'

Jamie was excited and went off to find Rosen to tell him about Smithy's hand-held shell shot. 'Find six good crew members who can throw a two-or three-pound coconut at least thirty yards.'

'Leave it to me, Skipper. I know just the young men to use.'

'Before you go, Rosen, I have something to tell you. We are only going to use the Swordfish to sail to England. We'll leave the Earl just in case those who have chosen to stay change their minds or at worst we all might get killed.' Rosen was in total agreement with him, knowing Mick would be a good captain. He would be able to sail to the North Island for food and water if they needed, and the young ones would be capable of crewing in a couple of years just in case the Swordfish didn't return. Over the next couple of weeks, everyone helped load the ship with supplies, continually moving her to deeper waters, as she got heavier and sat lower in the water.

Kate had been watching the weather and noticing they had recently had some heavy bouts of rain. She checked her calendar, and she was amazed to see it was Christmas Eve. Kate reminded Jamie, and he decided to have a feast to celebrate Christmas also their departure. The girls prepared food the following days and Jamie conceded to allowing beer to be drunk in moderation. Mick and Jamie sat down together to talk about the past and more importantly the future. 'Mick, my dear friend, I will miss you and Malley, the farmer. Make sure he plants more potatoes and carrots. I will miss the rest who are staying. You make sure you look after them and yourself as I am definitely coming back one day to see you all. Perhaps we will bring more people to live on these islands.'

'Set your mind at rest. I take good care of everyone and hope you do not leave it too long before returning. Come on, Skipper, let's have another beer.'

Jamie thought that was a good idea, and they clasped hands firmly.

They had more than just one beer and were becoming slightly inebriated when Sam and Kate came across. Pulling them up, they took them over to where several people were dancing. Swaying in time to the violin, they danced long into the night. Jamie got up the next morning and rang the ship's bell, having no recall as to how he had got back to the ship. The first person he saw was JB. 'So you are sober now, aren't you, Skipper? I had to carry you back here, or should I say row you back?' He stood looking Jamie up and down, grinning.

'Thanks, JB for that. We have to move fast to catch the high tide,' he said, clutching his head. It was throbbing, and he had never felt less like sailing in his life. They loaded all the last- supplies and barrels of fresh water, making sure the dog and cats were on board. Saying goodbye was hard, and the younger children were clinging to those they had become close too. Eventually, all those leaving managed to disentangle themselves and row out to the ship. Suddenly, little Tom started running into the sea towards the ship, crying hysterically, 'Please, please, Skipper, take me with you.'

Jamie could not bear it. He immediately ordered the crew in one of the boats to return and get Tom. When he finally came aboard, Jamie hugged him. He remained by Jamie's side, waving to those on shore until the ship had disappeared over the horizon.

They had been at sea for almost five long months, constantly on the lookout for land as they neared their destination. During the entire voyage, they had watched for pirate ships but had seen no sign of any, and one day.

Suddenly, a shout from the crow's nest told them of a big ship bearing down on them. The first mate rang the ship's bell as Jamie looked through his telescope. It was flying the skull and crossbones. That had been a thirty-gunner French cruiser. Shouting to his crew to prepare to fight, he raced around, preparing for a battle. JB and two of the crew quickly made ready Black Beauty for firing. Jamie told him he would let him know when the ship was in range. The captain on the pirate ship gave orders to fire a couple of shots in front of their bow when they got into range. He assumed the Swordfish was a merchant ship that would surrender easily. The pirate ship reached within the Swordfish range, and the Skipper shouted to JB to FIRE.

There was silence for a couple of s. 'What's wrong, JB?'
'It won't fire, Skipper!' said JB as he frantically kept hitting the bolt that ignited the gunpowder. 'Have you put a new flint in it recently?' JB hesitated, 'Oh god, no!'
'You had better do it right away. We have only a few minutes before they open fire on us Hurry!'
It seemed like a lifetime to Jamie whilst JB changed the flint. 'Ready, Skipper!'
'Then, ruddy, well, fire!'
Bang! Bang! Bang! JB carried on firing at the pirate's ship, just as the pirates ship was coming into range to return fire. JB was firing the delayed fuse shell; the pirate captain and his crew started laughing. 'They are trying to sink us by loading us with metal shots,' shouted the captain as two shells fell through the hatches into the hold. There was a massive explosion. One of the shells had exploded in their ammunition magazine. Everyone on board the Swordfish could see the ship begin to disintegrate and sink, and they also saw some of the pirates getting into boats. Jamie shouted to JB, "GOOD SHOOTING, but next time, make sure you check that ruddy flint.'
Ay, ay, Skipper, I will do. I will,' JB said as he wiped the sweat away from over his eyes. Jamie breathed a sigh of relief, feeling it had been rather too close for comfort.

Kate came running up on deck and shouted to Jamie, 'What are you going to do with those poor men?' as she pointed at the few pirates who had made it into two small boats.

'Kate, my love, we are only two days away from Tanzania, and Zanzibar is even nearer. That scum you see will be able to row to Zanzibar in two days.

At least, that's giving them a chance. It's more than they would have given us if they had captured this ship. They would have killed me and some of the crew, and they especially like young girls.'

'I see what you mean. I apologise for shouting at you.'

'Apology accepted. Now, let's get this ship back in order.'

That evening, over dinner, Rosen questioned Jamie, 'If the opportunity arose to capture the Sea Eagle, would you do it?'

'No, because the ship would be always be recognisable with its big eagle's head on the beak head. Even if we changed the flags on it, it would be easy to spot.'

Rosen understood what Jamie was saying but continued, 'Skipper, would you like to have another ship that would have more speed and gun power than this one?'

'Yes, I would. This ship was mainly meant for exploration, but perhaps the gold and valuables that we have taken from Zak will be enough to buy another ship when we return home. I still want to keep this ship to use for merchant shipping, as my father intended.'

They carried on talking late into the night, making plans for their current mission.

They sailed on unhindered and soon reached the harbour at Dar-es-Salaam. There were many other ships there as they docked, so Jamie decided to look for the Sea Eagle on foot around the quay. The crew noticed quite a few people staring at their ship as they were all quite young and with some young black men aboard. As Jamie was about to leave, Jada reminded him of the Mayfly and that it could be docked there. He told her he had not forgotten and kept watch for it. He started to walk along the harbour with JB and Sam. They were amazed at the amount of activity going on. There were ships of various shapes and sizes, being loaded and unloaded. Most of the cargo was trading goods, but they could not see any slaves, only a few blacks helping with the cargos. They searched all day for the Sea Eagle, but alas, it was not there. Sam found a young man who could speak English and asked him where she could find any slave ships. The young man replied, 'Do you see that pontoon over there, young lady?'

'Yes, by that cliff.'

'That's the one. They dock just behind that cliff, well away from us because a lot of sailors do not like how they treat the slaves.' She thanked him and walked across to Jamie, telling him where they could find the slave ships. Jamie looked up to the sky and noticed the sun started to sink below the horizon. He told them they needed to hurry before it got dark. Having got to the pontoon, just as darkness was falling, they walked around the back of the pontoon, and there, before their eyes, were three large ships. One of them was the Sea Eagle.

'We have found her, but it is too late now. Better to come back tomorrow morning and find out what she is up to.'

Rosen and Sam agreed and hurried back to their ship to tell the others.

The sun rose early the next morning, and Jamie told his crew to stay on board. 'Hermit, you are coming with me and look scruffy like me and don't bring your sword. We will find out who is in charge of the Sea Eagle and ask them if we can join their crew as we are looking work. That way, we should be able to assess whether they are on board or travelling across country, getting slaves.'

They certainly looked the part when they reached the Sea Eagle. Torn clothes and mud smeared on their faces. The only difference between them and the filthy seaman they approached was that they didn't smell as bad as them. Jamie spoke to the man,

'Do you work on this ship, sir?'

'What concern is it of yours?'

'We are looking for your captain, sir, to ask him for work on his ship.'

'You'll have to wait awhile. He and most of the crew are away on business. Should be back in about four or more weeks. Come back then, but only if you are any good with a sword, else you'll be wasting his time.' Jamie then enquired about the other two ships moored alongside. 'Perhaps we could ask if one of their captains could find us work as we have no money for food and cannot wait for your captain to return.'

'You're both wasting your time. They have gone with my captain as well.'

Jamie was elated to hear that all three ships had only a few sailors aboard and could not return to the Swordfish quick enough. They hurried back, and Jamie immediately gave JB the order to set sail and head due north. Within the hour, they had set sail and were about two miles out, heading towards a place between Dar-es-Salaam and Bagamoyo, with the intention of dropping anchor just offshore. Jamie called Rosen, Sam, and Kate to his cabin and pointed to a map he had been studying.

'Looking at this map, the only route I can find to Lake Tanganyika is this one. The slavers would have to walk from Salaam harbour and then take this route that goes through a place called Morogoro. It's not too far inland. If we could anchor somewhere near, it would not take too long to walk there.'

'I know just the place,' said Rosen. 'When I was young, my father took me fishing along this coast between the two towns of Salaam and Bagamoyo a number of times. I know a small bay we could drop anchor in shallow water. It's a very safe place.'

'That sounds just the place we need. Rosen, can you gather all those who lived in the villages near Lake Tanganyika, and I'll meet you on deck in a minute?. Ask JB to come along as well.'

Rosen left to go in search of those Jamie wanted to speak to, closing the door behind him. Jamie looked at Sam and Kate. 'You do realise this mission will be very dangerous?'

Sam replied, 'Yes, we do, Skipper, but you know we are the best fighters in the world, and I am sure we will succeed.'

'Let's hope so, Sam. Let's hope so.'

They followed Jamie out of the cabin, and they went on deck to find Rosen and the others. When they all arrived, Jamie questioned them regarding the route they had taken when they had been taken from their villages. They told him how long they had been allowed to sleep at night, how they had to walk four hours before they stopped to eat and drink and that had only been three times a day in the searing heat, and how they were always chained up even going to relieve themselves. One young man called Bubba said, 'We stopped at a water hole a few days after passing through the small town of Morogoro.'

Jamie asked him to describe the water hole. 'It lies at the base of a line of some mountains, alongside a dirt track and is fed from a spring that runs down the rocks into a small pool. We used it to drink and then to wash in. The water then runs into a small lake that the animals use, but by then, it gets very muddy and may have crocodiles in it.'

JB interrupted, 'What the hell is a crocodile?'

'I will tell him,' said Sam. 'My father had a stuffed head of one on our wall. As a child, I was scared to death of it. The crocodile is a reptile that only eats meat and grows to fifteen feet long and would eat you JB and your dog in one go.'

JB was horrified, and the others laughed at the expression on his face. Whilst they were all teasing JB, Jamie's mind had been turning over, making plans. He asked Rosen to assemble the rest of the crew as he wanted to put his idea to them all. They gathered around Jamie, some standing and others sitting on the deck.

We have all agreed that we are here to free those poor slaves'.

'I have made plans, but it all depends on the situation at thetime.' He outlined his idea, and they all agreed they thought it could work as long as the slaver's used the same dirt track and that there were a few hours in between each group.

Rosen looked around him. 'I think we will be fine, Skipper. The slavers should not be following right behind each other because they would have gone to different villages to take slaves. These villages are quite a distance apart. But I am sure they would still come back using the same old route. This is the safest way for them. If they took an unused track, they would face the risk of being attacked by wild animals. Also on this route, they could buy food, wine, and water, especially in Morogoro.'

'Thanks, Rosen, for this information. Rosen and me have agreed, when we havedropped anchor, we must move fast. We will cut across land, hoping no one will see us. Then after a few miles, we will pick up the dirt track that heads towards Bagamoyo and this water hole. That's where we will ambush these slavers.

Each of us will have to carry full packs of food and weapons but only enough water for the journey there, also whatever Kate needs to use for the slaves and the wounded. Rosen, you and your people will have to wear the quick release chains, and Smithy has made a few master keys to free the other slaves.'

The crew wandered off talking amongst themselves about the plan, and Jamie went back to his cabin, praying that everything worked out right. By the end of the second day, they sighted the small bay Rosen, had mentioned and almost sailed the ship on to the beach before dropping anchor. As it was late in the evening, Jamie decided to leave at first light and gave everyone last - instructions. He said to the eight young boys and girls, 'You must look after the ship while we are gone. Day and night, you must keep your eyes open, but never put your lives at risk. If for any reason you have visitors, just say your families are resting, but never try and fight them if they come aboard. Do you understand?'

They all nodded, but Jamie was praying that the visitors would not be pirates, so he decided to leave Hermit behind as he could use Black Beauty, just in case. He told him to make sure the young ones do what he had told them to. While the crew were having dinner, he decided to talk to them about other parts of the plan.

'Altogether, including myself, less Kate and her six women, we are ninety-one fighters strong, but as you know, Rosen and his thirty-nine young women and men will be in chains. They will only release them on my orders to fight the slavers. The rest of us will have to fight first, and hopefully, the three slave crews will not be walking together. Otherwise, this would mean we will be well outnumbered. Does anyone have any questions?'

'What are Kate and her six helpers going to do while this fighting is going on?'

'Good question, Sam. When we are ready to ambush the slavers, Kate and her six helpers will be hiding well away from us; together with the extra food we are taking for the slaves we hope to rescue any more questions? Yes, JB, what do you want to know?'

'How do Rosen, and the others who are chained get their weapons? When we all start fighting, we would not have the time to give them any. Can we use our red scarves?'

'The bundles they carry on their shoulders will be weapons concealed in sacks to look like they are carrying ivory, and we cannot use our red scarves. It would be too conspicuous. If that's all, then let's call it a day because we have to be up early tomorrow. Smithy, before you go, what is that contraption of a pistol you have on your belt?'

'It's my new invention. I have used the same design as your swivel gun. The only thing different is you have to load your shot by opening a catch on the side, then you put the tube shell in and close the catch. I have made the tube shell from a hollowed bamboo cane, and I have filled it with gunpowder and on the discharge end put the metal ball shot. To stop the gunpowder from falling out the other end, I used a small piece of silk dipped in lamp oil. When it is loaded, you pull the hammer back as normal and then fire. The flint inside the pistol sparks, the same way as before, and then bang. Open the catch, take out the empty case, and repeat it all over again,' said Smithy, proudly waving his gun about.

'Marvellous Smithy. This will be a lot quicker than loading it the old way as you can load the powder and shell altogether and load it from the side.'

'Yes, Skipper, it will be, but I have not had the chance to practise using it yet.'

'That could be a problem. You'll get the chance to find out in the next couple of days, but keep away from all of us when you are doing it please.' Jamie walked away, smiling to himself. At first light, after saying goodbye to Hermit and the younger ones they packed up their gear and waded through the shallow sea water

There were loads of shouts of 'Be careful, and Come back safe and kill those slavers'. Jamie picked up his telescope and told JB to bring his dog along as it might ward off any snakes or wild animals.

The journey took them through thick bush and open grasslands, and they saw many wild animals. The white crews were utterly astounded, never having seen animals like them. Rosen knew full well what they would come across on this journey. He made sure some of his young men took the lead and put some at the rear in case of wild animals and snakes as they were used to walk in that terrain. Even though they were all carrying heavy packs, they run at trotting pace until midday. They stopped to rest for a few hours to escape the heat of the sun and continued on their way when it cooled down. Rosen knew that at this pace, it would still take them no more than two weeks before they found the dirt track leading to Morogoro. At the end of the second week in the evening, they finally came across the dirt track. One of Rosen's men remembered this part of the dirt track and told Rosen roughly how far away they were from Morogoro and how far it was to the water hole. Rosen passed this information on to Jamie, so they decided it would be better to rest that evening and start early the next morning and continue walking that day until they found it. The sun was high in the sky when they came across the water hole, much to everyone's relief. They scouted around for the best place to ambush the slavers from and then took a well-deserved rest and wash.

Shortly afterwards Rosen told Jamie that one of his friends who were good at tracking had looked at the dirt track and told him that in the last few days, no large amounts of people had used it. There had only been a few people walking both ways in over a week.

This was very good news knowing the slavers had not passed them already. The water hole was an ideal place for an ambush. After they had rested for a couple of hours, Jamie told everyone to prepare. He had also noticed a small hill that would be an ideal place to watch for the approaching slavers.

By now Rosen had found a good place for Kate and her helpers to hide and settled them down with all the packs of goods. It was about

200 yards away in a ditch. There were a couple of big trees that would give the girls some shade as well.

After putting all their packs in the trench, Rosen and Jamie made final plans and prepared to set the ambush. Rosen asked a young man called Buba to tell them how the slavers operated. He told them the slavers always walked fully armed each side of the chained slaves. When they got to a water hole, half the guards cooled down in the water first and then they changed over, and the other half took their turn. They never let the slaves out of their sight. When they had finished, they let the slaves drink and wash but kept them chained. They would rest for about two hours before moving on depending on how hot it was.

After hearing Jamie gave instructions to everyone, regarding his plan in the hopes that there would be no mistakes.

'When the slavers are spotted, we will lead them to believe we have also just got here. We will wait for about half a mile up the dirt track. I will signal you when they get closer. Start walking slowly back towards this water hole, and do the same thing here as they would be doing, making them think we are just another slave gang. You have to get the timing exactly right. When the slavers and slaves are about to get here, you will move Rosen and his black troops away, still chained up to look like slaves. Shout at them. Even pretend to use a whip on them to make it look authentic. When you have finished washing and drinking, go about thirty yards away, and let the slavers get to the water hole. Ten of you will stay by the water hole, five on each side. Make it look like you are drying yourselves, but keep about twenty yards away from them. Sam, you will be one of the ten. This may distract some of the guards and give us a bit more time.'

JB shouted out, 'It will distract us all with her lovely figure!'

Sam blushed, but managing to compose herself, she answered back, 'This is no laughing matter. Some of you will die when we start fighting these bloody slavers.'

Everyone stopped laughing at JB's remark, a silence fell among them.

'Sam is right, so take what I have said seriously. When all our slaves have laid down about thirty yards away from the dirt track, they will be surrounded by our guards or should I call you my troops? When the time is right, I will shout out, Attack! Those of you acting as slaves will have to wait before you get up and undo your chains. You have to allow your guards at the rear to jump over you. Then you can start fighting the slavers as well. Is this clear to you all? I want no mistakes.' They all said they understood and were impatient to begin.

'We will have to spring this ambush at least three times against the different groups of slavers. We have to deal with them all before we return to our ship.'

The Skipper also told Rosen, 'I am going to climb up that small hill over there to watch for the approaching slavers, will you keep organising things down here.' Rosen set about practising the trap withthe fighters.

Jamie called out to Smithy, 'You go over there behind those big rocks and try out your new invention. Make sure you point it away from us.'

'Ay, Skipper, I certainly will.' Sam asked if it was all right if she went with Smithy.

By all means Sam, just make sure the gun works and let me know.'

Jamie climbed the hill, settled down amongst the vegetation, and pulled out his telescope. He had been on the hill for about two hours and still, there was no sight of the slavers.

He went back down to their camp. Passing the telescope to one of the men, he told him to keep watch and to shout loudly, no matter who was approaching.

Just after Kate asked if she should keep the dog with her, but Jamie pointed out that would be dangerous as it could give away their hiding place. It could alert the slavers that things were not what they seemed together with the fact as they were all quite young. Jamie told them all to get some rest, then asked Sam about Smithy's invention. She said it worked well, but he had only made two and only had a few shots left, but she had managed to persuade him to give her one. It was now getting a little dark. Rosen had already told the lookout up on the hill to come down. He told everyone to move nearer to Kate's trench. Jamie wanted to know why so far away from the water hole. Rosen pointed in the direction of a herd of elephants coming their way. 'Rosen, why are we gathered so close together in one place, would we not be better in smaller groups?'

'This is my country, and I learned the behaviour of these wild animals. When the sun goes down, the lions go hunting for food, especially near a water hole. This is why we must all keep together.'

'Give me a ship and open seas anytime,' retorted Jamie.

Rosen smiled, 'I am thinking along the same lines.' He put his arm around Jamie as they laughed together. Jamie posted lookouts throughout the night, but none of them got much sleep. Jamie woke them in the morning and told them to get something to eat from the packs and get into position near the water hole. It was a long and tedious wait, sweating as the day heated up. Suddenly, the lookout on the hill shouted to Jamie to come up and look. Jamie wasted no time in climbing up to him. Looking throughout his telescope, he saw a cloud of dust heading their way. He grabbed the lookout by his arm and dragged him down the hill, stumbling in his haste, telling everyone to get into place but warning them it might be a false alarm and just another herd of animals. They took up their positions as instructed, and Jamie, Rosen, and their 'slaves' ran towards the cloud of dust and stopped about half a mile away from the water hole. Jamie found some high ground nearby and looked through his telescope and yes it was the slavers and shouted.

'The slavers are coming now! Get ready to start walking back slowly, and then take up our planned positions for the ambush.'

They all knew exactly what to do. They started walking back slowly to give the slavers a chance to catch them up. Within the hour, the slavers were only a few yards away. They smelt them coming before they could see them. Jamie had counted about fifty guards. They all looked tired and disgruntled from walking in the heat. The poor slaves looked even worse as they were carrying heavy ivory tusks and large sacks. Jamie and his men reached the water just before the slavers, and they took up their positions. Jamie noticed a large man giving out orders and glancing at Rosen and his slaves suspiciously.

Rosen instantly knew this was their captain. All was going to plan, until the big dog McKay ran up and licked Rosen wagging its tail. The captain of the slavers realised instantly that the dog knew the black slaves. 'It's a trap,' he shouted to his men. 'Prepare to fight!' Rosen and his men released their chains after their guards had jumped over them, and pulling the swords from their bundles, they charged at the slavers. Jamie and his group fought alongside them. The slavers drew their cutlasses and fought with ferociousness Jamie had not expected. The slaves who had been captured and still chained were frightened and had huddled into a bunch at the side of the dirt track.

Jamie was face to face with a slaver; thrusting and parrying, the slaver stumbled, and in a flash, Jamie ran him through. Glancing over his shoulder, to his horror, he saw his ten men being forced back into the water hole, and one of them was Sam.

'Follow me!' he shouted to JB. They ran across the dirt track and came up behind the slavers, who were getting the better of his men. 'Look behind you scum!' screamed Jamie.

Some of the slavers did turn around to face them. Jamie and JB attacked as they heard Sam shout, 'What kept? Frightened of the competition?' In between driving the slavers back inch by inch, he called back, 'No, but I know you cannot swim, so I thought it would be a good opportunity for you to learn!'

'Very funny,' sneered Sam as she stuck her sword into the belly of a slaver. He fell down, clutching his stomach as she looked around for her next opponent.

'Stop bickering at each other,' yelled JB. 'Fight, will you?'

It wasn't long before, there were just a few slavers left alive, and they begged for mercy. Rosen was still in combat with the captain; for all of his size; the man was quite agile, but Rosen remembered him as the one who had taken him and his family captive two years before. Rosen was getting the upper hand as the captain tired. Rosen was relentless in his attack against this evil man. The captain was backing into some trees and had nowhere to retreat to as Rosen plunged his sword into the man with fatal consequences. He looked down at the dying man. 'May you rot in hell, you scumbags? That's for all the misery you have caused.' He pulled his sword out and turned away. The battle was over. They released the captive slaves and took them over to Kate. Rosen and his men used the chains to manacle the surviving Pirate slavers. These men were then gagged and led away into the undergrowth. Some of Jamie's men had been wounded, so the girls led them to Kate, and she tended their wounds. Fortunately, none had been killed or seriously injured. Several of the slaves had had injuries inflicted upon them, so the girls helped Kate with compresses and ointments. It was not long before, the lookout on the hill came running down with the news that there were more slaver's approaching. Everyone ran, taking up their previous positions. Jamie made sure the dog was tied up this time and climbed the hill to see how far away the slavers were. To his dismay, he saw two lots of slavers together. One was only a few 100 yards behind the other. Jamie called to Smithy to get some of his hand shells ready by the water hole just in case they needed them. 'Plan two!' yelled Jamie, and everyone took up different positions. The idea was for Jamie's men to split into two groups.

Not having enough would-be slaves, Rosen ran to the ditch where Kate had the newly released slaves and asked for volunteers. Some of the young men offered but refused to put chains back on until Rosen explained the release system.

'You are unarmed, as soon as the fighting starts get out of the way quickly,' instructed Rosen.

'Smithy, you stay here and make sure these poor slaves are not followed back to this ditch by the slavers. It would be disastrous for Kate and the girls,' said Jamie as he went to take up his position with Rosen's men at the edge of the water hole. The other group went up the track a short way and started to walk back. The first group of slavers overtook them, pushing them aside in their desperate need to get to the water. Their captain was a short fat man with earring weighed down by gold bracelets and chains. 'Get that lot out of my way,' he bawled at Jamie. Jamie obliged as the slaver's jumped in the water. He could see that the second group of slaver's were by now alongside Rosen's group. Taking a deep breath, he yelled, 'Attack!'

Even though Jamie's men were outnumbered and weary from their earlier fight, the months of practising paid off. They were starting to overpower the slavers, but suddenly the newly released slaves had run off into the bushes and were being chased by two heavily armed slavers. Smithy came out of nowhere, pointed his new revolver, and fired at one, killing him instantly. The second man lifted his pistol to fire back and watched Smithy loading his pistol with a bamboo cane. The slaver lowered his gun and, standing astride with his hands on his hips, threw his head back and gave an almighty roar of laughter. 'You are going to shoot me with a piece of bamboo cane. Do you have something to help get the splinter out afterwards?' He raised his pistol again and then hesitated. 'After you, young man,' laughed the slaver. There was a loud bang from Smithy's pistol, and the pirate looked at the big hole that had appeared in his chest. As he fell down, dying, Smithy shouted to him, 'Do you need something to get that splinter out with?'

He threw down the gun as he had used all his shells and ran to his heap of coconut shells. There was a girl running towards him being chased by a slaver brandishing his sword. She yelled at Smithy she had lost her sword. He grabbed a shell and lit the fuse. The girl knew what he intended to do and threw herself to the ground. Smithy took aim and tossed it as far as he could at the man. The slaver stopped, watching it fly through the air towards him. 'I'm not hungry. Thanks,' he said, letting out a bellow of laughter. It exploded as it hit him full on, but at least, he died with a smile on his face. The fight was in full swing Rosen's men were getting the upper hand all the slavers were beginning to tire. Jamie's crews were young and fit and soon got the upper hand as well. Sam shot one of the slavers, trying to protect the girls. Slavers numbers were dwindling rapidly as Jamie's men cut them down. When there were just a few slavers remaining, they surrendered and laid down their weapons. Jamie marched them to the other prisoners and chained them alongside the others, with Rosen ordering two of his men to stand guard over them. All those that were not wounded were organised into burying the dead slavers.

Jamie had not lost one man, several injuries, which Kate and the girls were tending, but no fatalities. Even slavers deserved a decent burial, thought Jamie, as he led them in a short prayer.

Afterwards, everyone who could help has been asked to help dig graves for the dead. This was quite away from the water hole. After they had buried the dead, the skipper read from the Bible to give them a Christian burial and said the Lord's Prayer.

Chapter 25

The crew made camp, and Jamie estimated they had freed about 500 slaves. Rosen had already found out from one of the villagers that no more slavers are heading their way. Kate and the girls were caring for the weak and wounded.

Rosen approached the chiefs from each of the villages, who asked them what they wanted to do. He gave them the option of returning to their villages if so he would help them build new huts. The other choice is to go with him and Jamie to find another place to live. There was much discussion amongst them all, then one chief asked Rosen if they could give him their decisions in the morning. Night fell quickly as it does around the equator so everyone settled down to get some much-earned rest.

There was much activity the following morning, with the natives collecting fruit and water to feed the vast number of people at the camp. When they had all eaten, the chiefs went to Jamie and Rosen with their decision. Rosen listened carefully as he would have to translate to Jamie. He was very surprised by their answer. 'Skipper they all would like to go back to their villages, but also eighteen of my men decided to go with them to help get the wounded back to their homes and to stay with them to help build homes, also they will help to teach the villagers how to protect themselves so that slavers can never take them again.' Jamie was not too surprised as Rosen was.

'Rosen my friend, if that's their decision then so be it, after all, I suppose this is their country.'

Jamie walked over to talk to the eighteen young men and women who wanted to leave, wishing them all the luck in the world, telling them he was proud of them wanting to help the villagers. He said it had been a privilege of spending more than two and a half years with them. They told him they had been honoured as well and asked if they could take the slavers' weapons with them. Jamie readily agreed.

Jamie decided to spend that day at the camp to give everyone time to recuperate as they all had a long trek in front of them, whichever way they were going. They spent the rest of the day dividing up the food, gathering fruit and water for their journey.

That evening, they found the time to mull over the battle. Some of them congratulated each other, but the villagers continued to express the surprise they had felt at the expertise with which Jamie's men and women had fought.

Sam seated herself next to Jamie. 'I see Smithy has found a girlfriend.' 'What about you, Sam? Why have you not found someone?'

Smiling back at him, she replied, 'I have decided to be like you. Keep them all at arm's length, or should I say bandaged arm length?' as she pointed to the bandage Kate had wrapped around his arm to keep the deep cut in his arm clean. She quickly moved out of the way as he went to give her a friendly slap.

'I will say this, Sam. Any man you end up with will be the luckiest man in the world. The way you fought yesterday, no other women in the world could fight like that as long as he never upset you.'

'Ah, Jamie, you do care about me after all,' she laughed as she rubbed her fingers through his hair 'get off, Sam,' as he pushed her away with a friendly push. There were many sad farewells the next morning as they said their goodbyes. The villagers thanked Jamie profusely as they turned away with eighteen of Jamie's men with them to walk slowly back along the dusty road, waving as they left.

Rosen made sure all the prisoner slavers were chained and carrying heavy loads for their journey back. He could not bring himself to have them lashed with the cruel whip, but McKay yapped and nibbled at their ankles instead.

They had been walking for a long time. The sun was getting hotter when Rosen turned off the dirt track to lead them through the undergrowth. Jamie asked him how he knew that this was the way that had come.

'You are a good captain at sea, but my men are good at finding their way on land.'

'But you do not have a compass, and there are no stars in the sky.' 'Look here, Skipper,' he said as he pointed down to the ground. 'You see those three stones. We laid a trail when we walked this way before. Also, can you see the broken branch on that small tree? We did that as well to most of the trees we passed. It will lead us back to our ship.'

Jamie realised he had underestimated Rosen. He had always known he was a leader with great abilities.

They decided to rest for a while to get out of the sun and found some leafy trees and bushes to give them some shade. Kate sat down with Jamie and remarked that she had been surprised at how few injuries their men had received and that no one had been killed. She praised Sam, saying it was thanks to her intensive training. Jamie agreed and said she was a very special young woman.

After two hours again they set off walking watching their prisoner's struggling carrying the heavy ivory to the delight of the slaves. It was three weeks before they reached their ship, to a warm reception from Hermit and the youngsters. Rosen and Jamie made sure the slavers were well guarded, and every so often Rosen would check that they were all been fed and watered. Then one of them said to Rosen, 'We will never do this again to your people. This walk carrying these heavy loads for three weeks has taught us a lesson.'

'I hope so. Our people carried those loads for a lot longer, not as you have done for just three weeks.'

'That's the reason we will never do it again, sir,' said this slaver.

When they all arrived at their ship, they all got a wonderful reception Skipper and Rosen went on board first just to make sure everything had gone well while they were away. Hermit had made all the young boys clean the decks, polish the brass, and do all the other chores needed to get the ship looking spotless. He was delighted to see Jamie and Rosen. 'There have not been any problems while you have been away, Skipper. Oh, sorry, I forgot, just one.' He started to laugh.

'What is that just one?' Jamie asked.

'You'll have to eat dried fish for six weeks. We caught so much while you have been away.'

Jamie sighed, relieved that everything had gone well in his absence. 'Tell me, Hermit, how are my two cats doing?'

'They are fine, Skipper like your dog McKay I see, your cats love the fish. You will find them skipper asleep in your cabin.' Jamie roared with laughter as he strode off to check his cats.

They set about preparing the ship to set sail for the following morning; then after they had eaten that evening, Jamie outlined his next plan.

'We are now going to sink those three slave ships using Smithy's coconut hand-held explosive. We will dock our ship in the main harbour and fill up with fresh supplies. Just before we leave, I will take Rosen and five of his men who are familiar with the explosive to blow up these three pirate ships. Anyone has a question?' Tooth raised his hand. 'Skipper, why can't you use Black Beauty on those ships? 'Tooth my friend all the other ships anchored in the harbour would see it was us firing on the three ships, and they may think they were under attack as well and open fire on us. We would have to contend with the soldiers' cannon placed in the fortress at the entrance of the harbour as well.' Tooth and the others agreed, not relishing the thought of being blown apart.

Jamie continued, 'We must act normally to give us the chance to stock up with the supplies we need. While you are all doing this, we will prepare to launch our attack. We will attack at night and sail the next morning.' He told them all to get some sleep but asked Rosen and his men to stay a bit longer.

'I take it these are the ones who can throw the coconuts?'

'Yes, Skipper, plus myself. After all, we do not have to put mud on our bodies for camouflage, do we?'

Jamie laughed. He liked Rosen, always quick with his humour. 'So it will be only me who must put mud on my body?'

'No, Skip, you will not be doing it. We will slap it on you willingly. Even Kate and Sam will not recognise you.' All seven men collapsed with laughter at the thought of seeing Jamie covered from head to toe in thick sticky mud. They released the slavers early the next day, and

Jamie pointed out the direction of Bagamoyo, as this was the nearest place for them to walk to. Kate made sure they had some food and water to take on their journey, for which they were all grateful. It was a hive of activity on the ship, everyone helping to load supplies, including the ivory. Eventually, they set sail for Dar-es-Salaam. With a good steady wind, they made good progress and arrived late in the evening. They docked the ship in the harbour, and Jamie told them he would arrange to buy cargo the following day. He spent the next few hours checking on the wounded.

Then he went to Kate's cabin and found her writing in her diary. 'I see you are still doing your diary. I think you will miss doing it if you decide to live back in England.'

'Yes, I will. I will also miss you, Jamie, along with everyone else. But the diary I hope to hand over to Sam. I will make her promise that she would carry on doing it, and maybe in a few months, she will be able to give it back to me, providing you all come back home safely from your next journey.'

'Kate, how sad this makes me. You should know by now I have feelings for you. I just hope you change your mind before we get back to England. I want you to sail with us always my love.'

He took her hand and kissed it gently, looking up into her eyes with longing. Wishing her goodnight, he turned sadly away. After he left her cabin she closed her diary, tucked it under her pillow, and went to sleep with tears in her eyes.

In the warehouse, the next morning, Jamie and some of his crew purchased supplies for their journey back to England. Loading would take a couple of days. They could use Rosen and his men openly, and they wouldn't seem out of place as the other ships were using black slaves. Later that evening, Kate and Jamie decided to go for a walk along the harbour as the sun started to set, glowing shades of red and orange as it sank below the horizon. They had only walked about 300 yards when two port guards stopped them.

'Where are you going? Do you not know it is forbidden here to walk around at night? Only those with our permission are allowed. The only exception is those helping to dock a ship. You can walk at night in that bay over there, but I would not advise it, especially with your young lady.' He laughed and pointed towards the jetty where the slavers' ships were docked. Jamie apologised, and both walked back to their ship.

'Well, Kate, that's mucked up my plan a bit. I'll have to think of another way to sink those ruddy ships.'

'I am sure you will think of another way as you always do.' Kate put her arm through his as they walked up the gangplank.

'It has been a most pleasant short walk. We must do it again sometime,' said Kate mischievously.

'Kate, it's not a laughing matter. I will bid you goodnight.'

Jamie summoned Rosen and his five men, who were going to help him blow up the three ships. He told them of his encounter with the port guards the previous evening and said to Rosen, 'Can you think of another way to sink those ships?'

Rosen thought for a moment. 'Skipper, tomorrow will be our last night here, so I will do a bit of night fishing in a boat but use coconuts for bait.' Having a big grin on his face.

'Rosen my wonderful friend you are spot on. That's the way we will do it. The only thing is we will have to move our ship and sail to just inside the entrance near the fortress tomorrow evening, and drop anchor. It would be the shortest way to row back. Then early the next morning, just before it gets light, we will help you to lower the smallest boat, and hopefully, you all will be able to find those ships in the dark. As soon as you get there, light the fuses and throw them and row like hell back to our ship. By that time, it will be getting lighter, and it will be high tide as well, and we will set sail. Will you and your lads be all right without me?'

'Skipper, we will manage fine. We are used to the dark. Just light a small oil lamp for us to guide us when we return. There is one more thing. Could Smithy make the fuses last longer, to give us time to row back to you

'I will get Smithy to start doing it today. One thing more, you will have to board our ship around the other side so no one sees you. The blasts from those ships will definitely light up all the harbour. I am also going to instruct JB and his mates to prepare to fire Black Beauty, just as a precaution in case those cannons lined up at that fort decide to open fire on us. I am sure it will be fine because there will be no connection between us and the explosions on the three ships.'

Later that day all the extra cargo had been loaded, and it was now time to get their plan organised. Smithy had made longer-timing fuses and two oil lamp covers. They would need the lamps to light the fuses but did not want them shining at night to give away their position even if they looked like they were fishermen. Then the crew released the docking ropes then using the light breeze to slowly sail just inside the entrance of the harbour as planned then dropped anchor. Time was moving fast, and it was getting late into the night. The moon was visible now and again, as the clouds scudded past it, giving an occasional glimpse of light shining over the water. Rosen was calming his men down as they were becoming a little nervous. But he reminded them that those ships had been used against their people. It seemed to have the right effect and made them determined to carry out the destruction of the ships. Just before high tide in the early hours of the morning, they prepared to put their plan into action.

The six young men rowed off, disappearing into the darkness knowing exactly where the pirate's ships were docked.

Nobody on board the Swordfish had slept well, and they were praying for the safe return of their comrades. After what seemed like hours, they heard Rosen's voice coming from the portside of the ship. They were quickly pulled up on to the deck boats as well with the help from the light of the moon.

As they clambered aboard, there was a massive explosion, followed by another and another. The night sky lighted up. There were shouts and cheers from the crew, but Jamie told them to keep the noise down so as not to lead suspicion to them. It was too late. The soldiers upon the garrison could see them quite clearly lit up by the blazing ships.

The Swordfish had raised anchor and sailing out the harbour, the soldiers assumed they were firing at ships in and around the harbour. Believing them to be an enemy of the state, they prepared to open fire on them. There was a lot of scrambling about at the garrison as most of the soldiers had been asleep.

Jamie shouted to Curly, who was at the helm, 'Steer the ship close to the cliff face, as near as possible. Quick, let's get the hell out of here.'

He reasoned that if they sailed close to the cliffs, it would be almost impossible for the cannons to fire on them. 'JB, are you prepared to fire on my command?' 'Yes, Skipper. Just say when.'

Jamie ordered all unnecessary crew below decks as he knew the soldiers would fire their muskets. 'Curly, you have to go as well. I will steer the ship now. And you, Sam, it is too dangerous here.'

'Not on your life, Jamie. I am staying here. We have always fought together, side by side.'

Two cannon shots came hissing through the air, just managing to hit the canvas sails, leaving two big holes. This was followed by musket fire. Jamie heard Sam scream. 'Are you all right, Sam?'

'Yes, fine Skipper just a little scratch. Just get us the hell out of here!'

By now dawn was breaking, and the light was shining across the waters of the harbour. The lieutenant in the garrison could just make out the ship and to his horror saw it was a merchantman. He ordered his men to cease fire believing he had made a mistake and the one cannons on the Swordfish would not have been sufficient to cause such damage. As luck would have it at that same moment, Jamie ordered JB to fire, but JB had just been shot. It was only a scratch, but he was bleeding badly and was being helped by his mate.

'Sorry, Skipper, give us a few seconds, and we both will be ready.'

Those few seconds probably saved a lot of lives. The fire from cannons and muskets had stopped all of a sudden. Jamie reacted immediately, 'JB, stop! Do not fire yet!'

JB had the hammer ready to strike the firing pin. If he had fired the Black Beauty with its rapid-fire, the lieutenant would almost certainly have realised it was them who had sunk the three ships and would have continued firing at them. Jamie yelled, 'All hands on deck!'

To the relief of those sheltering below deck, they hurried on deck and helped to sail away from the harbour, they had caught a fresh breeze and sailed well away from the garrison.

When they were well underway, Jamie ran down the wooden steps to Kate's makeshift sick room to see his two injured 'How are they both?'

Kate pulled him to one side. 'JB is fine, but I am worried about Sam. She has a splinter lodged behind her shoulder blade. I have to cut it out, and I have not done anything like this before. It doesn't help with the ship heaving in this wind.'

'Kate, my love, you are the only one who can save her life. Please, please try. I will drop anchor as soon as I can, so you can try and remove the splinter. I know you can do it.'

They walked over to the bunk Sam was lying in, and it was obvious she was in a great deal of pain. Jamie tenderly took her hand. 'Sam you stupid woman why did you not go below when I told you, now look what has happened to you, my dear friend.'

Silent tears rolled down his cheeks as he gripped her hand tightly. 'Ouch, you are hurting my hand. You do care about me then Skipper?' Sam was trying to grin at Jamie even though she was in pain. 'Sam I care about each and every one of my friends, young lady.'

They smiled at each other.

'I have to go now. I will leave you in the capable hands of Kate.

We have to drop anchor soon to repair the canvas, the skipper shouted to his crew as he came up on deck.

Kate remarked to Sam that Jamie liked her more than he was saying. Sam lay back in the bunk and knew that she liked Jamie more than she was saying as well.

Back on deck, Jamie sought out Rosen and explained the situation, Rosen replied.

'We are only a day away from the town of Kisiju. My village is before there, so we could drop anchor and repair the sails. We can sail the ship right up to the sandy beach, and there may be survivors from the last slave raid who could help us,' suggested Rosen.

'That sounds like the best place to stop, and get poor Sam back on her feet., Maybe, they can help repair our ship, then, we can stock up with water and fresh fruit as well before going to England.,.'

With all sails set to catch the wind, they made excellent progress and were soon Docking on the sandy beach. Rosen and Jada went looking for their friends while Jamie instructed some of his crew to repair the sails and rigging. He told the rest of them to enjoy themselves on the beach and then went below to see how Sam was holding up.

Pulling Kate to one side he asked. How is she doing?'

'Getting worse I have to take that splinter out now. Can you make her drink the green berry juice, please? She won't take it from me. She says she does not mind the pain.'

'Leave it to me,' said Jamie as he went over to Sam. Beads of perspiration are trickling of her face. Jamie took a piece of cloth and tenderly wiped them away. 'Sam, drink this juice now. That's an order or else. Looking up at him, she smiled, 'Or else what, Skipper?' 'Or else, I won't marry you.'

'Who said I want to? But putting it like that, then I will drink it' Jamie watched her as she drained the cup and within a few minutes fell asleep. 'Sorry, Kate it was the only way I could think of doing it. 'Never mind now get out of here, and let me and my girls get on with getting that splinter out.'

Jamie waited on deck for news of Sam, pacing up and down until the rest of the crew were worn out watching him. At last, Julie, one of Kate's girls, came on deck. 'All went well. She is fine but needs to rest. She is still sleeping, and Kate will be up shortly to speak to you all.'

Everyone cheered with delight. Jamie stopped pacing and sat down on a wooden barrel and sighed with relief. Kate then came up and told them much the same but said, 'Sam is very weak and now has a fever. I must go back to look after her and no visitors for a while.'

Meanwhile, Rosen and Jada had found several survivors who had rebuilt the village. One of them told Jada that her mother and father stopped there every few months looking for her. She was filled with delight and asked then when they thought her parents would next return. They thought in about two months, and she could not thank them enough. Rosen told the villagers about the slavers and hoped they would not have any more problems from them. Rosen and Jada helped them gather fruit, and they went back to the beach and lit a fire, cooking a freshly killed pig to celebrate. The crew came ashore, everyone was dancing and the playing of drums. Everyone joined in the celebrations. Jamie left the festivities and went to check on Sam, but Kate stopped him before he reached the cabin.

'Jamie, she is very sick. She is in a coma and has a high fever. I have to keep her warm to try and make her sweat out the fever go back and enjoy yourself. There is nothing you can do.'

Jamie walked slowly back to the beach, not feeling in the least inclined to join in when JB came running up and asked if they could drink some wine. Jamie nodded, not caring whether they were drunk or sober. He was so worried about Sam and could not get her out of his mind. It began to dawn on him that he felt about Sam the same way he felt for Kate. He knew Kate would not sail with him again, and the thought of losing them both was unbearable. Wanting to be on his own, he went to his cabin and opened a bottle of his good wine. He had just finished his first glass when two of the girls walked into his cabin and started to drag him out. 'You can finish your bottle of wine on the beach Skipper Kate's orders.'

Rosen noticed Jamie was miserable and went across to him. Putting his arm across Jamie's shoulder, he asked, 'Why the long face?'

'It's poor Sam. She is in a bad way with a fever.'

'If she is no better in the morning, I will ask the local witch doctor to look at her if you like. He is good at removing fevers.'

'The witch, what doctor?'

'Jamie, you have had too much to drink. Let's wait till morning and see how she is then.'

Most of them slept on the beach that night. Jamie had gone to his cabin in the early hours of the morning and slept fitfully. He tossed and turned, lying awake, thinking about Sam. When he felt he could lie there no more, he went to find out how she was. Kate told him she was getting worse and the fever was very high. She thought it might be blood poisoning. Jamie hurriedly left Kate and went to search for Rosen and found him in his village with his friends. He told him Sam was worse and asked him to go and find the doctor he had mentioned.

'I will go now and fetch him. He knows all about poisons as well. I will meet you back on board the ship.'

Jamie rushed back to the ship to give the good news to Kate. The waited by Sam's bed and it felt like a lifetime. It wasn't very long before Rosen knocked on the door and ushered in his companion. Kate and Jamie stood there in astonishment.

The witch doctor was painted from head to foot in different colours, and the parts that weren't covered by this rainbow were strung with large leaves and old bones. He also had a large discoloured bone stuck through his nose. He was carrying a large wooden feathered staff. Kate grabbed hold of Rosen. 'Does this…this man knows what he is doing?'

'Yes, Kate. He cures a lot of people who have a poisoning of the blood with his medicines.'

'I just hope you two know what you are doing, right Jamie, come outside for a minute please.' Once outside, Kate looked at him squarely in the eyes, her fury mounting. 'What kind of a doctor is this thing you brought in to help our poor Sam?'

'Kate, just wait and find out first if he is any good, please,' Rosen said. 'He cures everyone in his village, so give him a chance.'

'What with his magic wand? I hold you fully responsible if anything happens to her.'

'I am sure she will be fine Kate.' Now he was not sure.

'Worse more likely, with whatever medicine he gives her! Honestly, Jamie, you make good fighting plans, but this time, you are unbelievable.' While they were arguing outside, Rosen could hear them. When the witch doctor had finished, they decided it would be safer for the two of them to leave. Rosen and the witch doctor could still hear them shouting at each other even when they reached the beach. Kate and Jamie were arguing furiously when they heard a voice shouting at them from Kate's cabin. 'Shut up! I am trying to rest.'

They stopped shouting and stared at one another and then pushed each other out of the way in the haste to get into the cabin. Sam was sitting up on the bunk, looking very well indeed.

'I might have known it was you two. You sound like an old married couple.' Sam put her arms out, and they rushed and hugged her.

'Welcome back, Sam. We both thought you were going to die,' said Jamie.

'What and leave my two lovely friends without saying goodbye? Not on your lives. After all, I have to give Kate some competition in winning this handsome young man next to me.'

They all started laughing. 'Just like my old Sam,' Jamie said grinningly. 'Kate, am I forgiven?' 'Of course, but only if I am as well.' They hugged each other.

'Come on, you two, not while I am here.'

'It's good to see you feeling better,' said Jamie. 'But I am going to sort out my crew.' He kissed both Sam and Kate on the cheek and left to tell the crew that Sam was recovering. Kate sat down on the stool next to Sam's bunk and reminded her that it would soon be Jamie's eighteenth birthday. 'Let's make it a good one,' suggested Kate.

'I should be feeling a lot better tomorrow. I will try and make a big bread cake with fruit for him. My mother used to make them for me when I was a little girl.' She started to cry remembering her mother. Kate passed her a cloth, and Sam wiped her face. Kate continued with her plan as she changed the subject to distract Sam.

'You do that, and I will tell the others to get things ready for a feast on Saturday. That's if we can keep it a secret from Jamie.'

Chapter 26

Preparations were well underway over the next few days, getting the ship ready for the long journey back to England. Sails were mended, rigging repaired and checked, and water barrels cleaned and refilled with fresh water with a little rum mixed in. Jamie watched as provisions were loaded as he wanted to set sail by Saturday or Sunday. Being Friday, Rosen was searching the beach for Jamie and came across Sam and Kate cooking something on a fire. 'What are you cooking? It smells lovely. 'Sam replied. 'It is a birthday bread cake with fruit for Jamie's birthday tomorrow.'

' Oh I have something to tell him I hope it won't spoil his day.'

'Tell him what, Rosen?' said Sam.

Rosen could not look at them. Holding his head down, he said, 'I am going to tell him my people and Jada want to stay here and live and I do as well. I have many friends here, and it will be easy to see my family from time to time. With all I have learned from you all, I can be of value here.'

'Goodness, this will be a surprise for him, Rosen, but I am sure he will understand your decision for staying,'

Kate agreed but asked him to wait until they were eating that evening, so she and Sam could be there to give him support.

That evening at dinner, Rosen found the courage and told Jamie of his decision, explaining that Jada and his men had decided to stay too. Jamie was surprised and sad. He hesitated for a moment before answering him. He stood up and picked up a glass of wine. Raising his arm, he said, 'Attention, everyone. Rosen and his gang are leaving us, so on behalf of us all, we wish you a wonderful long life here. Let's all drink to Rosen and his men and Jada, of course.'

Everyone stood up and raised their glasses and joined Jamie in wishing them every success. Some of the younger ones were sad as Rosen had become an important part of their lives.

Later that evening, Sam put her arm around Rosen and said 'That was not so bad, was it? Jamie understands. After all, you have done everything you wanted to do. You found your families, stopped the slavers, and sunk their ships. Now, you can build a new life here safely.'

'Thanks for that, Sam," Rosen said sadly as he wiped his eyes. 'Come on, you big guy, stop crying,' she whispered in his ear. 'Tomorrow you can fetch all your friends to this beach to celebrate Jamie's birthday, and you can wish us a safe journey and bid us farewell. You might bring some of that lovely wine your friends make.'

Saturday arrived, and Jamie was up early, checking everything was ready to set sail that afternoon. He was just going to go to Kate's cabin when he was stopped by Sam.

'What is the matter, Sam? Why can't I go down to the cabins to see Kate?'

'Er...er...because four young ladies are in her cabin and have come down with a fever. So Kate said no one is allowed in there in case it is contagious.' 'Well, I upset her the other day. I had best do as she says.'

He wandered off in the other direction to check the cargo. Sam went straight to see Kate and told her the lie she had told Jamie. They both started laughing.

'Well done, Sam. Trust you to think of that.'

Jamie caught up with JB and some of his crew, who assured him everything, was ready to set sail. He looked over the bow at the beach and noticed a lot of activity. 'What's going on down there, JB?'

'I believe Rosen and his villagers would like to say farewell in the traditional manner with food and wine on the beach before we sail off this afternoon.'

'That will be fine, but we have some girls down with the fever. I will go down to see Rosen and explain what has happened.'

Jamie went to the beach, where he found Rosen giving directions to everyone. He could see who was going to be chief in that village. 'We may have to postpone sailing for a few days as we have some girls down with a fever. It would be just until they are feeling better, or perhaps we could use your witch doctor again to give them a quick cure?' Jamie said jokingly.

'No, Jamie! Not again please.' 'I was just joking, Rosen.'

'Thank god, you were,' replied Rosen as he joined in Jamie's laughter. 'Skipper, I must go to my village and get ready for this feast. It is too late to stop it now. Here comes Sam. I'll leave you to it.'

Jamie turned around and saw Sam walking towards him. Sam, how are you feeling?'

'Good, thanks Skippy sorry Skipper, the shoulder is healing, well, thanks to that witch doctor.'

'Now you are getting better Sam I just wondered if you remember something I said to you before you fell asleep.'

'Knop Skipper, I don't remember a thing.' She had remembered but didn't want Jamie to feel embarrassed or obliged to feel he should marry her. Jamie sighed with relief. He did not want to be committed at this moment in time. He still had important decisions to make about his future.

Sam smiled at him alluringly, fluttering her eyelashes. 'What was it you said to me?'

'Um…nothing of any importance I just wished you luck.' Jamie walked off feeling very embarrassed, and behind his back. Sam gave a big grin.

At midday, the girls asked Mitch to show Jamie something down in the bottom hold so they could take the cake to the beach without him seeing. When they got to the lowest hold and looked, Jamie said to Mitch, 'I cannot see anything wrong here, so why am I here?'

'I just wanted you to check all the ivory and everything is to your satisfaction.' 'Mitch, you must be joking. I should have never been asked to check again. I have already done this once today. So, you fool, let's get back on deck now!'

As Jamie and Mitch came up the wooden ladder from the hold, they looked across to the beach to see everyone gathered. There was a loud cheer as they called out, 'Happy birthday, Jamie.' Even the villagers who could not speak English had learned how to say happy birthday over the last few days. Jamie was overwhelmed as Mitch led him down the gangplank to the beach. They showed him the cake Sam had made especially for him. He joked about her having hidden talents but laughed as she produced a sword to cut it with. As quick as a flash it was all in slices. They passed the cake slices around, and the feast began.

As Jamie went across to Kate, several of the girls, including Sam, came and kissed him. As he reached Kate, she pulled him close and gave him one almighty kiss. 'Well! I wish I had a birthday every week.' She smiled at him and kissed him again. He asked about the sick girls. Kate told him the cake had been in her cabin, the girls were just a disguise and Mitch had been in on it too. Jamie laughed and called out to Mitch. 'I will get my own back on you one day.'

The villagers had started to dance, movements that had been passed down through the generations. Traditional costumes from long ago swirled and dipping as they stomped and swayed to the beat of the drums. The wine was flowing freely, but Jamie did not care. They were having fun but so sad at leaving their friends. Jamie shouted out to some of his crew. 'Has anyone seen Rosen please?'

Sam then pointed out Rosen. 'That's him with the mask on,' she said with a slur, having drunk a little too much of the local wine. Jamie called out to Rosen, who came and sat down beside him. They talked for a long while, reminiscing about the past few years. They talked about their achievements and their sadness at leaving one another.

Kate with the help of Jada was in deep conversation with the witch doctor, asking him about the herbs he used. She particularly wanted to know about his cure for hangovers, knowing she would need it the following day for the crew. When she understood what the concoction consisted of, she told her girls to promise not to reveal what was in it. This would only be until the last drop had been taken.

Kate thought I will tell them all in the morning what was in it. Perhaps they might think twice before getting drunk again. Addressing her girls, Kate said. 'Before they all drink this tomorrow, I want you to drink some too.'

'Not on your life,' replied one of the girls, grimacing. 'Don't worry. It will look the same, but it will be only fruit juice.'

The girls giggled, but Kate told them in the morning, they have got to line up first before the rest of them when she administered the medicine to them on the beach so as not to raise any suspicions.

As Kate expected, they all woke with hangovers. Some had slept on the beach, not being able to find their way back to the ship. She rang the ship's bell loudly. 'Wake up, you lot. I want everybody who drank last night to meet me on the beach for your hangover medicine. You are all going to need it because we sail this afternoon.'

The crew were not impressed as they staggered to the beach. Kate's girls lined up first and drank theirs, hardly daring to smile. Then it was the turn of the rest of the crew. They moaned and grimaced, saying it tasted horrible. Rosen and Jamie were the last to drink it and tried hard not to pull faces just to show the others how brave they are.

Kate then announced she would tell them what was in the medicine. She wasn't going, to tell the truth, and thought she could have a bit of fun with this. 'The medicine you have just drunk was made by the local witch doctor. It's made from the juice of a worm and crushed spiders' legs.'

Several of the crew turned green and started to be sick, but Kate continued, 'It also has pulped mushrooms that grow from cows' droppings.' By now, the entire crew had run down the beach to be sick, and Kate and the girls were holding their sides from the pain of laughing so much. The girls now realised why Kate had dished out the medicine on the beach. When they had all recovered a little, hangovers almost cured, Kate told them all what was really in the witch doctor's potion. Fortunately, they saw the funny side of it but still threw Kate and her girls into the sea as penance. Tom and the other younger boys had been watching this from the ship as they had taken the medicine having had no wine, but it made them think twice about overindulging in strong alcohol.

Everyone was now filling a lot better. Jamie caught Kate by the arm. 'The crew are saying they are feeling well enough to sail when I give the word. That medicine or rather your description of it did the trick nicely.'

She laughed. 'Next time I pull a stunt like that, I'll make sure I haven't got this wretched skirt and petticoats on.'

Jamie laughed with her and pulled her close, hugging her tightly. He gave the orders for those going with him to be ready to leave in two hours so they could catch the high tide. This gave them time to say their goodbyes to Jada and Rosen along with his men. Everyone was shaking hands and hugging. It became quite emotional, especially when Sam and Kate reached Rosen. Jamie promised Jada that if he spotted the Mayfly, he would let her family know where she was. Free and safe!

Rosen gave Jamie a beautiful seashell, which had been given to him when he was a little boy and had buried it just before he was taken captive. Jamie was delighted and said he would always keep the shell in his cabin. In return, Jamie presented Rosen with a gold chain that he had been given by his friend Temp. Rosen said he would wear it always until they next met. Jada gave Sam and Kate a big hug and Jamie a kiss. It was too much for Jada and Rosen as they turned away with tears.

Jamie called his crew to embark. They pulled up the anchor and hoisted sails. Sadness was felt by all as the ship disappeared into the sunset homeward bound.

Chapter 27

Jamie had plotted a course back down past the Cape of Good Hope, hoping there would be no bad storms at that time of the year. He explained to the crew it would be quicker on this return journey as they would have the wind behind them most of the way, instead of having to tack as they had on the outward journey. They also had less crew on board and no animals, so they wouldn't have to stop as frequently to load supplies and hopefully would not have any encounters with the likes of Zak and the pirates.

After their evening meal, Jamie called Sam to one side. 'Can you give those eight young ones some vigorous training lessons on fighting and sailing until we get back to England?'

'Sure skipper' replied Sam.

Kate had overheard Jamie's request. 'They are very young. They could hurt themselves.'

'No they will not Kate. I will make men out of them, but if you like, I will start the training gently,' said Sam, winking at Jamie.

As Jamie left he closed the door after him, leaving Sam and Kate alone, he hoped they would not argue over this.

They made excellent progress. The wind held, and the sun beat down on them as they crossed the equator. Kate and the girls spent much of their time making uniforms for them all, and the younger ones trained hard with Sam. They were all excited at the thought of seeing England again. They all enjoyed a lovely Christmas of dried fish but made the most of it.

They sailed well away from the French coast; soon they were sailing into the English Channel all of them now filling the cold but it did not matter now.

Everyone was on deck, were all excited as they entered Portsmouth harbour just after midday. Spider had heard from other sailors that Jamie's ship was docking and rushed down to the quay to meet them. Jamie, Kate, and Sam were the first to disembark, and Spider clasped Jamie to him. He then stood back and held him at arm's length. 'My goodness, you have grown into a handsome young man, and you girls are now beautiful young women.'

Jamie was keen to hear the news of his shipping business and his family's house. Kate was eager to hear about her grandparents.

'Everyone and everything is fine. Do not worry. I will tell you all in good time, but firstly, I will get the workers' wives to give you all some English wine and home-cooked food. Then I will tell you everything that has happened while you have been away.'

The women brought food to the harbour and set it out on long tables. The crew, which now consisted of only the workhouse children, who had now developed into young men and women, tucked in heartily while Spider told Jamie about the events in England.

Jamie then told Spider about his run-in with Zak and Edwina and some of the escapades they had been up to but promised to go into more detail later as there was so much to tell.

Kate was impatient to see her grandparents, as was Jamie to go home, he ordered a carriage to take the three of them to the village. He told the crew to remain on board until he returned the next day. Sam said she would prefer to stay for the time being as she wanted to help three young boys to find their parents. She explained it might take a few weeks but asked not to sail without her as she wanted to join him on his next voyage.

'Sam, that's very kind of you to want to help them. Take as long as you like. I am not thinking of leaving for a while and would never go without you anyway.'

'Thank you, Jamie. I appreciate that, just one more thing. Can you take young Tom along with you? He keeps asking to go with you.'

'Sam, of course, I will take him. Can you fetch him now as the carriage is approaching?'

She rushed off and hauled Tom back to the carriage, he was beside himself, with excitement. Tom saw Jamie's two cats and asked him. 'Can I look after your cats for you, sir?'

Jamie replied, 'Yes, young man, but just call me, Skipper, please.'

'Yes, sir. Sorry, Skipper.'

As they approached the village, Jamie said to Kate, 'I will tell the coachman to stop at your grandparents' house first.'

'Are you coming in?'

'Not just now. Tom and I are off to the big house to find out what the surprise is that Spider mentioned.'

Kate being so excited knocked on her Grandparents door, longing to see her only family again. Her grandmother answered the door and stood aghast at the sight of Kate. They threw themselves into each other's arms and cried, so delighted at the sight of seeing each other. As the carriage pulled away, Jamie turned to see Kate still in the arms of her sobbing nana.

Within minutes, the carriage was trotting up the long driveway towards the Manor. It was the middle of January, and Jamie and Tom felt the cold penetrate through their outer clothes. They had become accustomed to hot climates and were finding the lightly snow-covered landscape chill their bones. The branches on the trees on either side of the drive were glistening with a light frost, but Jamie felt calm and happy to be back in familiar surroundings.

As they reached the front door, Tom looked up at Jamie and asked if he could pull the bell. The door opened, and there was his nanny, Mary. She screamed in delight, hugging him so close he could scarcely breathe. Tom stepped into the hall and looked around. He was dumbstruck; never before had he seen such luxury and splendour. One of the housemaids noticed he seemed a little lost and came forward. Putting her arm around him, she said, 'And what's your name, young man?'

'It's Tom Missus, and I have to look after these two cats.'

'Well, Tom, leave them here and come along with me to the kitchen. I think we can find something nice for you there.'

Tom followed her through the hall and down a passageway to the kitchen, all the while staring around him in amazement Not long after Tom was on his way to an early night's sleep, he was fast asleep in the first bed he had ever seen and slept in.

Mary had taken Jamie into the drawing room and made him comfortable, fussing over him and wanting to know everything that had happened to him since she had last seen him. They talked long into the night. Tiredness overcame Jamie. Mary lit a candle and led him up the stairs.

'Before you retire, my son I would like to show you something,'

She lit a candlestick holder, and they both went upstairs, Mary took him through a door just off the hallway, down another corridor that led to the west wing. She opened a door and walked in, shining the candlelight around.

'I hope you don't mind, but the school at the vicarage stopped running, so we have made this into a classroom for the village children and have taken in some orphaned children as well.'

Jamie was stunned and did not know what to say. Mary then quietly opened another door leading off from this room, telling Jamie to be very quiet. She shaded the candle holder as she led him into the room. To his astonishment, he could see beds lined around the room.

'Jamie my son the boys are on this side. There are twenty of them, and there are ten girls on the other side,' she whispered. They backed out of the door quietly, closing the door behind them.

'Dearest Jamie, I hope you don't mind. They are all orphans they had nowhere to go since the workhouse shut down. Your uncle would not continue to support it. I am sure your mother and father would have approved, and we are teaching them the skills needed aboard a ship—sail making, carpenter, cooking, and all manner of things.'

'That was probably the best thing Zak has ever done in his life. Mary, this is wonderful. I agree that Mother and Father would have welcomed this as I do. You and Spider have done a wonderful job. Thank you from the bottom of my heart. Everything Edwina stole from this house will be returned.' Mary was happy that Jamie approved and kissed him goodnight before they went back to bed in the main house.

At the breakfast table, the next morning, Tom asked Jamie if he could go to the stables with the horseman to help him.

'Yes, you can, but be careful they can kick you.' Tom scampered off excitedly; Mary came into the dining room to clear their plates, followed by another young girl.

'Hello, Lizzie,' Jamie said as he smiled at the girl.

She looked down at the floor, embarrassed he had remembered her.

She graciously replied. 'It is so nice to have you back, sir.' She hurriedly cleared the plates off the table,

'Mary I see also you have kept nearly all of my father's servants.'

'Yes, most of them stayed on even after Edwina and Zak left. They have looked after the house with me now I have returned. I have let them keep the money they received from selling the game and vegetables they grow on the land here. They always believed you would come back one day.'

Jamie was so overwhelmed by their loyalty and decided to compensate them by giving them some of the gold coins from the ship.

As Jamie was about to leave the dining room to visit Kate and his mother's grave when he bumped into thirty young children on their way for breakfast. Mary introduced him, and they politely wished him good morning.

She hustled them into the breakfast room as several servants arrived with bowls of steaming porridge, followed by slices of bacon. 'Jamie, do not bother to hurry back. I will look after young Tom. He can stay and learn with the other children.

Oh, I nearly forgot to tell you. Next to your mother's grave is a headstone for your father and next to them is our dear old friend… Temp.' Jamie held her arm as she wiped away a tear. He was torn between sadness and anger at the death of his dear friend.

It was not long before he was knocking on Kate's, door, she showed him into the parlour. Her grandmother greeted him warmly, 'You have become a very good-looking young man and how tall you have grown! Our Kate has become a beautiful young woman too. Thank you for looking after her for us and bringing her back safely.'

He blushed at her praise but composed himself. 'It was rather the other way round, I believe, madam, she looked after me.' They laughed as Jamie looked around for Kate's grandfather.

'Where is your grandfather Kate?' 'He is not too well. We have made him stay in bed, but think it's only a chill.' she showed Jamie a chair. Kate's grandmother bustled about serving tea and homemade biscuits. He told them both about the children who were now ensconced in his house and about the school. Kate was delighted and said as soon as her grandfather is better, she would go and see Mary. He drank his tea and stood up; he thanked them for their hospitality, saying he was now off to visit his mother's grave.

He walked along the lane towards the church, pulling his scarf around him. The weather felt cold and damp. The slush from the thawing snow splashed up over his boots as his thoughts went to the time he met Kate there, and how long ago it seemed. There were no wildflowers to put on his mother's grave this time, but he knew the snowdrops would be pushing through the frozen ground soon. On arriving he stood looking at the three headstones with great sadness.

He felt the nearness of his father and Temp and said in a prayer. I love you all I will carry my memories of you all my life. I only wish that I could have saved you all from dying.

He was on his way out of the churchyard, he noticed a young man of about his age standing before a headstone.

Understanding the solitude one needed when visiting a loved one; he left without speaking to him.

Mary had lunch prepared when he returned to the house, and he told her he was going to take the carriage and go to the harbour to see Spider and would not be back until late. He wrapped up warmly and climbed on to the carriage. Taking the reins, he set a steady pace and soon arrived at the harbour to find Spider, who had kept his crew busy. JB asked him how long it would be before they set sail again.

'JB, we only just got here. It will be several months at least. Just keep training them all in the evenings, and keep doing the work during the day, and I will pay you all a shilling a week to spend in town.'

'Well, Skipper, that's different. Yes, we will,' JB grinned.

Spider had walked over and heard what Jamie said. 'I could have made them work for much less than that.' JB took off before Jamie had a chance to change his mind.

'Come on, Spider, let's go to the office to talk about this shipping business, and how is my dog doing?' Spider started laughing. 'Your flipping dog poo-poos everywhere.'

Laughing back, Jamie said, 'Well, it keeps everyone on their toes.'

Both of them were still smiling when they sat down in the shipping office, and Jamie looked around him. 'Spider, you have done a wonderful job here, so I would like you to be my partner.'

Spider was speechless for a moment. This was so unexpected. 'Jamie, I have kept this business going out of my love for you, Jim, and Temp. I never expected this generous offer.'

'Well,' said Jamie, 'what's your answer?'

'Yes most definitely.' Spider jumped up and shook Jamie firmly by the hand. 'I will be proud to accept this offer.'

'Spider in the next few days, we will go and see Mr Westgarth and make you a legal partner in the business. There are a few other things to sort out. Firstly, everything Edwina and Zak stole from my house is on the ship. Could you arrange for them to be returned? Also, I have a hold full of ivory, which I would like you to sell. You know all together with the remainder of the gold I got from Zak, and by Temp, I believe we could afford to buy a new ship to replace the Earl.'

'I agree. We do need another ship for long journeys. Is there anything else?'

'I made a promise to a young lady called Jada. Her parents sail on the Mayfly. Her father is the captain. If you see it, can you inform them she is free and alive and well? I will leave you the name of the place she is living at.'

'I will keep an eye open for this ship. I have seen it docked here before. Jamie, you have done a wonderful job with your crew. They look so smart with their uniforms and that red scarf around their waists when they train.'

They continued discussing the business. Spider had kept immaculate accounts, which he showed to Jamie. He was astounded at the profit they had made while he had been gone, realising that Zak had been stealing from the business and lining his own pockets.

Jamie then went to the local constabulary to report the deaths of Zak and Edwina. The constable listened patiently as Jamie relating the events that led to their deaths and informed him that as there were no bodies to prove his story, he would not be able to claim the reward. Jamie took his hat and left the constabulary and left to go home, not caring about the reward but glad that Edwina and Zak were finally out of his life.

Kate had still not been to the house to see Mary after three days, so Jamie assumed her grandfather was still ill. Finding himself at a loose end, he walked back to the graveyard. The young man he had seen on his last visit was just leaving. 'Good morning, my name is Jamie Heslop.'

The young man held out his hand in greeting, 'I'm Daniel, but most people call me Dan.'

'I'm pleased to meet you, Dan .sadly I noticed you have lost two of your friends.'

'No, it is my mother and father. Only my father is not buried there. It is just a headstone in his memory. He was lost at sea.'

'What a coincidence! My father was also lost at sea, and they have put a headstone here for him next to my mother.'

They sat on a bench and continued to talk. Dan asked Jamie when his mother had died, and Jamie replied that he had been only six years old at that time. He also told him the events of his father's death and how he believed he had been murdered and about Temp's death. When he had finished, he asked Dan about his family.

'Jamie I am so sorry such a sad story. Mine is much the same, but they were not murdered. My mother died a year ago of a broken heart, because my father, who was a merchant seaman and had been lost at sea. It happened late one night a few years ago during a storm. They said he fell off the mainsail. They threw things into the sea after him that floated in the hopes he could cling to one of them. Unfortunately, they could not find him and no one since has ever found a body or heard anything more of him.'

'Yours is also a sad story, Dan. Where are you staying?'

'Over there next to the vicarage in that cottage,' replied Dan as he pointed to a small thatched cottage. 'I am staying with my aunt until I find work for my late father's merchant ship. We moved here from Ireland several years ago that's where I was born we moved here and rented a place in Portsmouth.

Jamie wanted to see Kate, so he said goodbye to Dan, telling him he would look out for any work he could find for his' ship.

As he walked to see Kate, his mind mulled over what Dan had said about the floats that had been thrown for his father. He wondered if anyone had done that for his father. Kate answered the door. 'I am sorry I have not been to see Mary, but my grandfather got worse, he has been very ill. Fortunately, he is feeling much better.'

'Kate, my love, it is fine. Perhaps tomorrow, I will come to see you and take you to see Mary.'

She nodded eagerly and said that would be a lovely idea. Jamie then went on to tell her of his meeting with Dan. He left Kate, promising to collect her the next day, still deep in thought about his father's death.

As he was eating breakfast the following morning, he asked Mary who taught the children to read and write.

'That's me. The tutor left some six months ago because we could not pay him. Although I am not very good at teaching, there is no one else who will do it.'

'Mary, this is too much work for you. I know just the person who may help you. I will get her straight away.' He put the last piece of bread in his mouth and ran down the drive and across the village green. He knocked on Kate's door; her grandmother answered it.

'Good morning, Jamie. Come in. Do you want to speak to Kate?' Being a bit out of breath he answered. 'Yes, please. How is your husband doing?'

'He is a lot better thankyou since our Kate has been looking after him.'

'Yes, she was also brilliant at looking after everyone who was ill on board the ship.'

Kate entered the room, looking lovely in a warm ruby red dress with her hair tied back with a matching ribbon. 'He asked her if she would accompany him back to Compton Manor to see Mary'.

'I would be delighted to, Jamie. My grandfather is a lot better today. I will just get my cloak.' As they walked up the drive, Kate observed that although the trees were bare and there were no flowers at that time of year, everything in the grounds looked neat and tidy. The leaves from the autumn fall had been swept away, and the dead branches pruned back.

'Mary and the servants must have put a lot of work to keep things this neat.'

'No, Kate Mary has been too busy looking after the children. It's one of the things I want to talk to you about, but first, let's go inside and have a cup of tea.'

Lizzie let them in and went to make them both some tea, they went into the small drawing room with a fire blazing in the hearth.

'My darling Kate you are the most beautiful compassionate woman in the world, and I think I am in love with you. I want you to be by my side everywhere I go.'

'Jamie, thank you for those lovely words, but I do not love you. I think the world of you but have come to realise that the affection I feel for you is more of a brotherly nature. Also, I have not changed my mind. I want to live on land, not at sea. Sam likes you very much. Perhaps maybe she even loves you. She would be the ideal woman for you, and I have seen you looking at her with love in your eyes.'

'I do like her a lot, but it is you I love and do not want anyone else.'
'Stop, Jamie. You are not the person I want to spend my life with.'

Kate dare not look at him as her love for him goes deep into her heart but knows she would only make him unhappy by keeping him away from his first love—the sea.

'So you have decided to stay and settle down here. Would you consider living here in my house?'

'Jamie sorry, I would not live in your house with you.

'No, no, you misunderstand. Mary needs someone to teach the orphans how to read and write.'

'That's different I would love to do it.'

'Then come and tell her yourself.'

They both walked along the passageway leading through to the west wing and knocked on a door.

When they entered, Kate was surprised to see about forty children sitting listening to Mary.

'Excuse me for interrupting, but this young lady would like to ask the teacher something.'

Mary told the children to go and play outside for a little and greeted Kate warmly. 'My dear, is it really you, how are you? My, you have become a lovely young woman!'

'Thank you, Mary. You look lovely as well. I am here to ask you I wondered if I may help you to teach these children.'

'Help me! OH, Kate. Would it be possible for you to do it on your own?'

'Why? Yes. Mary, I love teaching. If you like, I could even begin next week.'

'That's lovely Kate I will make sure that everything you need will be ready,' Mary being very relieved.

Jamie whispered in Mary's ear, 'This job is only until I get her to sail with me again.'

Kate was delighted with the situation. Not only would she be doing something she loved but would also be with her grandparents. ; I will walk you home, Kate. At least, next week, I will see you every day when I come home from the shipyard.'

'No, you won't, Jamie. I intend to continue living with my grandparents. It will only be a short walk here every day.'

After Jamie left Kate at her cottage, he wandered off towards the churchyard, disgruntled that his plan had not gone quite as he had hoped. On the way, he met Dan, who was just leaving.

'Hello, Dan, may I have a quick word with you?' 'Yes by all means. What is it about?' 'When you told me about your father falling overboard, you said the crew threw things into the sea for him to cling to.' 'Yes, I did say that why you ask Jamie?' 'I have been wondering Dan if it was possible for a man to be saved like this.'

Well yes, I had heard of one man who was rescued clinging to floating objects, by a merchant ship on its way to County Cork in

Ireland about three or four years ago picked him up. My poor father did not have this man's luck. Why do you ask Jamie? Do you think it could be your father?'

'No, I don't think so, although it was about that time my father was lost, he would have been in touch with me after a few weeks. Do you know what this lucky man's name was?'

'Nobody knew his name because apparently he had been hit over his head or knocked it as he fell overboard and suffered from loss of memory. It was around that time when my father docked his ship in Cork harbour and the ship that docked alongside us was the same ship that had found this sailor in the sea a few months earlier. That's why I know a lot about it.

Everyone was talking about him and wondering where he came from. I never saw this man and never bothered to find out what he looked like. There was no reason for me to find out.'

'Thanks, Dan, you have made me wonder if there is a chance it could have been my father. I am going to try and find out more about it. Thanks again.'

Jamie went to the harbour and found Spider in the office. 'Spider, I have met a young man called Dan. He asked if we have any work for his merchant ship.'

'Not if you are going to buy another ship and if you don't sail off anywhere in a hurry.'

'Well, that all depends.'

'Depends on what?' Spider said Smiling at him. He was to tell Spider about the sailor who fell overboard and was rescued off the coast of Ireland and that it was about the same time his father went missing.

'You go and get JB, and I will fetch Mr Thompson, and we will talk to them in this office and try to establish what really did happen that night in the storm.'

It didn't take them long to find JB and Mr Thompson. They sat them down in the office and explained the situation.

'JB, what time did my father fall overboard the night of the storm?' 'It was probably about two hours before dawn.'

'Did you see my father get hit on the head?'

'Yes, I think he was hit with something like a lump of wood or metal. I think it must have been wood the way the man lifted it quickly.'

'Mr Thompson, did you or any of the crew throw anything into the sea after you knew someone had fallen overboard?' Jamie was praying to hear the answer he wanted. 'Yes, we did.'

'Did you remember what sort of things they were?'

'Aye, we threw some empty barrels that I managed to cut loose and also some ten or so glass floats that were tied together. I remembered your father had brought them from a Norwegian ship in Cuba just before we set sail.'

Jamie was filled with hope as JB and Mr Thompson wished him luck. When they were on their own again, Jamie said to Spider,

'When Sam gets back, I am going to Ireland and the harbour of County Cork. It could well have been my father who was rescued, and I won't rest until I find out who the man is.'

'You do realise the sea was very cold when your father fell overboard. Anyone who fell overboard could only survive in it for a couple of hours at the most.'

'I know, but my father was a very good, strong swimmer, and if he found those floats early enough, he could perhaps have climbed on top of them and out of the cold sea.'

'I suppose you could be right about that. I will make sure everything is ready to set sail when Sam returns.'

'Thanks, Spider, and put a hold on buying a new ship until I return from Ireland. I think we should take the offer of using Dan's ship.'

'That's fine. We have plenty of crew to man her.'

'Spider, just one more thing, can you make an appointment with Mr Westgarth for us both? I will use the same crew again. The only thing is Kate might decide to stay here. Where is Smithy? I have not seen him around.'

'In his second home, the blacksmith's shop and the local foundry, making something you will like. So he says.'

'Whatever is he up to now? Just make sure he is here when we sail.'

Jamie hurried back to the village to tell Kate his news, the first thing he told her was what he had been said about his father.

' Kate I wonder if it could be my father, but then why has he not got in touch with me by now.'

Kate replied that his father may have a loss of memory that could last one day, one year, or forever. This made him even more determined to go to Ireland to find out.

'Kate, would you like to come and meet Dan?'

'Yes, I like too.' She thought this was a lovely idea as they were neighbours. There was a cold wind blowing, so Jamie waited while Kate wrapped herself up in a woollen cloak and scarf.

They hurried across the green to his house, Dan opened the door. He stared at Kate openly as Jamie introduced them to each other. Kate blushed under such close scrutiny.

'How do you do, Kate? My goodness, Jamie has spoken of you but never mentioned how beautiful you were.'

Kate blushed even more and pulled her scarf up further to hide her embarrassment. Dan pulled the door wider and asked them in. He offered them tea as they sat down. Kate was mumbling that Jamie was a good friend, but Jamie felt disgruntled that Kate was not explaining that their relationship was more than that, at least in Jamie's eyes. Jamie told Dan he was going to Ireland to try to find the man Dan had told him about just in case it was his father. He asked Dan if he wanted some coastal work for his ship until Jamie returned from Ireland. Dan was delighted but said he would have to find a crew, hardly taking his eyes from Kate. Jamie explained he had enough crew to man his ship, they both shook hands on the agreement.

Jamie was in a rush to leave, all he wanted to get Kate out of there as fast as possible, wishing he had never taken her with him, as he walked her home he said to her.

Dan seems to like you. I may have some competition.' 'Don't be so stupid, Jamie. I am not interested in him at all.'

Chapter 28

The coming weeks Jamie worked in the shipping office with Spider being impatient for Sam to return, but not wanting to leave without her. He was shuffling papers back and forth across the desk one day when all of a sudden the door flung open.

'How are you, handsome?'

'Sam, I am so glad you're back.' Jamie rushed over and hugged her tightly.

'Hold on their skipper. You are squashing me. Did you miss me?'

'It's nothing like that. We need to set sail as soon as possible.'

'Aren't you going to ask me how I got on first?'

'Oh sorry, how did it go?'

'I managed to find the parents of two of the children, and they promised me faithfully to care for the third child and search for his parents and would look after him until they found them.'

'That's fantastic, Sam. Well done.'

'We will go to my house now, so you can have some food, and then tomorrow, we will catch the evening tide.' He rushed outside to tell Spider to get everything ready, as they would be leaving the next day.

'Skipper, it will take nearly all night just to load all the boxes Smithy is taking with him.'

Jamie frowned thinking what the hell has he been up to?'

Sam and Jamie set off in the carriage to Compton manor as they got halfway up the long driveway they saw Dan and Kate at the front steps. They seemed to be in deep conversation and enjoying each other's company. Jamie was irritated. He pulled up the reins and jumped down. Kate and Sam greeted each other warmly. 'Who is this young man you have found?' questioned Sam.

Kate introduced Dan as Jamie's friend. Sam raised her eyebrows, thinking it looked as if he was more Kate's friends as Jamie changed the conversation quickly, as a little jealousy was creeping in.

'I have got some good news for you, Kate. Sam has managed to find the parents of two of the children.'

'That's Wonderful, Sam! I always thought you would.'

Jamie told Kate they were sailing tomorrow evening and asked if she would like to sail with him to find his father. Kate not saying a word one way or the other avoided the question. Dan asked, could he accompany them tomorrow, as he wants to talk to Spider about his ship? Jamie replied, 'By all means, Dan.' they said their goodbyes, and Kate and Dan continued down the drive and back to their cottages. When Sam and Jamie entered the mansion, Tom came to greet Sam and Jamie hugging his legs. 'Skipper Jamie, is it all right if I stay here with Auntie Mary when you next sail?'

'I am sailing off tomorrow, Tom, and of course, you can stay, but on two conditions: Look after my cats, and learn as much as possible, and when you are older, you can work for me.' He shouted out, 'Yes, yes, Skipper, I will,' Then he runs off to tell Mary his good news before it was his bedtime.

When Kate arrived back at her grandparents' cottage, she thanked Dan for escorting her home and bid him goodnight.

She had a lot on her mind and after eating her supper, she asked to be excused said goodnight to her grandparents and started to make her way upstairs, her grandmother asked her if she was feeling well? Kate turned around and said she was fine, hurried up the stairs to her bedroom before her grandmother could question her more. Her grandmother, however, was concerned, as Kate seemed to have something on her mind.

Kate's grandmother was really worried about Kate and got up from her bed to check on her. It was way past midnight and her grandmother could see the light of a flickering candle under her door. She knocked gently on her door and whispered her name.

Kate's voice uttered 'Yes nana'.

'May I come in '?

'Of course nana'

Kate's grandmother sat on her bed and asked her what was wrong. Kate was a bit reluctant to tell her at first. 'Nana I do not know what to do tomorrow and it hurts me inside'. Her grandmother cuddled her tightly and said 'You know you can tell me anything child' Kate sighed and took a deep breath. 'Its Jamie nana, his friendships means more to me that I care to say'.

Her grandmother sat in silence waiting for Kate to say what was in her heart. Kate sighed again.

'I have to make a decision nana if to sail with Jamie and all my friends tomorrow'.

Her grandmother could see she was having a hard time trying to say what she wanted to say.

'Meeting Jamie has changed my life and my love for him has intensified as we grew older, but our lives seem to be going in different directions, a home and family is my heart's desire. Should I give up my love or sail off with him again and put aside my dreams'?

Her grandmother was almost in tears. 'Kate you are a wonderful daughter to me, it pains me you have to make this awful decision, but seems to me you have already made your mind up and I cannot influence you in any way as it has to be your decision and yours alone'.

'I know nana, thank you for listening to me'

Her grandmother nodded her head. 'I will not come to see you off tomorrow child, because I don't want to see you upset'.

'I understand nana'.

'Now try and get some sleep child as you have to be up early in the morning'. Her grandmother kissed her forehead and said good night.

'Nana, I'll try, good night.'

As Kate lay down in her bed, she hoped the decision she had to make in the morning would hopefully come easy to her. Nana said one more thing before closing the door

'May God guide you my love in your dreams tonight,'

Kate rested her head upon her pillow and closed her eyes. Even though she spent a sleepless night, tossing and turning, as she knows the decision she will make would greatly affect her future.

Next morning, she packed her bags and was ready, just after saying goodbye to her grandparents with kissing and tears, Jamie and Dan arrived. Then after they helped her into the buggy and her bags, then waved to her grandparents, set off at a steady gallop heading to Portsmouth, when they got there the ships loading was well underway.

Straight away Dingle and Teresa joked with Jamie, 'When we get to Ireland, we will translate into English for you.'

'Get away before I slap you both,' laughed Jamie.

When near the time they were to sail Jamie noticed that Mary, Tom, and most of the servants had arrived in the carriage to see them off. He felt honoured that so many people cared, and by some many friends and felt a lump in his throat.

Kate asked Sam, 'Would you carry on writing in my diary? But most of all look after our captain for these few weeks. Promise me you won't read it.'

'Kate, my dearest friend, I was hoping you would come with us.'

'No, sorry, Sam, but I have yet to tell, Jamie.'

'Well, Kate, you keep your diary please, and I have a stack of papers and will write daily in it for you to read when we return, and yes, I will look after him, and I promise not to tell him how much you love him.'

Kate was surprised. 'You have been reading my diary!'

'No, of course, I haven't,' replied Sam. 'But it's written all over your face.'

They both kissed and hugged one another with Kate giving Sam instructions to use a girl called Julie to take her place, looking after the sick.

By now, Jamie had walked over and interrupted them, 'Are you ready to go, Kate?'

'No, Jamie, not this time.'

'But when I saw you with your bag this morning, I presumed you were going to come with me. You never said a word about it on the way here. Perhaps when I get back in a few weeks, hopefully, you will have missed me so much you might change your mind and come on the next trip?'

'I am so sorry, Jamie. The bags are for the girl Julie, and it is full of medicines. But I wish you a safe journey and look forward to seeing you all when you get back.'

'Kate, my love, because you have kept an account of everything that happened on our journey in your diary, would you also be kind enough to look after the ship's logbook. It is full now, and I need to start a new one. It contains all the information about the ship's journey, including weather conditions, the crew, cargo, and all manner of things I am obliged to record.'

Kate flung her arms around Jamie, holding him tightly. He felt too choked to be able to speak, and as she released her hold, he wiped the tears from her face.

'Jamie, my dearest friend, look after yourself and get back here safely.'

She turned away, not trusting herself to follow him to the ends of the earth.

Spider noticed how emotional Jamie was and put his arm around him. 'Jamie, cheer up. Women always make us men sad. She will change her mind when you get back. Just wait and see.'

'I hope so, Spider. I'm not sure I want to live without her.'

Trying to change the subject, Spider said, 'I have met your friend, Dan, and have come to an agreement with him using his ship, while you are away. He seems a nice young man.' Jamie was only half-listening when Spider said, 'You see that ship docked over there. It arrived last night from Asia. It had stopped at Zanzibar, and the captain has told me there is a price on your head and the Swordfish. The slave trade has dropped by a huge amount.

He recognised your ship as there were only a very few built to that specification. Every French corsair ship is looking for you. Most of the bounty money has been put up by Mr Bourbonnais. You must have made a big impression over there. 'OH, I nearly forgot Mitch has a surprise, awaiting you in your cabin.'

'Thanks for telling me that, Spider. It's cheered me up already, but not that surprise.' Spider slapped Jamie on the back, smiling over his face.

'Well, Partner, have a good journey, and fetch me back some Irish cheese.' 'I will, so I will,' said Jamie in the broadest Irish accent he could manage. They were still laughing as Jamie called the rest of his crew and there dog McKay to board the ship and cast off.

The ship started to move slowly with everyone on the quay waving frantically. Mary put her arms around Kate. 'You like my Jamie a lot, don't you?'

'Yes, I love him with all my heart, but I cannot bear days like this when he leaves.' 'I understand. Kate, It would break my heart as well if it happened to me.'

Above all the shouting, as the ship is drifting away, Dan shouted to Jamie, 'Wish you the best of luck, my friend. See you back here in a few weeks.'

'Thanks, Dan. By the way, what is your family name? I might need it when I get there.'

'My friend, it is RILEY.

LITTLE DID THEY KNOW IT WILL BE ANOTHER TWO OR THREE YEARS THEY WOULD NOT BE BACK.

www.ingramcontent.com/pod-product-compliance
Lightning Source LLC
Chambersburg PA
CBHW071655090426
42738CB00009B/1538